ANXIETY

Its Components, Development, and Treatment

ANXIETY

Its Components, Development, and Treatment

STANLEY LESSE, M.D., MED. SC. D.

Editor-in-Chief, *American Journal of Psychotherapy;*
President, Association for the Advancement of Psychotherapy;
Neurological Institute of the Presbyterian Hospital of New York;
Faculty of Neurology, College of Physicians & Surgeons,
Columbia University, New York, New York

GRUNE & STRATTON New York and London

GRUNE & STRATTON, INC.
757 Third Avenue
New York, New York 10017

Library of Congress Catalog Card Number 70–120305
International Standard Book Number 0-8089-0663-1

PRINTED IN THE UNITED STATES OF AMERICA

(PC-B)

1595088

To
Margie, Marcia, and Margaret,
but especially to Margie

PREFACE

This book is basically devoted to a systematic phenomenologic study of anxiety in terms of its components, its development in response to various types of stress, and its amelioration in response to various therapies.

Some monographs are derived from unintended beginnings, have long periods of incubation, and emerge only after passing through a long, circuitous route. To say the least, this description applies to this particular book. The original, and at first glance initial, conceptual stimulus that finally evolved into a study of the phenomenologic aspects of anxiety came about in late 1950, while I was still a senior resident at the Neurological Institute of New York.

At that point, after years of training in surgery, pathology, and neurology, I was scheduled to begin a neurosurgical residency. However, I had become intrigued by Wilder Penfield's reports of his studies on "evoked memory." As a result I dropped my plans to become a neurosurgeon and became a resident in psychiatry at the New York State Psychiatric Institute under Dr. Nolan D. C. Lewis. I simultaneously began formal psychoanalytic training.

These were planned stepping-stones for my admission to the department of research psychiatry, which was under the direction of the late Dr. Paul Hoch, who invited me to join his department and to participate in the very active psychosurgical program then in progress. I presented a detailed research plan by means of which I intended to study the effects of electrophysiologic stimulation of the temporal lobes of actively hallucinatory schizophrenic patients under local anesthesia. The results of these studies would then be compared with the pseudohallucinations recorded by Penfield in his work with epileptics. Dr. Hoch was receptive to my plan, and I became a member of his department in 1952, first as a U.S. Public Health postdoctorate research fellow and later as senior research psychiatrist.

These were my salad days in psychiatry, and very shortly after I entered the clinical research department I was confronted with the realization that I had to develop a method by means of which extremely anxious, agitated, chronically decompensated schizophrenic patients could be prepared to undergo craniotomy, cortical stimulation, and lobotomy— procedures that took two to four hours—under local anesthesia. The technique that I developed, after months of experimentation, for the control of massive anxiety in an experimental setting is described in detail in Chapter 12.

These preoperative studies entailed a broad, multidisciplinary, phe- nomenologic investigation of how severely anxious schizophrenic patients responded to marked or massive stress of various types. In a parallel vein, a broad spectrum of treatment techniques ranging from supportive and psychoanalytically oriented psychotherapy, on the one hand, to oral and parenteral drug therapy and psychosurgery, on the other hand, were utilized to ameliorate these extreme levels of anxiety.

In retrospect these were very exciting and challenging days, for we were also studying the hallucinogenic properties of intravenous mescaline and oral lysergic acid. These drugs presented me with unique tools for the study of rapidly increasing anxiety and its secondary consequences. In late 1953 our laboratory was among the first in the United States to investigate the tranquilizing effects of the phenothiazine drugs (chlor- promazine was the preparation that was available). This new medium of psychotropic medications added a fascinating dimension to the study of the rapid amelioration of anxiety. In 1955 I was awarded a Doctor of Medical Science degree by the College of Physicians & Surgeons, Columbia University, a degree based primarily upon the psychosurgical aspects of my research program.

By early 1953, about six months after I had begun my research project, my central goal had broadened from the original study of the effects of electrophysiologic stimulation of the temporal lobes of chronic schizo- phrenic patients to the step-by-step phenomenologic investigation of the production and amelioration of anxiety, its components and secondary clinical manifestations.

In 1954, shortly after oral chlorpromazine was made available for re- search purposes, I became interested in the use of psychoanalytically oriented psychotherapy in combination with chlorpromazine in the ambulatory treatment of patients who manifested extreme anxiety. This was an attempt to increase the spectrum of patients with severe psychologic ailments who could be managed on an outpatient basis and also to increase the efficiency of psychotherapeutic techniques. The initial, detailed descriptions of the methodology and results of this combined technique were presented in 1956 before several psychiatric societies, and the first papers were published in 1956 and 1957 (Lesse, 1956, 1957).

In April, 1956, the Association for the Advancement of Psychotherapy (AAP) invited me to present a paper dealing with my new combined technique. This talk proved to be the introduction to a new, and perhaps the richest, phase of my medical life. The chairman of that meeting was Dr. Joseph Wilder, one of the founders of the AAP. I presented clinical evidence to the effect that the more anxious patients were at the moment chlorpromazine was administered, the more favorable their response.

During that AAP meeting I became acquainted with Dr. Wilder's pioneering work with the Law of Initial Value, in which he pointed out that the change in any function of an organism resulting from a stimulus depends to a large degree on the prestimulus level of that function. This applied to both the intensity and direction of the response. During the past fourteen years a close personal and professional relationship has developed between Dr. Wilder and me. Our many discussions about basimetry, which is the study of the effects of the Law of Initial Value, in part influenced my studies of placebo effects and psychobiologic rhythms, particularly in relation to anxiety. The results of these studies are summarized in Chapters 10 and 11.

Following the 1956 talk I was invited to join the Association for the Advancement of Psychotherapy. My fourteen years of membership have included eight years as president and eleven years as editor-in-chief of its official organ, the *American Journal of Psychotherapy*. These have been the most rewarding years of my medical career, for they exposed me to the broad eclectic spirit that was engendered in psychotherapy and psychiatry by this organization. One of the high points of this fourteen-year association has been my close work with Dr. William Wolf, one of the truly versatile medical scholars from whom I gained an appreciation of the importance of reaching for a balanced optimum and avoiding the blind pursuit of the ever-elusive maximum.

Twenty years have passed from the time I first became interested in evoked memory to the publication of this monograph on anxiety. During this entire period my wife Margie has been my most enthusiastic assistant and my most reliable aide. In the early days she was a willing draftee as my sole researcher, secretary, typist, medical artist, and chartist. Though the passing years have lessened her technical roles she has remained my chief confidante and critic, a never-failing source of patient and gentle encouragement.

STANLEY LESSE

CONTENTS

1

PURPOSE AND METHODOLOGIC DESIGN

The subject of anxiety has been considered in the literature from many viewpoints and prejudices. These have ranged from the philosophic to the sociologic, to the psychologic, to the biologic. Usually the investigators, whether individuals or teams, have dealt with but one aspect of anxiety, each focusing on a very narrow fragment of the problem and often magnifying his particular approach so that his concept takes on the magnificence of a law or dogma.

In general, some have dealt with the stresses that produce anxiety; some have dealt with defenses, positive or negative, secondary to anxiety. Usually, after a relatively small number of clinical observations, the authors have burst into a veritable garden of theory that at first glance may appear to have substance, but that on closer examination is found to be limited in scope. Unfortunately, many of these limited constructs have become dogma and have acted as intellectual soporifics. One author after another has climbed on the bandwagon and has followed this or that prophet. The trend to quote clinically unsubstantiated theory and treat it as fact is one example of the pseudoscientific bent that is characteristic of so many studies in psychiatry and its allied fields. As in all instances where philosophy coupled with poor documentation holds sway there has been general disagreement as to definition and validity of interpretation.

Cattell and Scheirer (1961) have written about the measurement of anxiety and the neurosis. They emphasize the need to apply scientific attitudes and principles in order that the individual may understand and master himself as he has mastered other things in his environment. It is their claim, and rightfully so, that psychiatry is still focused on premetric rationales. They claim "that so long as intuition and personal insight,

1

rather than measurement and replicable experiment, remain the basis of clinical theory and practice, psychiatry will remain an art and will not become a science" (Cattel and Scheirer, 1961, p. 2).

I cannot disagree with their claim. However, I would like to point out that the metric method has not contributed all that it should to the knowledge of psychological understanding. Indeed, one must question at times whether the documentation thus far recorded as part of the metric period is valid. One reason for this is the fact that most metric systems have failed to evaluate the initial values prior to beginning an experiment or therapeutic regime.

Those who have written about the measurement of anxiety have been preoccupied with static evaluations of a fixed moment of anxiety. They have failed to consider anxiety in relationship to time, rate, or direction. For example, what is the effect of rate of change of anxiety on the production and amelioration of symptoms and signs? Psychiatry, psychology, and the socioanthropologic sciences are in some ways in the prewheel neolithic period of scientific development in comparison with physics and its applied branches, such as engineering. How primitive physics would be if time, rate, and direction of energy change were not as yet recognized let alone not employed in theory and research. For example, in aeronautic engineering, since World War II, the problem of piercing the sound barrier has been of great moment. As yet only military aircraft have accomplished this feat. The first supersonic civilian aircraft are expected to become operational in 1972. These problems will be minute as compared to the challenges that will present themselves when the question of travel closer to the speed of light becomes imminent. However, as I have already noted, we in the psychologic disciplines have not even seriously considered the problem of rate of change. A few halting steps in this direction will be made in this book.

Though I freely admit that my work is primitive in that I know very little about rate of change in relationship to anxiety and other psychologic phenomena, I plead with the reader to throw away the intellectual shackles and blinders that have bound our thinking and observations and attempt to think in terms of dynamic observations that include a study of time, direction, and rate of change.

The huge sums of money that have been expended by various research foundations in an attempt to give a scientific basis to psychiatry have tended to build a hierarchy of gadgeteers who have stressed methodology without producing reliable replicable data. Ultimately, the technique suggested and described by Cattell and Scheirer (1961), in which multivariate data gained by means of multivariate techniques are exposed to factor analysis, may produce a greater amount of reliable data concerning anxiety and its relationship to psychological disorders in general.

My study is long on observation and short on statistical data. Insofar as possible all terms have been defined operationally. The preexperimental and pretherapeutic levels of anxiety have been taken into consideration, which has not been done in any other extensive clinical psychiatric work. Without this preexperimental and clinical evaluation, any study must be relegated to the realm of art rather than science. This will be discussed later in detail in the chapters dealing with the placebo effect and the Law of Initial Value.

My studies can be checked readily by any observer if the definitions and methods outlined in this book are followed. The definitions and techniques of evaluation, which will be described in detail, serve as crude but meaningful instruments of measurement that can be utilized by clinicians or those engaged in clinical research. These definitions and techniques are equally adaptable to studies performed in patients' homes and those done in the more artificial setting of the office or clinic. The techniques described here can also be refined ad infinitum and utilized by the experimental psychologists who investigate human behavior in the laboratory.

All the observations included in this study have been collected by me. This is at once a disadvantage, for all the failings and untempered prejudices of one man are reflected in the data. However, many studies have testified to the fact that multiple observations by multiple clinical observers using various clinical rating scales do not necessarily show greater reliability (Cattell and Scheirer, 1961, p. 4). Once again, I do not doubt that test instruments properly applied by clinically trained persons eventually will surpass the rating scales of clinicians in reliability and usefulness; but that day does not yet appear to have arrived.

The purpose of this eighteen-year study is the description of the interrelationships among the various components of anxiety and between these components and other clinical psychiatric symptoms and signs as anxiety increases or diminishes in intensity. At any given moment these interrelationships can be measured more accurately by specific tests, but no test or battery of tests thus far devised has been able to plot these dynamic interrelationships from moment to moment. Though various tests can record static relationships between two or more factors at a given instance with great accuracy, these data may not be valid the very next moment as the anxiety changes in intensity. Anxiety is as fluid as time and must be considered in dimensions of time, quantity, quality, rate, and direction of change.

This book does not discuss specifically the delineation between normal and abnormal anxiety. All the patients included in this investigation were abnormally anxious by any definition. In all instances the anxiety present in these patients was of such magnitude as to seriously interfere with their capacities to adapt to their environments. This work considers whether different sources of stress produce different interrelationships among the various components of anxiety and between these and other clinical psychiatric symptoms and signs.

In all instances I have been concerned with overt manifestations of anxiety. My techniques have not depended on questionnaires that, in turn, depend primarily on the individual's awareness of himself. The intensity of anxiety in these patients was so severe that it was rarely possible for them to intentionally or unintentionally distort their behavior. At no time did the measurements of the degree of anxiety depend on the patients' evaluations of their own feelings. These measurements were based entirely on my evaluation of their overt clinical state.

Some may criticize this research because too few dimensions relating to anxiety have been defined. This criticism has great validity. However, I request the reader to concern himself purely with the dimensions that are defined. *At all times the concept of the changing intensity of anxiety is the important point. Thinking in terms of a static quantity of anxiety is to think negatively as far as the aims of this study are concerned.*

GENERAL PURPOSE

In general the purpose of this investigation was the systematic study of certain overt expressions of anxiety. The subjects were patients with severe psychiatric illnesses.

The changing clinical patterns in these patients were studied in relation to the quantitative gradation of anxiety as defined according to four components, namely, motor, affective, autonomic, and verbal.

These components were studied intensively as the degree of anxiety was increased in response to various types of stress and then as the level of anxiety was decreased in response to various therapies. To be more specific, I focused on the following problems:

1. The nature of these four components of anxiety and their interrelationships as the quantitative degree of anxiety increases.

2. The relationship of these four components of anxiety to the appearance of other clinical psychiatric symptoms and signs as the level of anxiety increases.

3. The problem of whether different sources of stress alter the interrelationships among these four components of anxiety.

4. The problem of whether different sources of stress alter the interrelationships between anxiety and the appearance of other clinical symptoms and signs.

5. The question of whether the sequence of clinical symptoms and signs follows a reproducible pattern or whether it is purely a chance relationship.

6. The nature of these four components of anxiety and their interrelationships as the level of anxiety is decreased in response to various types of treatment.

7. The study of the relationship of the components of anxiety to the amelioration of various clinical psychiatric symptoms and signs as the quantitative degree of anxiety is decreased in response to various therapeutic techniques.

8. The interrelationships of various psychiatric symptoms and signs as the level of anxiety is ameliorated.

9. The study of the quantitative degree of anxiety in relationship to complex psychologic mechanisms, such as dreams and hallucinations.

10. The study of anxiety in relation to psychosomatic processes as the level of anxiety is increased and decreased quantitatively.

11. The study of anxiety in relationship to placebo effects.

12. The relationship of anxiety to the Law of Initial Value.

13. The detailed study of a psychotherapeutic technique for the management of catastrophic anxiety in a research setting. More specifically, this study deals with the preparation of schizophrenic patients for craniotomies and lobotomies to be performed under local anesthesia.

14. The application of the knowledge gained in the above studies in the treatment of severely ill psychiatric patients. More specifically, this application will concern the indications and technique of psychoanalytically oriented psychotherapy in combination with various psychotropic drugs.

METHODOLOGIC PROCEDURES

THE STUDY OF MOUNTING ANXIETY

The phenomenon of mounting anxiety was studied in four groups: (1) schizophrenic patients prior to their undergoing craniotomies and lobotomies to be performed under local anesthesia; (2) schizophrenic patients undergoing craniotomies under local anesthesia; (3) schizophrenic patients given stress-producing psychedelic agents; and (4) patients suffering severe socioenvironmental stress. The test procedures were as follows.

1. Schizophrenic patients in preparation for craniotomies and lobotomies performed under local anesthesia. Forty-three severely ill schizophrenic

patients were evaluated intensively by various techniques in preparation for prefrontal lobotomies, which were performed under local anesthesia. This investigation was carried out between October 1952 and November 1954. All but one of the patients has been ill for more than three years. Some had been ill for more than two decades. The patients were screened by a multitude of psychiatric techniques including interview, conferences, drug studies, and psychologic testing. Only one patient was so severely deteriorated that the anticipation of an intracranial operation did not cause marked trepidation.

2. Observation of schizophrenic patients during the performance of craniotomies under local anesthesia. Patients undergoing large craniotomies requiring one or more hours to expose a specific area of frontal cortex offered a unique opportunity to study patients under maximum stress. Forty-three schizophrenic patients were included in this aspect of the investigation. The anxiety generated in response to the various technical procedures that were a part of the craniotomy technique was recorded by various means. I was in direct visual, verbal, and tactile contact with the patient at all times. Figures 1.1 and 1.2 show how the patient and I were in close proximity, shielded by drapes from the remainder of the research team. Figure 1.3 shows the neurosurgical team during an operation. I was able to record, in a very intimate fashion, the overt clinical changes that occurred with regard to the various components of anxiety

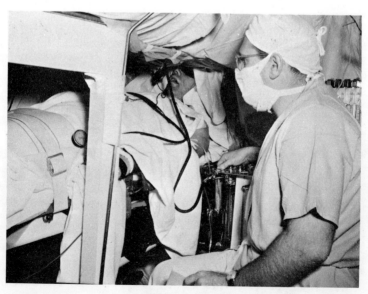

FIGURE 1.1

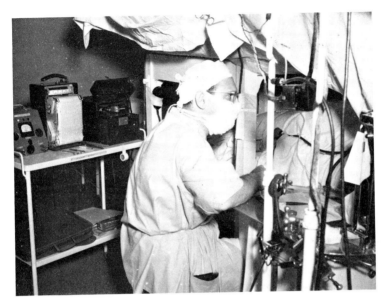

FIGURE 1.2

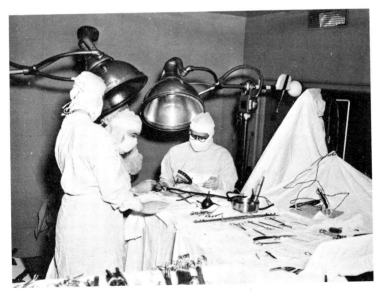

FIGURE 1.3

and to the appearance of secondary symptoms and signs in response to the stress of the various surgical procedures. In addition, continuous recordings of my conversations with the patients were coordinated with other recordings, such as continuous psychogalvanometric tracings, vital signs that were checked at two-minute intervals, and continuous electrocortical tracings that were taken before, during, and immediately after the lobotomy.

3. Patients exposed to stress-producing psychedelic agents. Twenty-five schizophrenic patients were given intravenous mescaline or oral lysergic acid (LSD-25). Some patients had two or more tests; a few received both mescaline and lysergic acid. In all, forty-one test procedures were carried out. These afforded a unique opportunity to investigate patients under extreme stress and the anxiety resulting from the stress. The vast majority of the patients who had craniotomies and lobotomies performed under local anesthesia also were given intravenous amobarbital and intravenous amphetamines as part of the test procedures. The results of these studies will be included in Chapter 12, "The Study and Management of Catastrophic Anxiety."

4. Patients exposed to socioenvironmental stress. Between 1952 and 1962 I treated 574 patients by various techniques. I saw most of them in private practice: (a) in an office setting, (b) in a general hospital, or (c) in a private psychiatric hospital. The vast majority were seen in my private office. Approximately 100 were patients in the Facial Pain Clinic of the Neurological Institute of the Presbyterian Hospital of New York. Without exception, all the patients manifested marked overt anxiety secondary to the stresses resulting from their exposure to routine or extraordinary environmental demands. In addition to anxiety secondary to environmental stress, some of the patients were plagued by somatic illnesses.

THE STUDY OF DECREASING LEVELS OF ANXIETY

Decreasing levels of anxiety were studied in (1) schizophrenic patients undergoing craniotomies under local anesthesia; (2) schizophrenic patients undergoing prefrontal lobotomies under local anesthesia; (3) patients given intravenous phenothiazines to block the severe anxiety produced secondary to mescaline and lysergic acid; (4) extremely anxious schizophrenic patients given intravenous phenothiazines; (5) patients given electroshock therapy; (6) patients treated by psychotherapy in combination with psychotropic drugs; and (7) patients treated by intensive reconstructive psychoanalysis.

1. Schizophrenic patients during craniotomies performed under local anesthesia: (a) psychotherapeutic techniques and (b) intravenous medications (barbiturates and amphetamines). As noted above, forty-three

schizophrenic patients were studied intensively during the performance of craniotomies. As anxiety mounted various therapeutic procedures were utilized to contain and ameliorate this anxiety.

2. Prefrontal lobotomies performed under local anesthesia. A total of thirty-four schizophrenic patients, in a fully conscious state, were lobotomized under local anesthesia. The clinical changes occurring during and immediately following the lobotomies were recorded in detail.

3. Intravenous phenothiazines used to block anxiety produced secondarily to mescaline and lysergic acid. Intravenous phenothiazines, primarily intravenous chlorpromazine, were used to block and ameliorate the anxiety produced by the use of mescaline and lysergic acid in twenty-five patients. The step-by-step changes that occurred were recorded.

4. Intravenous phenothiazines in the management of extremely anxious schizophrenic patients. Seventy-six very anxious schizophrenic patients were treated with intravenous phenothiazines. All but seven were treated with chlorpromazine. The clinical manifestations as the level of anxiety was ameliorated were recorded.

5. Electroshock therapy. Two hundred severely agitated patients were included in this study. The interrelationships of the various components of anxiety as the level of anxiety was decreased by this technique were observed, as was the relationship of anxiety to the amelioration of other clinical psychiatric symptoms and signs.

6. Psychotherapy in combination with psychotropic drugs. A total of 350 patients were treated with psychoanalytically oriented psychotherapeutic techniques in combination with oral tranquilizers, primarily chlorpromazine. This technique permitted an excellent stage for the observation of psychodynamic and psychopathologic changes as the level of anxiety was reduced. Psychodynamic changes that formerly took several weeks to months to occur transpired in a matter of days or one to two weeks. (The patients included in this study were in general too ill to be cared for on an outpatient basis by brief psychoanalytically oriented psychotherapeutic techniques alone, especially during the initial phase of treatment.)

7. Intensive reconstructive psychoanalysis. Thirty patients who manifested marked anxiety as part of the clinical syndromes were treated by intensive psychoanalytic means. They were seen three or four times per week for a period of one year or more. The changes that occurred in response to these procedures were compared with the more rapid techniques noted above.

MULTIPLE THERAPEUTIC PROCEDURES

It should be noted that many of the patients were exposed to more than one type of stress for the production of anxiety and that many patients were treated by more than one therapeutic technique. For example, most of the patients who were exposed to craniotomies and lobotomies also received intravenous mescaline or lysergic acid. Some of the patients who were not lobotomized also received the hallucinogens. In a similar fashion, the patients who were eventually lobotomized and received the hallucinogenic agents prior to lobotomy were also given intravenous chlorpromazine. Some of the patients who eventually received electroshock therapy received intravenous phenothiazines in an effort to temporarily relieve extreme levels of anxiety. Some of the patients who were treated by psychotherapeutic techniques alone or in combination with oral phenothiazines eventually required electroshock treatment. In some instances this occurred after an intiial improvement in patients who at a later date had severe exacerbations that necessitated electroshock. Some patients who originally had received electroshock therapy later were treated by psychotherapeutic means in combination with psychotropic drugs to control subsequent exacerbations.

SUMMARY

I stated earlier in this chapter that the purpose of my study was the observation and description of the interrelationships among various components of anxiety and between these components and other clinical psychiatric symptoms and signs as the intensity of anxiety increases or diminishes. The sources of stress to which the patients were exposed were multivariate, whereas the selection of therapeutic methods employed to ameliorate the anxiety and secondary clinical manifestations was eclectic, to say the least. The succeeding chapters present a step-by-step description of my observations.

2

OPERATIONAL DEFINITION AND EVALUATION
OF THE SEVERITY OF ANXIETY

One's definition of any phenomenon, including anxiety, immediately colors all the results of one's research. It sets strict limits as to the quality and quantity of data that will be permitted to seep into the research scene and to become available for evaluation. Psychiatry is replete with prejudicially censored material representing obsessively held intellectual and emotional scotomata that are distinguished by nothing more than a qualitative label.

Thus, with regard to anxiety, a plethora of qualitatively defined labels flamboyantly flash on and off with neon-like brilliance announcing "This is sexual anxiety." "This is separation anxiety." "This is interpersonal anxiety." "This is social anxiety." "This is instinctual anxiety." "This is free-floating anxiety." "This is oral anxiety; this is anal anxiety; this is general anxiety." "These are inferiority feelings" (implying that this is anxiety). "This is anxiety stemming as a threat to the conscious from the collective unconscious." "This is true anxiety for it is an expression of an organism in a catastrophic stiuation." "This is fear and not anxiety."

All these labels have a degree of truth. Of necessity they overlap and mingle in a wordy continuum, and the observer is left with a confused image of what anxiety really is. From this maze, the psychiatrist or psychologist chooses a definition of limited and usually inadequate scope, a choice that is dependent in great measure on his emotional and intellectual preferences.

These qualitative conceptualizations of anxiety raise more questions than they answer. Have they been verified? Which is correct? If one accepts a specific definition, how is it to be utilized? All this points to one final burning question implying the frustration of the ages, namely, "So what?" or in the words of a former popular ballad, "Where do we go from here, boys, where do we go from here?"

A definition, to be pragmatic, must lend itself to reportability and measurability. Anxiety, indeed, can be studied as a psychophysiologic phenomenon observable by routine clinical means.

Usually anxiety is referred to as an intense unpleasurable affect. It has a somatic as well as a psychologic aspect. In its popular connotation it is characterized as an experience of anticipated dread, a reaction to unreal or imagined danger, this danger being internal or external.

The term *fear* was originally confused in the German language with *anxiety*, and this confusion was carried into English when Freud's works were translated. *Fear* is popularly described by psychiatrists and psychologists as a foreboding of danger or trauma from a real, usually external, danger with the implication of a greater immediacy and a sense of being temporary or limited in duration. To summarize, *anxiety* is usually considered as being secondary to internal psychological or psychophysiological mechanisms, implying a more unreal base, whereas *fear* is attributed to more immediate or acute external or realistic stress

These traditional conceptions are in many way farcical, for in reality is it rare to observe pure anxiety or pure fear as defined above. From a practical standpoint, the terms *fear* and *anxiety* may be used interchangeably, for more often than not that which the observer records is a fusion of both. At any given moment, immediately prior to a given internal or external stress, real or imagined, there is a base-line level (initial value) of anxiety in the human animal that determines in great measure what his reaction to a given stress will be. This prestress threshold depends on genetically derived generalities modified by conditioning resulting from repetitive adaptation to one's environment.

The more one delves into the vast literature on fear and anxiety, the more one records contradictions, overlaps, and paradoxes. For example, in a recent edition of *Psychiatric Dictionary* (Hensie and Campbell, 1960, p. 292) one notes the following definition: "Fear may be of a twofold nature, namely, real fear and neurotic fear. The latter arises whenever an instinctual urge is felt which is unacceptable to the conscious mind and creates the feeling of fear, if the demand for expression is too great." This definition of *neurotic fear* is indistinguishable from a definition of anxiety.

The confusion between fear and anxiety deserves further attention. As it is popularly conceived, anxiety usually supplies a matrix for fear. On the other hand, it is conceived that fear triggers repressed anxiety. As commonly defined both have an anticipatory quality. For example, from a practical basis, in the instance of an individual with severe precordial pain, how much of the reaction is fear (the realistic dread of impending death) and how much is the expression of the accumulated anticipations gathered over a lifetime?

The boundary line between healthy and normal anxiety and unhealthy or abnormal anxiety also is often obscure. Normal anxiety is said to signal impending danger to the ego and as such leads to healthy defense mechanisms. This is a retrospective concept. It raises questions as to how reliable any given signal may be in relation to real and imagined dangers. Often warning signals may fire off in the absence of real danger. That which is normal at one instant may be abnormal the next instant.

Empiric observations by all observers substantiate the concept that there is a normal aspect to anxiety, a phenomenon that indeed does signal and stimulate various defense mechanisms. However, one also observes that this same healthy anxiety often may gain momentum and finally reach a point at which realistic defense mechanisms break down. These are then replaced by a succession of unhealthy defense mechanisms, which are the symptoms and signs noted in psychologically ill patients. These abnormal defense mechanisms, in the same manner as the normal defense mechanisms, may be looked on as processes of containment that prevent further increases in the level of anxiety.

OPERATIONAL DEFINITION OF ANXIETY

In all my studies, anxiety has been defined in the broadest possible fashion, namely, as *a sociopsychophysiologic phenomenon experienced as a foreboding dread or threat to the human organism whether the threat is generated by internal real or imagined dangers, the sources of which may be conscious or unconscious, or whether the threat is secondary to actual environmental threats of a biosocial, biophysical, or biochemical nature.*

It will immediately be seen that this definition does not take into account any of the differences between anxiety and fear. The definition was purposely very broad in its scope because as yet there are no clear-cut clinical, biochemical, or psychophysiological parameters available for the study of anxiety. Also, in the acute experiment it is not feasible to differentiate between the fear of the experimental situation and the emergence of unconscious fears, especially on a quantitative basis. During the course of this book, the reader may interpret some experimental examples as suggesting situations of pure fear, whereas others may interpret them as situations representing pure anxiety. After an intensive eighteen-year study, I still have not been able to recognize a state of pure fear or pure anxiety. It is safer, at this time, to abolish the distinction between the terms.

In this study there was no question that I was concerned at all times with abnormal anxiety. My work was made easier by the fact that I was dealing almost exclusively with patients manifesting marked or even extreme anxiety. This made the definition more distinct. Some observers might read into this statement that my operational definition of anxiety was similar to that of the late Kurt Goldstein (1940), who defined anxiety as "the subjective experience of the organism in a catastrophic condition." Though Goldstein's definition does hold for a great number of my patients, I do not subscribe to its total implication, which reflects too greatly his preoccupation with brain-damaged patients.

EVALUATING THE QUANTITATIVE DEGREE OF ANXIETY

Anxiety, to be discussed and evaluated, must be overtly manifested, and it is overtly manifested anxiety with which I have concerned myself. I will describe anxiety according to certain parameters that are common expressions of this psychophysiological phenomenon. The components or elements or parameters by which I have characterized or defined anxiety are stated earlier as follows: motor, affective, autonomic, and verbal.

These components are readily observed, described, and measured. Their fluctuations can be followed. Their presence is independent of the nature of the anxiety-producing stress.

All these components may not be manifested with equal intensity in every patient. Indeed, it is the gross exception when equal expression of all the elements is seen. At times one or more components may not be noted at all, and anxiety in these instances must be described in terms of the component or components that are overtly present. If none of these four components is observed, then according to my definition of the term, the patient is completely free of anxiety.

I am not implying that other parameters are not possible. If one defines and employs parameters different from those I have chosen, one might infer that a given patient is more or less anxious than stated according to my definition. However, I will state uncategorically that *any significant and readily applicable definition that can be used in a wide range of clinical and/or research settings must include the parameters used in this book.*

Some may hold that I have been very cavalier in my handling of the parameters of anxiety. Be that as it may, these were the only elements I thought I could readily measure at the very outset of my experiments, and they were continued in all of the studies for the sake of consistency and comparison.

I would like to stress that any definition of the character or degree of anxiety is momentary and is subject to change day to day, hour to hour, or even minute to minute. In every individual patient the definition of degree of anxiety must include the element of time in relationship to the onset of the stressful situation or in relationship to the onset of the therapeutic process.

THE COMPONENTS OF ANXIETY

MOTOR COMPONENT (TENSION)

The term *tension* is used in this work as being synonymous with the motor component or phase of anxiety. It refers specifically to that aspect of overt anxiety mediated through the pyramidal and extrapyramidal nervous systems, which, in turn, manifest themselves through the striate muscles of the body.

In the psychiatric literature, and indeed in the lay literature, the terms *tension* and *anxiety* have been used interchangeably. A considerable amount of confusion has resulted. It reminds one of the confusion in the field of neurology with regard to the term *petit mal epilepsy*. (From the description offered by many neurologists it is impossible to distinguish as to whether one is referring to fragments of a grand mal seizure or whether one is referring to a transient loss of consciousness commonly associated with three-per-second spike and wave electroencephalographic paterns.) If the term *tension* is restricted to mean the motor component of anxiety" one semantic confusion in psychiatry can be overcome.

Under ideal experimental conditions, the motor component of anxiety can be recorded by means of electromyographic tracings. This technique was not employed in these studies because the instrumentation was not available to me when my study began. Also I used only those clinical techniques that could be readily utilized in any office, clinic, or experimental laboratory. My recordings of the amount of tension present at a given moment were based on the degree of active and passive movement and the increased muscle tonus evidenced by the patient. Direct neurologic techniques of careful visual observation and palpation were used to record these manifestations of tension. The data gathered in this manner could then be roughly quantitated, and the degree of tension at any specific moment in different patients could be compared. This also enabled me to evaluate the fluctuations of the degree of tension in a given patient and the relative changes noted in two or more patients.

Clinically then, the intensity of the motor component is designated in the following manner:

Key

   1. Calm: no overt restlessness or tremor; no increase in muscle tonus to palpation.
   2. Slight: very little restlessness; increased movement that is usually intermittent; patient cannot sit still for long periods of time; "fidgety"; the restlessness may appear just in the upper or lower limbs; tremors, if present, usually are fine and intermittent; increase in muscle tonus is usually transient.
   3. Moderate: frequent restlessness; hyperactive; "constant fidgeting"; intermittent pacing; all limbs usually involved; tremors (usually constant), fine or coarse; increased muscle tonus (passive movement may be difficult).
   4. Severe: patient in panic; thrashing about wildly (incessant movement); tremors (coarse and fine involving all parts of the body); marked increase in muscle tonus (some patients are almost completely rigid and fixed).

All these descriptive phenomena included under the designation of the motor component of anxiety are not necessarily present in equal degree under a specific designation of intensity.

AFFECTIVE COMPONENT

The layman's conception of an anxious person focuses mainly on the affective aspect of anxiety. Laymen commonly describe it in terms of the individual "looking anxious" or "sounding anxious." If pressed for further details they say that the person looks "drawn" or "taut," that his "face is a mask of fright or terror," or simply that he "looks scared."

With regard to how the anxious person sounds, the layman commonly says that "he sounds scared" or "he sounds nervous" or "he sounds terrified" or "he talks too loud" or "he speaks too low." I have taken the common expressions of anxiety and grouped them together under the affective component. I have roughly graded their intensities in order that comparisons might be made among the different patients at a given time or in the same patient at different times.

The grading of intensities also enabled me to record the vicissitudes in the affective component in a single patient and among different patients. The intensity of the affective component is designated as follows:

Key

   1. Calm: facial muscles appears relaxed; voice denotes no evidence of alarm or fear in tone, quality, or volume.
   2. Slight: facial appearance of apprehensiveness that is slight, usually intermittent or transient; voice denotes "concern," usually transiently or intermittently; there may be slight elevation in the pitch or intonation and a slight increase in volume (much less commonly the volume is decreased); voice may be tremulous.
   3. Moderate: facial appearance of apprehensiveness that is quite constant; voice denotes obvious apprehension, usually with an elevation in pitch to a point of being shrill; volume is usually considerably increased, often to the point of shouting (much less commonly the volume is decreased and the patient may speak only intermittently).

4. Severe: patient in panic; facial expression of terror even to the point of grimacing; voice denotes agonizing terror, usually shrill, shouting, or screaming (at times patient is mute).

I note, once again, that all the descriptive qualifications included under the affective component of anxiety are not of necessity present at the same time, or if present at the same time may not be of equal degree as designated under these four quantitative levels. In general, the greater the degree of anxiety, the more numerous, constant, and intense are the qualitative factors of the affective component.

AUTONOMIC COMPONENT

The autonomic component refers specifically to that aspect of overt anxiety that is mediated through the autonomic nervous system. There is a large body of information in which various experimenters have attempted to relate physiologic change to alterations of emotion, including anxiety. There has been no clear-cut work done in which the quantitative degree of the autonomic phase of anxiety has been related to the intensity of the other components of anxiety. Lacey (1956) considered the Law of Initial Value in his studies of autonomic data. He suggested plotting a stimulus or response as a function of prestimulus level. This was a valuable contribution; however, the great bulk of material in which autonomic studies have been correlated with emotion has been contradictory in spite of the use of polygraphic recordings. Much of this contradiction lies in the fact that the initial values were not considered.

During the past decade there has been a greater concentration on "clever" electrophysiological gadgets than there has been in logical experimental planning. Electronic recordings have been "pawned off" in lieu of solid clinical understanding.

It is most difficult to devise a reliable method of accurate evaluation of the degree of change in the quantitative degree of autonomic functioning in response to stress or therapy. This is particularly so if one is not using polygraphic techniques. In my studies vital signs, including pulse, respiration, and blood pressure (systolic and diastolic), were recorded at two-minute intervals in all patients who were given hallucinogenic agents. In some of these patients psychogalvanometric studies were also performed. Vital signs were taken every five minutes for all patients who also had psychogalvanometric studies performed.

An evaluation of this material does not lend itself readily to being quantitated on a four-point scale as was done for the other components of anxiety.

With regard to the autonomic phase of anxiety, I will concentrate on the relationship of the autonomic changes to alterations in the other components and in relationship to the appearance and amelioration of other psychiatric symptoms and signs.

VERBAL COMPONENT

The verbal component of anxiety refers to that aspect of overt anxiety expressed through the pressure of speech, meaning the total number of words spoken over a given period of time. I am not referring in this instance to the quality, tone, or expression of speech, which was referred to and included under the affective component.

Evaluation of the verbal component required a very clear appreciation of what the usual pattern of speech was in a given individual during a relatively calm or calm period. In many of our patients it was not possible to observe such a preexperimental period.

The verbal expressions of those patients undergoing craniotomy and lobotomy under local anesthesia were recorded in their entirety. In this way the verbal production could be compared with the simultaneous recording of motor functioning, affective change, and autonomic change. This detailed comparison among the various components of anxiety was also possible in many patients who received hallucinogenic agents. In these two groups the recordings could be played back time and time again in order to obtain fairly accurate evaluation. The evaluations of the pressure of speech made in the other patients was not based on recordings but rather on empiric clinical evaluations.

In all instances, the intensity of the verbal component was designated as follows:

Key

1. Calm: conversational pattern.
2. Slight: rapid speech, usually intermittent or transient; less often intermittent or transient blocking of speech.
3. Moderate: frequent and rather continuous periods of rapid speech; difficulty in curbing flow of words; less commonly a rather persistent blocking of speech.
4. Severe: patient in panic; extreme logorrhea; unable to stop flow of words (in very rare instances patient became mute).

SUMMARY

The final evaluation of the quantitative degree of anxiety is based on the consideration of all four components described above. The highest level attained by any single component determined the final designation as to the intensity of anxiety. For example, if a patient had a motor component of two, an affective component of three, and a verbal component of two, the final designation as to the level of anxiety would be three. Another example might be that of a patient with a motor component of four, affective component of three, and verbal component of two; the final level of anxiety in this case would be four.

If one fails to consider the various components of anxiety, there will be definite errors and a clear concept of the intensity of anxiety will not be appreciated. Too often, psychiatrists measure only the affective component of anxiety and, to a lesser degree, the verbal component and neglect the other aspects.

I would like to reemphasize a point that was stressed in Chapter 1: namely, that anxiety is not a static phenomenon, rather, that it is fluid and must be considered in dimensions of time, quantity, quality, rate, and direction of change. This technique of evaluation is an attempt in the clinical application of this conceptual scheme.

3

THE INTERRELATIONSHIPS AMONG
THE COMPONENTS OF MOUNTING ANXIETY

In this chapter, as in the chapters that follow, my aim is to describe in detail a quantitative change in the degree of anxiety. I am not concerned here with theoretic constructs of any type, be they philosophic, psychologic, anatomic, neurophysiologic, or biochemic. I am not concerned with the semantic differences between emotions and feelings, the theories of the arousal of feelings, distinctions between emotion and perception, the relationship between emotion and memory, or the relationship between emotion and thought.

I am concerned here purely and simply with the step-by-step clinical description of the changes that occurred in an individual when he or she manifested an increased degree of anxiety in response to different kinds of stress. The patients included in this study were, for the most part, exposed to severe or even extreme stress. Therefore, the total degree of change .measured was not minute and did not require an elaborate stretch of the imagination to be recorded. Indeed, when considered as a whole, the changes were gross and readily discernible. Some aspects of the changes were transient or fleeting phases and required more intimate observation for their recording.

It will become clear that I am not speaking about rarities or individual oddities when I speak of these transient phases. The patterns and phases of patterns I describe are those seen in the vast majority of overtly anxious patients. Exceptional trends or curiosities will be noted only in passing and will not be confused with the basic, frequent, reproducible clinical patterns.

Why is there a need for a detailed description of what happens as a patient manifests mounting anxiety in response to stressful stimuli? It would seem that the psychiatric and psychologic literature is replete with papers dealing with many aspects of anxiety and that among these aspects there must be some that describe in detail the step-by-step changes that occur as the degree of anxiety mounts. Actually, though there are many clinical and laboratory observations dealing with anxious patients, there are almost none that afford a clear picture of the patient as he becomes increasingly anxious and of the relationship of other clinical psychiatric symptoms and signs to the quantitative degree of anxiety. Not even those papers dealing with autonomic changes occurring as the result of stress, in which polygraphic recordings are presented, correlate the quantitative degree of anxiety with the polygraphic recordings. Particularly, they do not correlate the polygraphic recordings of autonomic functionings with the other components of anxiety and with other clinical psychiatric symptoms and signs.

As I pointed out before, there are but a few clinical and research studies that consider the initial quantitative degree of anxiety let alone the fluctuations in the degree of anxiety. Without these prestimulus or pretherapeutic descriptions it is impossible to evaluate, compare, or reproduce the descriptive material with any accuracy. In Chapter 11, "The Law of Initial Value," I will indicate the importance of a knowledge of the prestimulus or pretherapeutic level of anxiety.

I also should like to point out that there are many studies recorded in the literature in which very minor degrees of stress are used in order to produce anxiety. This particular type of study does not adequately evaluate the changes that occur in the quantitative degree of anxiety. However, based on these very limited objective data, elaborate generalizations and theories have been drawn that have confused two generations of psychiatrists and psychologists.

THE NEED FOR DISCRIMINATE OBSERVATION

Anxiety, in its overt development, is not a gross, mass phenomenon. It is a highly organized psychophysiologic process and follows rather definite patterns that are predictable in the vast majority of patients. In failing to describe in detail the development of the "anxious state," the massive psychiatric, psychologic, and physiologic literature dealing with anxiety has implied that anxiety is a psychophysiologically amorphous phenomenon without characteristic laws of development.

As a result of this traditional view of anxiety as a phenomenon without definite patterns of clinical development, psychiatrists and psychologists viewed anxiety en masse, so to speak, and have been traditionally blinded to the fact that anxiety is a patterned process having orderly relationships with other psychic processes. This statement should not come as a shock. Why would one suppose that psychic functioning would be any less organized than cardiovascular, gastrointestinal, or renal functioning?

This blind spot in psychiatric thinking is unfortunate, because it is important for clinicians and research workers alike to recognize these basic biodynamic mechanisms from both a diagnostic and a therapeutic stand-point. It is doubly unfortunate because the information is readily available to all observers if simple, direct but discriminate powers of examination are used.

SUBJECTIVE ANXIETY

The subjective phase of anxiety cannot be measured by direct means. Our knowledge of it is mainly through personal experience, which cannot be accurately compared with the experience of others. Our semantic parameters in describing subjective anxiety are vague and primitive. Sub-jective anxiety is usually portrayed in such vague terms as "anxious," "tense," "nervous," "jittery," "on edge," "jumpy," "restless," "uneasy," "excited," "frightened," "scared," and "shaky."

Some formal psychologic tests purport to indicate the presence and degree of this "inner anxiety," but it is not known whether these tests reflect overt anxiety or the covert anxiety that precedes the overt expression. For example, it is not known how often covertly manifested anxiety precedes or follows the overt manifestations. Even using the broad concepts employed in my studies as parameters, I am unable to answer this question from the material I have collected during the past eighteen years.

I do not imply that the relationship between reported and nonreported anxiety cannot be studied, but that such a study will necessitate the use of many more subtle and epicritic parameters than those used in this study. This is purely a technical problem that should and, I am sure, will be solved. More refined psychologic and perhaps biochemical parameters will become available. Perhaps some of the work in multivariant factor analysis may help. The present biochemical parameters are too gross and unstable to be reliable in such an investigation. Eventually, however, the biochemi-cal parameters may offer some simple and direct information relative to the question posed here.

It further may be postulated that, as soon as one can describe and measure the minutiae of what is now the subjective, or nonreported, phase of anxiety, then by definition these minutiae will become phases of overt anxiety. The corollary of this would be that all subjecive expressions of anxiety will eventually be seen as components of overt, or reported, anxiety and that ultimately all anxiety that is subjective will be at the same time objective.

Perhaps this will be so at some distant period, but this theoretic possibility is not my concern in this book. Mine is the infinitely less sophisticated problem of describing overt anxiety in terms of four very general parameters based on the systematic observation of hundreds of psychiatric patients over a period of more than eighteen years.

OBJECTIVE ANXIETY

As an introduction to this subject, it would be well to state that the results of all my studies employing the various research techniques outlined in Chapter 1 indicate that *there is a direct relationship between the quantitative degree of anxiety and the formation of other clinical psychiatric symptoms and signs.* The symptoms and signs, such as phobias, obsessive-compulsive states, hypochondriasis, psychosomatic difficulties, paranoid delusions, hallucinations, indeed all clinical psychiatric symptoms and signs, appear to be secondary defense mechanisms against the pressures of mounting anxiety. This statement in itself is not new; it was suggested, though not proven, by Freud.

The vast majority of patients, no matter what the nature of the original stress, demonstrate definite evidence of mounting anxiety before there is any evidence of other clinical psychiatric symptoms and signs. Statistically speaking, this means that, of a total of more than 600 patients studied in this research project, more than 80 percent demonstrated signs of increased anxiety as the initial response to stressful situations of various types (see Table 3.1). This does not mean that all the components of anxiety described in Chapter 2 were present before the appearance of other clinical symptoms and signs. It does mean that in more than four fifths of the patients one or more of the components of anxiety were clearly observable before the introduction of other clinical symptoms and signs into the overt clinical complex.

Table 3.1 demonstrates that signs of anxiety precede other symptoms and signs in the clinical scene no matter what stressful situation is used. Twenty-one (84.0 percent) of the twenty-five patients receiving mescaline or lysergic acid demonstrated this pattern. Similarly, forty (93.0 percent) of the forty-three patients undergoing a large craniotomy under local anesthesia also manifested increased anxiety prior to the appearance of other clinical symptoms and signs. Finally, 519 (83.2 percent) of the 624 patients who appeared for psychiatric care owing to decompensation secondary to socioenvironmental stresses also revealed this clinical relationship.

The samples in the instances where hallucinogenic agents or craniotomy under local anesthesia were used as anxiety-producing forces are not large. However, the results of these two experimental techniques, particularly craniotomy under local anesthesia as the stress-producing force, were of such magnitude as to make them of great moment. I also would like to point out that many of the patients receiving hallucinogens received one or both of the drugs one or more times, so that many more than twenty-five experiments were carried out.

TABLE 3.1. Appearance of Overt Anxiety Prior to Other Clinical Signs and Symptoms

Sources of Stress	Number of Patients	Patients Manifesting Increased Anxiety Prior to Other Symptoms or Signs	
		Number	Percent
Mescaline and LSD-25	25	21	84.0
Craniotomy under local anesthesia	43	40	93.0
Socioenvironmental	624	519	83.2

The observation of forty-three craniotomies performed on schizophrenic patients under local anesthesia represents a unique experimental group in the vast psychiatric literature. It was accomplished by a highly integrated staff of more than ten people working together for more than two years. The fact that almost all the forty-three patients studied during the craniotomy demonstrated definite evidence of increased anxiety prior to the appearance of other symptoms and sings is a significant observation. All signs of change were readily available to me by direct observation and by equipment recording various components of anxiety. These situations were very stressful, and the changes recorded were very definite and by no means subtle.

I believe that the 93.0 percent figure recorded in patients undergoing craniotomy is the most accurate of those I have quoted because my observations of these patients during the experiments were constant and uninterrupted over a period of several hours. It is my firm opinion that, when more refined clinical and mechanical recording techniques are available, it will be found that an increased level of anxiety precedes the appearance of other symptoms and signs in all instances, no matter what the source of the stress.

But, thus far, I have referred only to the fact that mounting anxiety precedes other clinical phenomena in the vast majority of instances. This observation raises questions as to which aspect or component of anxiety appears first. What are the interrelationships among the various components of anxiety and their relationships to the appearance of such other clinical data as phobias, obsessions, compulsions, and hypochondriasis? I found, as all students of psychologic behavior should expect, that mounting anxiety is an orderly, well-documented, reproducible process.

MOTOR COMPONENT (TENSION)

I have indicated previously that the term *tension* is used in this work as synonymous with the motor component, or phase, of anxiety. In Chapter 2 I presented, in detail, my method of evaluating the quantitative fluctuation in the intensity of the motor component (tension) in a given patient. For the reader's convenience, I will repeat the classification briefly:

Key

1. Calm: no overt restlessness; no tremor; no increase in muscle tonus to palpation.

2. Slight: increased movement that is usually intermittent; unable to remain still for long periods; may involve upper or lower limbs; tremors, if present, usually are fine and intermittent; slight increase in muscle tonus, which may be inconstant.

3. Moderate: increased movement (hyperactivity) that is usually constant and usually involves all limbs; tremors are more frequent, may be coarse, usually involve upper limbs but also may involve head and mouth; increase in muscle tonus (passive movement may be difficult).

4. Severe: patient in panic; thrashing about wildly, incessant movement; tremors, coarse and fine, of all limbs and face; marked increase in muscle tonus to the degree that some patients are almost completely rigid and fixed.

An increase in the motor component of anxiety heralds mounting anxiety in the vast majority of patients in response to different types of stress (see Table 3.2).

For example, of the twenty-one patients who received mescaline or LSD-25 and who manifested anxiety prior to the appearance of other psychiatric symptoms or signs, seventeen (81.0 percent) demonstrated an increase in the motor component prior to the appearance of other components of anxiety.

The studies of patients undergoing craniotomy under local anesthesia are even more striking. In these experiments thirty-five (88.0 percent) of the forty patients manifesting increased anxiety prior to the appearance of other clinical psychiatric symptoms and signs demonstrated an increase in the motor component as the heralding sign of anxiety.

Referring to Table 3.1 it will be noted that 519 of the 624 patients who were psychiatrically ill as a result of socioenvironmental stresses demonstrated increased anxiety prior to other symptoms and signs. It was felt that adequate clinical data were available in only 454 of these 519 patients to determine the order of appearance of the motor component of anxiety in relationship to the other components. Of these 454 patients 385 (84.8 percent) showed an increase in the motor component prior to the appearance of other signs of anxiety.

These figures show a high order of concurrence independent of the source of stress. They suggest that the aspect of anxiety mediated via the pyramidal and extrapyramidal motor fibers into the striate muscle system is the pathway through which the clinician and the experimenter, with a great deal of assurance, can expect the initial indications of overt anxiety to be manifested.

TABLE 3.2. Frequency with Which Motor Component (Tension)
Is the Initial Manifestation of Anxiety

Sources of Stress	Number of Patients Manifesting Increased Anxiety Prior to Other Symptoms or Signs	Patients Manifesting Increase in Motor Component Prior to Other Signs of Anxiety	
		Number	Percent
Mescaline and LSD-25	21	17	81.0
Craniotomy under local anesthesia	40	35	88.0
Socioenvironmental	454	385	84.8

It is self-evident that careful observation of the patient is necessary to detect the earliest signs of increased tension. If the patient is not under continuous, careful visual and tactile surveillance, the opportunity to follow the complete development of the symptom or symptom complex is lost. Of equal importance is the fact that, if the earliest manifestations are missed, the opportunity to treat the patient while the level of anxiety is low and prior to the formation of other symptoms and signs may be lost. This statement follows a general rule of medicine, which in essence states that "the earlier the lesion is discerned and appropriate treatment instituted the easier and more successful are the results."[1]

---

[1] I am fully aware that there is no *always* in medicine and that there are exceptions to this statement (that is, permitting a cellulitis to localize before approaching a lesion surgically). However, many psychiatrists and nonmedical psychotherapists have no meaningful appreciation of the general biologic dictum that the sooner the effects of any trauma are treated, the better the results.

I have previously noted that the degree of tension was based on the study of muscle tonus, tremors, and active and passive movement. A knowledge of basic neurophysiology would lead one to predict, even expect, that an increase in muscle tonus will precede the appearance of tremors or restlessness. This was in reality what was observed in all the patients who were under close, constant observation during the period of mounting anxiety. This increase in muscle tonus prior to tremors or restlessness was noted in all forty-three of the patients undergoing psychosurgery and in those patients receiving intravenous mescaline. These changes are subtle and will be missed by the observer unless palpation is one means of clinical observation. Of course, electromyographic recordings would readily detect these changes because they reflect the earliest involuntary neurogenic discharge into the striate muscle end organ.

Tremors that are the result of involuntary, uncoordinated, simultaneous contractions of agonist and antagonist muscles were less commonly noted than restlessness, except in those patients in whom free movement was inhibited. For example, if free movement was inhibited by repeatedly instructing the patient before and during the experiment to remain still, tremors became very apparent. They rapidly lessened and usually disappeared when permission to move was given. During psychosurgical procedures free movement in all the patients was restricted by virtue of their being strapped to the operating table. In those instances where free movement was restricted, the increase in muscle tonus was followed by a rapid development of tremors, usually beginning in the upper limbs, that spread over the body to include the neck, face, back, and lower limbs.

In instances where there is a marked and rapid increase in anxiety all manifestations of the motor component may develop clinically so rapidly as to prevent a chronologic differentiation in the appearance of its components. When the level of anxiety is relatively low, the various phenomena may be transient or intermittent. Their constancy, in general, is proportionate to the level of anxiety.

It will be pointed out later that the degree of tension may spontaneously decrease with the appearance of the affective and other components of anxiety. The decrease in these instances is usually slight and transient; on rare occasions, it may be rather marked and persistent. More commonly, however, the degree of tension increases after other aspects of anxiety appear in response to continued severe stress.

Conversely, inhibition of the expression of the motor component by verbally ordering the patient to remain still or by strapping the patient may often be followed by a marked increase in the other components. Similarly, if one blocks the affective or verbal expressions of anxiety, an increase in the motor components and in the autonomic phase usually results. In summary, I found that *for a given quantum of anxiety there appeared to be reciprocal quantitative relationships among the various components of anxiety.* This finding will be elaborated on later in this chapter.

The multiple methods by which tension may be reduced can be simply alluded to at this point but will be described in detail in Chapter 12. In certain patients the purposeful introduction of physical pain will temporarily reduce tension. In other instances, permitting the patient to cause the therapist pain also may temporarily decrease the motor component.

Similarly, encouraging an increased expression of the other components, such as the affective and verbal aspects of anxiety, may transiently have the same effect. Further, if one encourages the expression of a secondary defense mechanism, such as a phobia or an hallucination, the overt expressions of tension can be reduced. These mechanisms of tension reduction are most dramatically seen in acute experimental situations where they can be titrated and manipulated in the attempt to control anxiety.

AFFECTIVE COMPONENT

In Chapter 2 I described the measurement of intensity of the affective component according to the patient's facial expression and the tone, quality, and volume of the patient's voice. The method of quantification was described in detail. The evaluation technique is reviewed here briefly.

Key

1. Calm: facial muscles appear relaxed; voice gives no evidence of alarm in quality and volume.
2. Slight: facial appearance of apprehensiveness that is slight, usually intermittent or transient; voice denotes "concern," usually intermittent or transient with a slight elevation in pitch or intonation and slight increase in volume (much less commonly the volume decreases); voice may be tremulous on occasion.
3. Moderate: facial appearance of apprehensiveness that is quite constant; voice denotes obvious apprehensiveness; it is often high pitched or even shrill; volume of voice is usually considerably increased to the point of shouting (much less commonly volume is decreased).
4. Severe: patient in panic; facial expression of terror to the point of grimacing; voice denotes agonizing terror; it is shrill, shouting or screaming (in rare instances it may be volume decreased in volume to the point where the voice is not audible).

I would like to point out once again that all the descriptive qualifications included under the affective component of anxiety are not necessarily present at the same time or present in equal degree under these four quantitative designations. In general, the greater the degree of anxiety, the more numerous, constant, and intense are the qualitative factors included under the affective component.

In the previous section, on tension, I reported that *in response to stress an increase in the motor component precedes the appearance of the affective component of anxiety in more tyan 80 percent of all patients studied, no matter what type of stress was employed.* This pattern held for all diagnostic categories, whether the patient was psychotic or neurotic, whether the patient was diagnosed as having schizophrenia, an organic mental syndrome, a manic-depressive psychosis, or a type of characterologic disorder.

Expressed in another way, *mounting affect either heralds the presence of anxiety or clinically appears at about the same time as the motor component in less than one fifth of all patients.*

When the change in affect precedes the onset of tension, it is very dramatic. For example, one patient, shortly after the intravenous administration of mescaline, appeared apprehensive and shouted incoherently. At the same time she remained seated in her chair and disclosed no clinical evidence of increased muscle tonus. This continued for more than five minutes before she demonstrated increased muscle tonus, restlessness, and other overt signs of mounting tension. (I should mention that there were definite changes in autonomic dysfunction during the period of the increased affect in the absence of increased tension.) In line with this observation I will point out later that *there is an intimate temporal relationship between affect and autonomic change.*

I have noted a similar sequence of events during the performance of craniotomies under local anesthesia. In these instances there was the additional factor of the patients being restrained on the operating table by straps that inhibited the free display of restlessness, which tends to accentuate the affective component.

I must repeat, however, that this precedence of a mounting affective component prior to the appearance of the motor component is the gross exception to the general rule.

If the affective component is deliberately or unintentionally inhibited, the motor aspect of anxiety may be accentuated. This inhibition of affect may occur in several ways. For example, if the patient is admonished to "remain quiet and speak calmly" one may note an increase in motor tonus, tremulousness, or restlessness. Usually this increase in tension is transient, but it may persist for many minutes.

I would like to point out that if affect is inhibited, the motor component is not the only aspect or phase of anxiety that may be increased. For example, *it is most unusual to inhibit the affective phase without producing an increase in the autonomic parameters.* Similarly, if the patient is admonished to "speak quietly" or is told forcefully to "stop being so excited" a marked increase in the pressure of speech, meaning the speed and rapidity of speech, may be noted. This is another example of how expressions of anxiety, when inhibited in reference to one component, will be manifested overtly by an increase in another component.

In an attempt to inhibit affect, one may inhibit just the vocal aspect, the patient then may express affect purely through facial expressions to the point of grimacing. (In reality, as I have mentioned before, facial expression represents a specialized aspect of the motor component.) If facial expression is blocked by admonishing the patient to "stop making faces" the affect can be limited so that it is expressed solely through a marked increase in the quality and volume of the patient's voice.

Any attempt to inhibit the affective phase out of rhythm, so to speak, with its normal relationship to other components of anxiety is usually only temporarily successful if the sources of stress are not decreased or removed. If one attempts to inhibit the affective phase for more than a brief period while permitting an increase in the source of stress, an explosion finally may occur, with the patient shouting and thrashing about wildly. This may come about precipitously and suggests that the predilection to express anxiety by means of a specific component may cause a covert building up of anxiety when this specific component is forcefully inhibited for a period of time.

At a later point I will indicate that a few patients with obsessive-compulsive or paranoid manifestations will, while fighting to conceal any overt facial or verbal expressions of anxiety, disclose the intensity of anxiety by a spilling-over process resulting in the accentuation of the motor aspect.

One can manipulate the relative intensity of the motor and affective aspects in some patients under acute experimental situations. For example, it can be done following the administration of lysergic acid or mescaline. I indicated before that in some patients, as the affective phase emerges following the phase of the motor component, the latter may seem to decrease in intensity. Usually this decrease is slight and transient.

A much more common process, if the source of stress is maintained at a steady level or is increased in intensity, is for the degree of tension to continue to increase without any apparent interruption paralleled by an increase in the affective phase.

In response to sudden, overwhelming stress a few patients will demonstrate an apparent simultaneous rapid emergence of all components of anxiety in an en masse crescendo pattern. This pattern is also not common; usually the elements that make up anxiety will be observed to develop step by step.

Later in this chapter, I will continue with the chronologic relationship among the affective, autonomic, and verbal components of anxiety in response to continued stress. I will emphasize that an increase in the autonomic phase appears to parallel an increase in the affective phase to the point that it was difficult to determine which took precedence over the other. Only when the affective aspect was inhibited did the autonomic expression take precedence or become dominant over the affective expression.

The verbal aspect is in almost all instances the last of the four components of anxiety, studied in detail in this investigation, to appear as anxiety juggernauts under the pressure of persistent sources of stress.

At this point, before proceeding to a consideration of the autonomic component of anxiety, I would like to interject an important corollary pertaining to the affective component, namely its relationship to the appearance of other clinical psychiatric symptoms and signs.

THE AFFECTIVE COMPONENT'S RELATION TO THE APPEARANCE OF
OTHER SYMPTOMS AND SIGNS

One of the most striking observations and perhaps one of the most significant clinical observations made during this entire study was the fact that the *various psychiatric symptoms and signs, such as phobias, obsessive-compulsive states, hypochondriasis, psychosomatic complaints, paranoid delusions, and hallucinations, in almost all instances begin to manifest themselves only after the definite appearance of the affective component of anxiety*.

This observation was constant no matter what order or kind of stress was employed to produce anxiety. An appreciation of the relationship between the existence of the affective component and the emergence of other symptoms and signs is of prime importance if the physician is to understand fully psychodynamic developments in a specific patient and if he is to be in a position to offer treatment at a moment of his own choosing.

Without this awareness symptoms and signs may develop under the very nose of the psychiatrist and become a fixed part of the patient's psychic defense mechanisms before the therapist is fully aware of their existence and especially of the degree of anxiety associated with them. I cannot point out too forcefully that there is a certain momentum to anxiety, just as there is a momentum to an accelerating vehicle. The greater the momentum, the more defenses necessary to contain the anxiety.

The various psychiatric symptoms and signs are compensatory attempts by the psyche, indeed, by the entire biodynamic *Gestalt*, to blunt or absorb this force. If these compensatory mechanisms are sufficient, the biodynamic force we call *anxiety* will be absorbed and contained. If they are insufficient, psychic anarchy occurs.

My clinical material is sufficiently complete to permit a correlation between the affective component of anxiety and the emergence of other clinical symptoms and signs in approximately 500 patients. This is summarized in Table 3.3.

TABLE 3.3 Frequency with Which an Increase in the Affective Component of Anxiety Precedes Other Symptoms and Signs

Sources of Stress	Number of Patients Manifesting Increased Anxiety Prior to Other Symptoms or Signs	Patients Manifesting Increase in Affective Component Prior to Other Symptoms or Signs	
		Number	Percent
Mescaline and LSD-25	21	19	90.5
Craniotomy under local anesthesia	40	36	90.0
Socioenvironmental	476	418	87.8

It will be noted that the sources of stress appear to have little bearing on the relationship. Nineteen (90.5 percent) of the twenty-one patients to whom mescaline and/or lysergic acid were administered, and who manifested increased anxiety prior to the appearance of other symptoms and signs, demonstrated an increase in the affective component prior to the onset of these secondary defense mechanisms. Similarly, thirty-six (90.0 percent) of the forty patients undergoing a craniotomy under local anesthesia, who had evidenced signs of increased anxiety before demonstrating other symptoms and signs, manifested an increase in the affective component of anxiety prior to these other symptoms and signs.

In Table 3.1 I noted that 519 of the 624 patients in whom socioenvironmental factors were the sources of stress manifested mounting anxiety as indicated by an increase in one or more of the four components prior to the appearance of other symptoms and signs. The histories of 476 of these 519 patients were considered adequate for a study of the relationship between the appearance of other symptoms and signs and the affective component. Four hundred and eighteen (87.8 percent) of the 476 patients demonstrated a dfinite increase in the affective component prior to the appearance of the other symptoms and signs.

Derivation of Statistics

The statistics used in this aspect of the study may very well be confusing to the reader. I have already noted in Table 3.1 that in my study of mounting anxiety I considered that only 519 of the 624 patients who became emotionally ill owing to environmental stresses showed increased anxiety, as indicated by one or more of the components of anxiety, prior to the appearance of other clinical symptoms and signs. This conclusion was gathered from patients' histories and by direct examination.

The remaining 105 patients were not included in this study. They were a mixed group in that they undoubtedly included at least two categories of patients, namely, (1) patients manifesting anxiety prior to the appearance of other clinical symptoms and signs but for whom the histories and my direct observations were simply inadequate to record the relationship of the affective component to the appearance of these other symptoms and signs, and (2) possibly a few patients who were exceptions to the general rule, for reasons of which I am as yet unaware, and who manifested no affective component of anxiety prior to the formation of secondary symptoms and signs.

I have placed both these categories of patients in one group of 105 (16.9 percent) of the 624 patients who had become ill owing to external environmental stresses. I firmly believe, however, that in the vast majority, and perhaps in all, of these 105 patients I have merely failed to detect the signs of increased anxiety prior to the other symptoms and signs.

In all of the discussions dealing with the motor component of anxiety, as noted in Table 3.2, only 454 of the 519 patients who manifested increasing anxiety prior to other symptoms and signs were considered by history and by direct examination reliable in demonstrating a relationship between the motor component and other components. The other sixty-five patients, representing 15.2 percent of the 519, included two categories of patients: (1) patients who in reality did have an increase in the motor component of anxiety prior to the appearance of other manifestations of anxiety, but for whom my histories and direct examinations were inadequate, and (2) patients who were exceptions to the rule and in whom components of anxiety other than tension heralded the presence of anxiety.

Here also I have included both these categories in one group and have treated these sixty-five patients as if they were cases in whom tension was chronologically preceded by other components of anxiety in response to stress. In reality, I do not believe this to be so, but feel it was the safest and most conservative way in which to handle the problem.

In all the discussions dealing with the affective component in relationship to the appearance of other clinical symptoms and signs (see Table 3.3), only 476 of the 519 patients who manifested increased anxiety as the result of socioenvironmental stress prior to the appearance of other symptoms and signs were considered reliable in demonstrating this relationship. The remaining forty-three patients probably included at least two categories of patients: (1) patients in whom an increase in the affective component of anxiety did precede the appearance of other clinical symptoms and signs but in whom I failed to detect this fact, and (2) patients who were the rare exceptions to the general rule and in whom secondary symptoms and signs occurred prior to an increase in affect.

Here too, I included both categories in one group and treated them statistically as if all forty-three were part of the second category.

The reader may be confused also as to why I was able to include 479 of 519 patients in a study of the affective component in relationship to other symptoms and signs, though I included only 454 of these same 519 patients in the study of the motor component. The answer is simply that clinically it is easier to study affect than it is to study the motor component of anxiety if electromyography is not employed as a tool.

It is important to note that *it is uncommon, indeed rare, for such symptoms and signs as phobias, obsessive-compulsive states, hypochondriasis, psychoso-*

*matic symptoms, and hallucinations to appear when only the motor com-
ponent of anxiety has increased before there has been an increase in the
affective component.* However, because an increase in the motor aspect
precedes the affective phase in the vast majority of patients, as I have
pointed out in detail in Table 3.2, both the motor and affective expressions
of anxiety are clearly evidenced, with rare exceptions, prior to the appearance of other clinical symptoms and signs.

In Chapter 4 I will deal in greater detail with the emergence of symptoms
and signs in response to mounting anxiety, their relationship to one other,
their qualitative change in response to an increase in stress, and their
appearance in response to repeated bouts of anxiety.

AUTONOMIC COMPONENT

In Chapter 2 it was stated that the vital signs (pulse, respiration, and
blood pressure) and psychogalvanometric recordings were the autonomic
modalities studied in detail when hallucinogens and craniotomies performed under local anesthesia were the sources of stress. Vital signs were
recorded for the group of patients who responded with great anxiety to
environmental stress, but with no consistent pattern.

As I mentioned before, a reliable measurement of the quantitative
change in the autonomic component of anxiety was not possible in these
studies. All my attempts to correlate the autonomic changes on a quantitative basis led only to frustration and not to any accurately reproducible
data.

I will, therefore, stress the qualitative aspects (especially the chronologic
development) of the autonomic phase or component of anxiety in relationship to the other three components.

All the studies of patients who received hallucinogens and those undergoing craniotomies while in a completely conscious state indicate that *alterations in autonomic functioning closely parallel changes in affect.* I feel
that this is a most important correlation, for it implies a common or
closely related denominator between these two components whether it be
in their sources or in the psychobiologic mode of transmission.

The relationship between affect and autonomic change could be consistently noted in a given patient in response to repeated bouts of stress.
Some patients exposed to socioenvironmental stress, hallucinogens, and,
finally, to a craniotomy demonstrated this close temporal relationship
between the affective and autonomic components in response to all three
types of stress.

Because the change in the autonomic component paralleled a change in affect, autonomic change also preceded the appearance of other clinical symptoms and signs in most patients. This will be documented in detail in Chapter 4 and in Chapter 9, "Psychosomatic Disorders."

Some confusing problems did appear in the early phases of my study. For example, one patient ill for many years with a syndrome diagnosed as schizophrenia, pseudoneurotic type, in response to an initial dose of mescaline demonstrated the usual appearance of an increase in tension as the initial expression of anxiety followed by an increase in the affective and autonomic components. The patient thrashed about in a very animated fashion and almost destroyed a piece of research equipment. In a subsequent experiment, prior to giving mescaline, the same patient was admonished to "remain still." This admonition was repeated many times during and following the injection of mescaline. To my surprise, he appeared very calm with regard to neuromuscular activity. However, his pulse and systolic blood pressure increased rapidly and was paralleled by marked facial grimacing. As the systolic pressure rose to almost 200 millimeters of mercury I wondered whether the rise resulted from the patient's displaying so little motor activity. I told the patient that he could move about in his chair. He began to writhe and contort, manifesting an extremely severe amount of muscle tension, tremor, and restlessness. Within ten minutes the pulse and systolic blood pressure had dropped to slightly above normal limits.

Following this experience I performed many experiments to test the relationship between the various components of anxiety with specific reference to the autonomic phase. Some patients were ordered not to speak after the administration of an hallucinogen or during phases of a craniotomy. In many instances this produced an increase in the motor component of anxiety and an increase in autonomic change. As I mentioned before, it also reflected itself in grimacing, which may be considered as being a highly qualitative aspect of motor functioning as well as an aspect of the affective component aspect of anxiety.

Other patients were admonished not to speak and not to move. This usually resulted in a marked increase in the autonomic aspect of anxiety.

As with the motor and affective aspects of anxiety, as the source of stress was maintained or increased in severity, the autonomic phase of anxiety also usually increased.

Finally, I would like to record the fact that *schizophrenic patients in a state of catatonic stupor in some instances demonstrate a reversal of the usual chronologic pattern of anxiety development*. A change in the autonomic component of anxiety in a number of instances was the first manifestation of mounting anxiety in these patients, preceding any change in the motor or affective components. In three pateints exhibiting varying degrees of catalepsy, autonomic changes in response to increasing stress was the only manifestation of mounting anxiety. This was observed in two of the three patients as they were being interviewed. One patient demonstrated this pattern under the stress of an interview and later in response to hallucinogens.

It may be argued by some that a patient in a state of catalepsy already has a highly developed motor phase of anxiety. Some would disagree with this. Several other patients in retarded catatonic states, but not in cataleptic states, demonstrated the same apparent paradoxic relationship between the autonomic and motor components of anxiety.

VERBAL COMPONENT

As described in detail in Chapter 3 the verbal component of anxiety refers to the pressure of speech, namely, the number of words spoken over a given period of time, and not to the quality, tone, or expression of speech. These latter qualifications are related to the affective component. The following is a summary of the gradations of intensity included under the verbal component of anxiety:

Key

1. Calm: unhurried, conversational pattern.
2. Slight: rapid speech, usually intermittent or transient; less often there is intermittent and transient blocking of speech.
3. Moderate: marked increase in frequency and rapidity of speech that is quite consistent; difficulty in curbing the flow of words (less commonly there is marked blocking of speech).
4. Severe: patient in panic; logorrhea; cannot stop flow of words (in rare instances patient may become mute).

An increase in the verbal component was the last of the four components of anxiety to appear in response to stress. This very striking and consistent observation is illustrated in Table 3.4. Of the twenty-five patients receiving hallucinogenic agents twenty-one demonstrated a state of increased anxiety. Nineteen of the twenty-one patients whom I was able to observe adequately manifested an increase in the verbal component last. Two of the patients who were actively hallucinating at the onset of the experiment showed an increased pressure of speech about the same time that there was an increase in the motor component.

All the patients undergoing craniotomies under local anesthesia demonstrated an increased level of anxiety at some point during the operative

TABLE 3.4. Frequency with Which Verbal Component of Anxiety Is the Last of the Components to Appear

Sources of Stress	Number of Patients Manifesting Increased Anxiety	Patients Manifesting Increase in Verbal Component as Last Component	
		Number	Percent
Mescaline and LSD-25	21	19	90.5
Craniotomy under local anesthesia	43	40	93.0
Socioenvironmental	160	121	75.6

procedure. In forty (93 percent) of these forty-three patients the verbal component was very definitely the last expression of anxiety to appear.

I performed another series of studies on patients who came for psychiatric help owing to socioenvironmental pressures. I subjected 160 of these patients to questions and statements calculated to produce anxiety. Only the relationships among the motor, affective, and verbal components of anxiety were recorded. From my mescaline and craniotomy studies I expected a very high correlation with the verbal component being the last manifestation of anxiety. I found this to be so in 121 (75.6 percent) of the 160 patients. Once again, I do not believe this group of observations to be as accurate as those obtained from my studies of patients undergoing lobotomies or receiving psychedelic drugs.

As pointed out before, the motor, affective, and autonomic phases of anxiety in the vast majority of instances are increased prior to the appearance of other clinical psychiatric symptoms and signs. An increased pressure of speech may occur before, at the same time, or after the appearance of other symptoms and signs.

Most patients did not manifest this increase in verbal flow until after the appearance of secondary symptoms and signs. In other words, the secondary symptoms and signs might first appear with the patient speaking at a relatively normal rate of speed and only then an increased verbal flow might be noted.

I have emphasized previously in this chapter that an increased pressure of speech at times could be precipitated by curtailing the motor or affective phases. Once again it must be pointed out that the usual observation was that, as anxiety increased in response to continued or mounting stress, there was an increase in all of the components including the verbal component.

Summary

This chapter documents the fact that mounting anxiety is not a haphazard psychophysiologic process but is functionally hierarchically ordered. The various components of anxiety can be manipulated by different maneuvers, but at best the effects of these manipulations are transient or temporary.

In Chapter 4 I will deal with the interrelationships of the various secondary symptoms and signs in response to increasing levels of anxiety.

4

MOUNTING ANXIETY AND SYMPTOM FORMATION

In Chapter 3 I observed that there appeared to be a direct relationship between the quantitative degree of anxiety and the appearance of other clinical psychiatric symptoms and signs, a definite increase in the level of anxiety before these symptoms appear, and, in the vast majority of patients, a measurable increase in the affective component of anxiety before the formation of these symptoms and signs.

In this chapter I will refer to these symptoms and signs as *secondary defense mechanisms* or *secondary symftoms and signs*. The word *secondary* is used because it was my objective observation that anxiety is the primary clinical response to stress. My studies have confirmed that there is a mounting level of anxiety before the appearance of these phenomena, which appear to be automatic secondary psychic defense mechanisms whose purpose is to contain or reduce the level of primary anxiety that is the initial response to stress. The secondary defense mechanisms include such common clinical phenomena as phobias, hypochondriasis, conversion states, obsessive-compulsive states, psychosomatic problems, paranoid manifestations, illusions, delusions, and hallucinations.

There appears to be a threshold of anxiety, unique for each patient, beyond which the secondary defense mechanisms are called into play.

Exactly why each patient's threshold of anxiety is unique was not obvious to me in my investigations, and it remains one of the questions as yet unanswered in clinical psychiatry. However, it was a very definite and repeated observation.

Sometimes the overt degree of anxiety decreased following the appearance of a secondary symptom or sign, that is, it was noted to be less than it was prior to the appearance of the symptom. This was usually just a

39

transient phenomenon (ten to sixty minutes) in patients studied under the effects of hallucinogenic agents or during the performance of a craniotomy, when constant observations could be made. However, some patients became relatively calm following the appearance of one or more symptoms, this relative calm being maintained for longer periods of time (as long as several hours).

Similarly, this calmness or decreased level of anxiety could be noted in some patients treated in an office setting over a period of many days. For example, it was not uncommon for a very anxious patient to develop a phobic reaction and as long as the phobic situation was avoided appeared calmer than he or she had been prior to the formation of the symptom. Similarly, when compulsive patterns came into play, as long as the patient carried out the compulsion he appeared to be considerably more relaxed than before the symptom became evident.

At times this decrease in anxiety in response to the appearance of a secondary symptom may just involve a decrease in the affective phase of anxiety without a concomitant decrease in the motor aspect. On other occasions both the motor phase and the affective phase of anxiety may be reduced.

As mentioned above, *this relative decrease in the level of anxiety following the appearance of a secondary symptom is the exception rather than the rule, for the secondary symptom usually appears without any noticeable decrease in the quantitative degree of anxiety.*

The number of symptoms and signs that are formed seems to be related to the quantitative degree of anxiety. If the source of stress is maintained or increased in intensity, the number of symptoms that manifest themselves increases. It appears that, as the level of anxiety mounts, more and more of the secondary defense mechanisms are brought into play in an attempt to diminish or perhaps to buffer against the increasing anxiety. There appears to be a certain threshold of anxiety that must be overcome before a second or third symptom or sign becomes overt.

One could note that as some patients became more anxious a symptom would appear transiently and then disappear as the stress-producing anxiety decreased and then return once again as the patient was subjected to more stress. These clinical reactions could be titrated with great sensitivity and predictability in some patients who were undergoing craniotomies.

The above-mentioned patterns brought to my mind various mental images, such as an engineer attempting to stop the forward rush of a runaway locomotive by applying ever-increasing pressure on his brakes. Perhaps a better mental image would be one of a man rolling down a precipitous mountainside grasping for objects that would break his fall. He grasps for a rock that may or may not contain his fall; it may slow him down termporarily, but if it is not sufficiently strong he will continue to fall. He then grasps at a small bush. If this is sufficiently strong it will stop him or at least slow him down. If this does not hold him he will fall still farther. Perhaps he will grasp for a tree that will stop his fall. If none of these objects stop him he may fall over a precipice. This would be comparable to a break with reality in which psychic anarchy prevails, as in the instance of a severe state of schizophrenic decompensation.

I could not determine from my work why a specific symptom appeared at a particular time in a given patient who was under great stress. I could not confirm or disprove the multitude of theories as to symptom formation, theories that vary with each author's particular school ties. Stressful situations resulting in mounting anxiety trigger the appearance of a symptom or sign or a series of symptoms and signs. The nature of these secondary defense mechanisms that appear in response to the mounting levels of anxiety most likely is related to hereditary and congenital imprints and past cultural experiences.

It is extremely difficult in an acute experimental setting, which lasts at the very most for a few hours, to differentiate between the foreboding or terror of the immediate situation and the anxiety generated from past situations. Patients who had a history of hypochondriasis reacted more intensely to autonomic changes than did other patients. For example, patients with a history of hypochondriasis and in whom cardiac manifestations were prominent at times rapidly became terrorized when tachycardia secondary to the administration of hallucinogens appeared. One then noted unmistakable fear of the immediate situation blanketed by the conditioning of terror stemming from the past.

This also could be demonstrated for patients who had a past history of phobias. If, following the use of an hallucinogenic agent, a patient with a history of severe claustrophobia was to be confined in a very small area, an immediate reaction, often of catastrophic magnitude, could be precipitated. This effect was obtained in one patient who had received LSD-25 by suggesting that the room was becoming smaller. This verbal picture was sufficient to produce a state of terror. A similar experiment had been tried on the same patient in the absence of hallucinogenic drugs without precipitating the phobic response.

The long-held concept that a state of free-floating anxiety exists prior to the formation of various symptoms was confirmed. With the development of a particular symptom the overt free-floating anxiety may be completely or partially ameliorated.

An example of this phenomenon was noted in a patient undergoing a craniotomy under local anesthesia.

Case History

This patient had a history of obsessive-compulsive symptoms and signs. During the early phase of the operative preparation he demonstrated increasing muscle tonus and then restlessness. His voice and facial expression denoted the intensity of his anxiety. The patient's pulse rate increased from 82 to 130 beats per minute, and his respiratory rate increased from 20 to 38 per minute. When he was asked "Why are you so restless?" he answered "I don't know. I'm scared." "Are you afraid of the operation?" "No. Yes. But it's more than that. I'm afraid of everything. I'm afraid things are going to happen." "What things?" "Something may happen to my folks. I won't get my job back. It's even more than that. I'm scared of everything." "What things?" "I can't explain it. Everything. It feels as if something terrible will happen."

Fifteen minutes later, at a point when the periosteum over the calvarium was being incised and reflected, the patient counted aloud and at the same time counted his fingers and beat out a count with his feet. This obsessive-compulsive pattern was in the form of a repetition of numbers one to seven. As the patient carried on his ritualized obsessive-compulsive counting, his restlessness and heightened muscle tonus gradually subsided. The terror in his voice disappeared, and his facial muscles lost their tautness. The pulse rate decreased to 88 beats per minute and respirations dropped to 24. When the patient was asked "How do you feel now?" he answered "Much better. I'm not so scared now."

In a number of instances I deliberately encouraged the development of secondary symptoms during the course of craniotomies in an attempt to temporarily contain the patient's anxiety. At best these maneuvers were only successful for short periods of time in an acute experimental situation in which the sources of stress were severe and persistent. The pattern that commonly develops is the situation in which the free-floating anxiety is temporarily blunted by the appearance of a secondary symptom. As the sources of stress remain constant or become more severe, the free-floating anxiety, or pan-anxiety state, becomes more severe despite the presence of the secondary symptom. In some instances this process may be repreated several times in a given patient as additional symptoms appear.

These examples have practical clinical application as I will illustrate in detail in Chapters 14 and 15. In instances in which the free-floating anxiety is partially contained by or attached to a newly formed symptom psychiatrists and psychotherapists may be lulled into a false sense of security and are prone to exaggerate the level of apparent clinical improvement. In reality the improvement merely represents a changing of the form of emotional energy without necessarily representing a significant decrease in the total quantum of anxiety.

The first symptom to appear in response to an increased level of anxiety does not depend on the source of stress employed to produce the anxiety. For example, if a patient had a clinical history of a phobic reaction as the initial symptom, this same phobic response developed as the initial symptom in almost every instance, whether a psychedelic agent was later administered or the patient was finally exposed to a craniotomy under local anesthesia.

Similarly, *the sequence of symptom appearance in situations where more than one symptom was manifested in response to a stressful situation was the same for all types of stress in a given patient.*

Certain rules regarding the appearance of symptoms and signs were noted. Some symptoms characteristically emerge late in a symptom complex. Psychosomatic symptoms rarely exist as an isolated clinical psychiatric pattern, but rather they usually appear in a mosaic with other secondary symptoms and signs. Also, a psychosomatic symptom is seldom the first in the parade of symptoms and signs. It usually evolves only after other secondary defense mechanisms are present.

Characteristically, illusions and hallucinations appear last in a chain of symptoms. The only exception to this observation was noted in a few catatonic patients, whose first overt symptoms were hallucinations. If intense stress is maintained, increased anxiety results, and the manifest content of the hallucination becomes more primitive and fragmented. The hallucinations may then also involve other senses.

In subsequent chapters detailed elaborations of the relationship among anxiety, dreams, hallucinations, and psychosomatic symptoms will be presented.

Another phase of my studies was concerned with whether individual patients have essentially the same sequence of symptom appearance in response to repeated bouts of marked anxiety occurring secondary to recurrent stress of the same or different types.

My studies indicated that *the vast majority of patients show essentially the same sequence of symptom appearance with each bout of anxiety whether the same or different types of severe stress are used. The number of symptoms manifested roughly seem to depend on the quantitative degree of anxiety on each occasion.* The results of some of these studies are summarized in Table 4.1.

TABLE 4.1. Similarity of Symptom Appearance in Response to Repeated Bouts of Anxiety

Sources of Stress	Number of Patients	Patients Demonstrating Similar Response to Repeated Stress	
		Number	Percent
Craniotomy under local anesthesia	38	33	87.0
Socioenvironmental	208	171	82.2

Very clear results with regard to this aspect of the investigation were noted in schizophrenic patients undergoing craniotomy under local anesthesia. Thirty-eight of the forty-three patients investigated during the course of craniotomies had two or more episodes during which there was a marked increase in the level of anxiety in response to the stress of the operation. Thirty-three (87.0 percent) of these thirty-eight patients showed essentially the same sequence of symptom appearance with each bout of anxiety. I will describe in Chapter 5 how the individual periods of anxiety were ameliorated, but at present I reiterate the observation that the sequence of symptom formation was almost always the same with each occurrence of rising anxiety.

In a study of 350 patients who were followed during the course of psychotherapy in combination with psychotropic drugs, 208 had two or more episodes in which they manifested acute, severe psychiatric flare-ups. These observations could be compared with one another and with the material in the patients' histories. One hundred and seventy-one (82.2 percent) demonstrated similar responses to the recurring environmental stresses. The pattern of symptom appearance was essentially the same for all patients.

A knowledge of the patient's pattern of symptom appearance is of great importance to the psychotherapist for the earlier an emotionally ill patient is seen, particularly if he is seen prior to the formation of secondary defense mechanisms, the more readily he responds to treatment. The various symptoms were viewed by me as lines of defense. The greater the the number of symptoms that were evident, the more lines of defense against the stressful situation that had been called into play. The secondary defense mechanisms appeared to work by the method of anxiety containment, which when successful prevented a further increase in anxiety. Hallucinations, in part, appeared to function in the same way. However, I will point out in Chapter 8 that hallucinations appear to have a second relationship to anxiety, namely that of anxiety decompression.

5

THE INTERRELATIONSHIPS AMONG
THE COMPONENTS OF DECREASING ANXIETY

Quantitatively, decreasing anxiety is not a gross, mass phenomenon; rather, it is a highly organized process and follows rather definite patterns that are predictable in the vast majority of patients.

I have observed that the intensity of anxiety must be decreased first before a symptom or succession of symptoms disappears. There appears to be a certain threshold below which the degree of anxiety must fall before a symptom or sign will disappear. This threshold is unique for each patient. A transition period exists in which a symptom is relatively denuded of its original emotional impact prior to the complete clearing of the symptom. This phenomenon can be observed very dramatically when improvement is rapid as in instances in which intravenous psychotropic drugs, psychosurgery under local anesthesia, or psychotherapy in combination with psychotropic drugs is used to treat extremely anxious patients.

As one might expect from the patterns noted with increasing stress, the various components of anxiety are not ameliorated simultaneously in response to various treatments.

The process of decreasing anxiety, both in regard to the relationship of the various components of anxiety to one another and the relationship of decreasing level of anxiety to symptom amelioration, was observed in response to many different psychiatric treatments. The treatments that were used are: (1) intensive reconstructive psychoanalysis; (2) psychoanalytically oriented psychotherapy; (3) psychoanalytically oriented psychotherapy in combination with psychotropic drugs; (4) intravenous phenothiazines to block the effects of mescaline and/or lysergic acid and for the treatment of severely agitated schizophrenic patients; (5) electro-shock therapy; and (6) lobotomy performed on conscious schizophrenic patients under local anesthesia.

Though many patients were exposed to only one type of treatment, many were exposed to two or more therapies at different times. In this manner, the patterns and rates of response to different therapies in the same patient could be compared. For example, individual patients were treated on different occasions by (1) intensive psychoanalysis and psychotropic drugs; (2) psychoanalytically oriented psychotherapy and psychoanalytically oriented psychotherapy in combination with psycho-tropic drugs; (3) psychoanalytically oriented psychotherapy, psychoana-lytically oriented psychotherapy in combination with psychotropic drugs, and intravenous phenothiazines; (4) psychoanalytically oriented psycho-therapy, psychoanalytically oriented psychotherapy in combination with psychotropic drugs, intravenous phenothiazines, and electrochock therapy; (5) psychoanalytically oriented psychotherapy in combination with psychotropic drugs and electroshock therapy; (6) intravenous phenothi-azines used to block the effects of mescaline and/or lysergic acid and lobotomy under local anesthesia; (7) intravenous phenothiazines (in very agitated schizophrenic patients) and electroshock therapy.

Many of the patients who were lobotomized had long, detailed histories in which all types of therapy had been utilized prior to coming under my supervision. Because I did not observe these previous therapies I did not quote them in this book.

The relationship between a reduction of the intensity of the various com-ponents of anxiety and the amelioration of secondary symptoms and signs did not vary with the different types of therapy. Only the rate of improve-ment depended on the type of therapy used.

The rate of decrease in the quantitative degree of anxiety depended on a number of factors. First, as mentioned above, the type of treatment was extremely important. The rate of change secondary to lobotomies or intravenous phenothiazines was incomparably more rapid than with the other types of treatment. Changes could occur during the course of a lobotomy within a matter of minutes. Similarly, with the use of intravenous chlorpromazine a lessening in the degree of anxiety was noted to begin in approximately five to ten minutes. These rapid alterations permitted a panoramic view of the relationship of the various components to the secondary symptoms and signs.

Second, *the greater the degree of anxiety at the time treatment is insti-tuted the more rapid the rate of decrease in response to treatment.* If anxiety is rapidly mounting at the time treatment is instituted a decrease in anxiety does not occur as rapidly as it does if the level of anxiety had already reached the plateau before treatment is instituted. Similarly, if the level of anxiety is already spontaneously decreasing prior to treatment the rate of decrease is very rapid. These factors will be discussed in greater detail in Chapter 11, "The Law of Initial Value."

MOTOR COMPONENT

With all forms of therapy a definite lessening of the motor component was the first sign of a decrease in the quantitative degree of anxiety in the vast majority of patients (See Table 5.1.) This finding is confirmed in from 74.3 percent ot 89.7 percent of the patients observed, depending on the method of treatment used.

TABLE 5.1. Frequency with which a Decrease in the Motor Component (Tension) Is the First Sign of Decreasing Anxiety

Type of Therapy	Number of Patients	Patients Demonstrating a Decrease in Motor Component Prior to Other Components	
		Number	Percent
Psychoanalytically oriented psychotherapy plus drugs	241	179	74.3
Electroshock	206	168	81.6
Intravenous phenothiazines			
1. To block effects of hallucinogens	23	19	82.6
2. In agitated schizophrenic patients	79	67	86.1
Lobotomy under local anesthesia	29	26	89.7

The most striking observations, and I believe the most accurate, were those obtained in schizophrenic patients who were lobotomized under local anesthesia. Nine of the original forty-three patients had to be anesthetized for various reasons before the lobotomy proper was begun. However, of the thirty-four remaining patients only twenty-nine were sufficiently co-operative to enable an accurate evaluation of the relationship of the motor component to the other components of anxiety in response to the lobotomy. Each of the five patients not included in the statistics had developed a severe, acute organic mental syndrome either immediately prior to or during the initial stage of the lobotomy proper. This prevented an accurate evaluation of the various components of anxiety and their relationships to the other clinical factors in these particular five patients. In twenty-six (89.7 percent) of the twenty-nine lobotomized patients included in this aspect of the study a decrease in the motor component heralded clinical improvement (Table 5.1).

Three hundred and fifty patients were treated with psychoanalytically oriented psychotherapy in combination with phenothiazines. I felt that I could obtain accurate information concerning the motor aspect of anxiety in 241 patients. In 179 (74.3 percent) of these 241 patients the motor aspect of anxiety appeared to be the first to be decreased in response to treatment. I do not consider the findings obtained with this particular type of treatment to be as accurate as those noted during the course of lobotomy, because the clinical changes occurred much more slowly and the opportunity for continuous intensive observation possible with the lobotomized patients was not feasible with patients receiving psychotherapy in combination with tranquilizing drugs.

Electroshock therapy presented an excellent opportunity to observe the various components of anxiety in relationship to one another. Two hundred and six patients in a series of 234 who received electroshock therapy presented data that I considered reliable with regard to the various components of anxiety. One-hundred and sixty-eight (81.6 percent) of these 206 patients demonstrated that the motor componenet was the first to be decreased. They required three to five electroshock treatments, in the vast majority of instances, to effect a definite lessening of the motor component, although there were a few patients who showed definite changes after two treatments and, in rare instances, after a single treatment.

Intravenous phenothiazine therapy also offered an excellent opportunity to study the various components of anxiety. Twenty-three schizophenic patients of the original twenty-five who had received mescaline or lysergic acid had responded to these drugs with a marked degree of anxiety. Nineteen (82.6 percent) of these twenty-three patients, rapidly improving after receiving chlorpromazine intravenously, manifested a decrease in the motor aspect as the initial response to treatment.

In another group of seventy-nine very agitated schizophrenic patients who were given intravenous injections of phenothiazines as emergency treatment sixty-seven (86.1 percent) exhibited a decrease in the motor component prior to any change in the other components of anxiety. As in the instance of patients undergoing lobotomy under local anesthesia, the opportunities to evaluate these patients very closely was excellent and the changes that occurred were highly dramatic.

In some patients I could observe that tremors and active movements decreased in intensity as the initial indication of a decrease in tension. A marked decrease in muscle tonus was the last parameter of the motor aspect of anxiety to be reduced in intensity.

The decrease in tension was affected by several factors. Some patients in restraints during treatment evidenced a temporary increase in muscle tonus. A more rapid decrease in tension was noted in unrestrained patients. As I related in Chapter 4, some patients were admonished not to speak and to mask any facial expressions denoting anxiety. This, at times, caused a temporary increase in a motor component that had already begun to be ameliorated. However, this increase, if it was noted at all, was only transient.

I want to make it clear that the improvement in the motor component prior to the improvement in the other components was relative. As improvement was noted in the other components in response to continued treatment, further amelioration in the motor component continued.

In Chapter 3 I referred to the experiment wherein I deliberately caused pain to the patient or permitted or encouraged the patient to try to hurt me by forcefully squeezing my hand; this often resulted in a temporary and slight decrease in the degree of tension during the period of increasing anxiety. Indeed, as already noted, these techniques were used in some patients during the course of the craniotomy as a temporary method to contain mounting anxiety. The opposite effect resulted if physical pain was deliberately introduced during the lobotomy proper. *If pain was inflicted on a patient while the lobotomy was in progress, signs of improvement, such as a decrease in the components of anxiety secondary to the lobotomy, could be reversed so that all components of anxiety were again increased until the painful stimulus was removed.*

AFFECTIVE COMPONENT

A decrease in the affective component of anxiety follows a decrease in the motor component in response to all forms of therapy. This rule is independent of the clinical, nosological, diagnostic classification that may be applied to a patient's illness. The patients will evidence less restlessness, less tremor, and less muscle tonus before the tone, quality, or volume of voice or facial expressions, which mediate the quality of apprehension or foreboding that I call the affective component, are ameliorated.

There are exceptions to this rule, but they are infrequent (see Table 5.2). In Table 5.2 I have attempted to indicate the frequency with which a decrease in the affective component occurred before a decrease in the motor component. I have also attempted to note the number of patients in whom a decrease in the affective component appeared to parallel a decrease in the motor component. In this second group I do not really believe that the components decreased at the same time, but rather that this overlap is a reflection of the grossness of my clinical techniques of observation.

TABLE 5.2. Frequency with Which a Decrease in the Affective Component Precedes or Parallels a Decrease in the Motor Component

Type of Therapy	Number of Patients	Patients Demonstrating a Decrease in Affective Component	
		Prior to Decrease in Motor Component	Parallel to Decrease in Motor Component
Psychotherapy and drugs	241	8	54
Electroshock	206	5	33
Intravenous phenothiazines			
1. To block effects of hallucinogens	23	3	1
2. In agitated schizophrenic patients	79	4	8
Lobotomy under local anesthesia	29	1	2

It will be noted that the instances of overlap are greatest in those patients in whom my clinical observation was not continuous owing to the fact that treatment took place over a long period of time. For example, patients who received psychoanalytically oriented psychotherapy in combination with psychotropic drugs and patients who received electroshock therapy demonstrated a greater number of overlaps in comparison with those patients who received intravenous phenothiazines or who were lobotomized under local anesthesia. In these last two groups of patients my clinical observations were constant throughout the experimental procedures. To reiterate, in all types of therapy the number of patients in whom the affective components decreased prior to the amelioration of the motor component was negligible.

Facial expressions often became more normal before there was a change in vocal expression. Perhaps, as mentioned before, this is so because facial expression is merely a highly qualified version of motor activity.

If the patient is inhibited in any way from expressing the affective aspect of anxiety by restriction of facial or verbal expression the process of improvement can be reversed temporarily. A decrease in the affective component is usually paralleled by a change in the autonomic component. I can not positively state that the affective or autonomic component preceded one or the other. However, both components preceded a decrease in the verbal component.

Usually, as the patient improves, the affective component continues to decrease in intensity coinciding with the continued improvement in the motor component.

THE AFFECTIVE COMPONENT AND ITS RELATIONSHIP TO THE
AMELIORATION OF SECONDARY SYMPTOMS AND SIGNS

The secondary symptoms and signs did not begin to disappear until there was a definite decrease in the affective component of anxiety. It appeared that it made little difference how much improvement in the motor component had occurred; if the affective aspect was unchanged the secondary symptoms remained.

In many patients the affective component was decreased for a variable period of time before there was any disappearance of the secondary symptoms and signs. As I related previously, a given symptom or group of symptoms did not completely disappear until the degree of anxiety decreased below a certain threshold, which appeared to be unique for a given patient. There was a transition period in which the symptom appeared to be stripped of the original emotional impact. This period of emotional denudation varied from minutes to days depending on the patient and, of course, on the type of therapy employed.

A few clinical examples will illustrate these relationships.

Case Histories

1. A twenty-four-year-old male patient, whose diagnosis was schizophrenia, pseudo-neurotic type, had been ill for eight years and had been subjected to many types of psychiatric treatment including intensive psychotherapy, electroshock therapy, and various sedatives. Among his symptoms was a hypochondriacal preoccupation with his chest that at times assumed the quality of a somatic delusion. During the course of a craniotomy, the patient became very restless and showed an extreme increase in the affective component of anxiety. He grimaced and cried out in a terrified fashion that "the movements of his chest were restricted and that he was unable to breathe."

At that point the lobotomy was begun. When the medial half of the right frontal lobe was sectioned a moderate decrease in the motor component of anxiety occurred. The patient's affect in relation to the hypochondriacal preoccupation with his chest remained unchanged. When the medial half of the left frontal lobe was sectioned the patient's facial grimacing disappeared and the tone and volume of his voice improved. For a period of five minutes he continued to complain about his chest. However, these complaints now were made in a quiet fashion, stripped of all overt qualities of terror. After the lateral half of the left frontal lobe was sectioned he stopped complaining about his chest entirely. When he was questioned about his chest at this point, he stated, "It's fine!"

This entire lobotomy was accomplished in approximately fifteen minutes. The patient's complaints about his chest, denuded of the great affect, lasted for approximately five minutes. It was extremely dramatic to observe a patient who had been struggling with his bonds, crying out with great apprehensiveness, and terrified by the thought that horrible things were going to happen to his chest in a few minutes quickly showing muscular relaxation and calmly complaining about his chest in a very offhand, matter-of-fact fashion and finally ceasing to complain.

2. A twenty-six-year-old single male schoolteacher had a history of severe difficulty in social and vocational performance when he was placed under any stress. For six months he wrestled with the problem of whether he should marry a young woman whom he had dated for a year. He became extremely anxious. He was restless and paced incessantly. At times he screamed out loud and smashed the walls with his hands. He was completely incapacitated vocationally and socially. The patient was obsessed with the paranoid idea that his fiancée was unfaithful. His apprehension and periods of rage necessitated emergency hospitalization.

Shortly after admission, an intravenous injection of 75 milligrams chlorpromazine was given over a two-minute period. Approximately five minutes later the patient's wild thrashing rapidly decreased. He continued to cry out, "She's cheating! She's fooling around!" Eight minutes after the completion of the injection the marked apprehension denoted in the patient's facial expression changed and the shrillness and anguish of his voice disappeared. However, he continued to repeat softly, "She's fooling around. She's cheating on me." Little if any emotion now was associated with these words. Eleven minutes after completion of injection, the patient's complaints stopped. When he was asked how he felt, he stated, "I feel much better." When I questioned him twenty minutes after the completion of the injection he stated that he really didn't believe that his fiancée was cheating on him, but he knew that she had had sexual relationships with another man prior to meeting him and his feelings of insecurity were so marked that he was constantly apprehensive that she might find another man's attention more appealing to her, though he had no realistic grounds for his fears.

3. A thirty-nine-year-old housewife had a ten-year history of intermittent overt psychotic behavior characterized by referential trends and religious preoccupations. She became extremely agitated and did not respond to oral phenothiazines or to pheno-thiazines in combination with supportive psychotherapy in the hospital setting. Electro-shock therapy was instituted. She was given a treatment on three successive days. After her third treatment she was less restless, stopped pacing, and was able to sit quietly in a chair. However, on questioning, she continued to be obsessed with the idea that "the neighbors are against me and are telling the priest dirty things about me." The patient was then given three more treatments on alternate days. After the fifth treatment the affect associated with her delusion was markedly decreased. She did not spontaneously complain that the neighbors were speaking against her. However, if she were asked about this question, she answered in a very bland fashion, "My neighbors are still talking about me."

Following the eighth treatment the delusions disappeared even when she was questioned about them directly. She stated "No, I don't believe they are talking about me." This disappearance of delusional material was not owing to an organic mental process as evidenced by the fact that she was able to remember very clearly that she had had this particular delusional pattern prior to the institution of electroshock treatment.

4. A thirty-one-year-old woman had a long history of intermittent claustrophobia. Whenever there was a conflict involving her mother, the claustrophobic symptoms be-

came more marked. Psychoanalytically oriented psychotherapy was begun on a twice-a-week basis. During the first two weeks of therapy she became increasingly anxious following a very dramatic scene with her mother. The patient was started on oral chlorpromazine. After an initial dose of 100 milligrams per day, the dose was increased to 200 milligrams per day. After three days the patient was much less restless. On palpation I noted that muscle tonus was considerably decreased and all tremors had disappeared. However, she still cried out in fear when she came up the elevator to my office. On the fifth day following the institution of chlorpromazine she appeared more relaxed and spoke much more calmly. She stated that the elevator continued to terrify her but to a far less degree. On the twelfth day following the onset of drug therapy she failed to spontaneously mention the elevator. When this was called to her attention she stated calmly, "I was not conscious of the elevator today."

Table 5.3 indicates the frequency with which the affective component of anxiety is decreased before the amelioration of any secondary symptoms and signs. One notes that the total number of patients in whom my observations appeared adequate for the purpose of relating a decrease in the affective component to the amelioration of secondary symptoms and signs differs from the number of patients quoted in Table 5.1, in which I compared the motor component to the other components of anxiety. A greater number of patients treated with the combined psychotherapy-tranquilizer technique and electroshock therapy was available for evaluation because it is much easier to observe the relationship of the affective component to the amelioration of secondary symptoms and signs than it is to relate a decrease in the motor component to the other components of anxiety. This also accounts, in great measure, for the relatively higher percentages noted in Table 5.3 than in Table 5.1.

TABLE 5.3. Frequency with Which a Decrease in the Affective Component Precedes the Amelioration of Secondary Symptoms and Signs

Type of Therapy	Number of Patients	Patients Demonstrating Decrease in Affective Component Prior to Amelioration of Other Symptoms and Signs	
		Number	Percent
Psychotherapy and drugs	278	229	82.4
Electroshock	217	188	86.6
Intravenous phenothiazines			
1. To block effects of hallucinogens	23	19	82.6
2. In agitated schizophrenic patients	79	74	93.7
Lobotomy under local anesthesia	29	26	89.7

In Chapter 6 the relationship of the various secondary symptoms and signs to one another as the level of anxiety is decreased will be described in detail.

AUTONOMIC COMPONENT

The relationship of the autonomic component of anxiety with the other components and with an amelioration of secondary symptoms and signs was observed primarily in patients who had received intravenous phenothiazines and in patients undergoing psychosurgery under local anesthesia. I could not quantify the decrease in the autonomic phase with any reliability.

I consistently noted that a decrease in the autonomic component of anxiety paralleled a decrease in the affective component. A change in one usually was accompanied by a change in the other. This means that a decrease in the motor component (tension) preceded a decrease in the autonomic phase in almost all instances.

It also means that there usually was a decrease in the autonomic phase prior to the disappearance of secondary clinical symptoms and signs as a result of treatment. Once again, the rate change in great measure depended on the type of therapy employed. I also noted that those patients who had a very elevated level of autonomic function showed the most dramatic decrease in response to therapy in keeping with the Law of Initial Value. Patients treated with more than one type of therapy showed similar patterns of improvement with regard to the autonomic aspects of anxiety. As mentioned above, only the rate of change differed.

Some catatonic schizophrenic patients showed a different pattern of improvement with regard to the decrease of the various components of of anxiety. Several patients in catatonic stuporous states demonstrated a decrease in the autonomic component as heralding a decrease in anxiety. This was also seen in two patients in catatonic excitements who were given intravenous phenothiazines.

The following example is illustrative.

Case History

A twenty-three-year-old woman had a long history of uncontrolled bouts of excitement that appeared precipitously after prolonged family conflicts. She was admitted to the hospital in a wildly agitated state, dominated by auditory hallucinations in which she heard voices planning her doom. She was given 100 milligrams of chlorpromazine intravenously over a 4½ minute period. Three minutes after the completion of the injection, the patient's systolic blood pressure, which had been recorded at 210 milli-meters of mercury, began to drop. This preceded any change in muscle tension or any change in affect. The drop in blood pressure continued. Five minutes following the completion of the injection of chlorpromazine the systolic blood pressure was recorded at 152 millimeters of mercury.

At that point a very noticeable decrease in tension was noted, and two minutes later her facial expression and quality of vocal expression changed. For three more minutes the patient's hallucinations continued, but were denuded of overt affect. The patient, on questioning, blandly related the hallucinations. Eleven minutes following the completion of the injection the hallucinations stopped.

The relationship of the autonomic component and the amelioration of psychosomatic disorders will be discussed in Chapter 9.

The observations noted during psychosurgery with regard to the autonomic component of anxiety, I believe, are of great importance from a psychophysiological standpoint. A decrease in the affective and autonomic component of anxiety did not appear usually until the medial halves of each frontal lobe were sectioned. Neuroanatomically speaking, these cuts severed the projection fibers of the dorsomedial nucleus of the thalamus as they radiate to the orbital aspect of the frontal cortex. These fibers radiate to areas 9, 10, 11, and 12 of Brodmann. (Area 8 will not be considered, although it receives dorsomedial thalamic projections, because it differs from the others in being grossly motor in function.) These projection fibers to the orbital gyri of the frontal lobe are systematically organized as shown by McLardy and Davies (1949) and Meyer and Beck (1954). The thalamic nuclei that project to the medial orbital regions of the frontal lobe contain the magnocellular portion of the dorsomedial nucleus. This nucleus receives fibers from the hypothalamus and from the periventricular system.

The changes that occurred in autonomic and affective functioning were very dramatic when these medial sections of the frontal lobes were made. The improvements occurred within two to three minutes after the completion of the section. These changes raise the question in humans of the relationship of affective change to autonomic functioning mediated through the dorsomedial nucleus of the thalamus and hypothalamus. They suggest that the transmission of affect may be the same, in great measure, as that of autonomic functioning as an expression of higher neural activity.

I do not want the reader to gain the impression that I believe that the hypothalamus or the thalamoreticular system is the center of emotion. This type of thinking would be a return to the naive, neuroanatomic theorization prevalent for almost fifty years. However, the data that I presented suggest a very close relationship between affect and autonomic change.

In general, as the patient continued to improve all components of anxiety tended to improve. In other words, the motor component continued to improve although it was the first modality to show a degree of amelioration.

If, during therapy, the patient was restricted with regard to his movement or was admonished not to express anxiety verbally or facially, the process of autonomic improvement could be reversed and a temporary increase in autonomic functioning could be precipitated. However, as soon as the patient was permitted free motor and affective expression he again showed an improvement in the autonomic phase. Once again this illustrates the close interrelationship among the various components. They serve as a mechanisim of overflow or compensation for one another.

VERBAL COMPONENT

The verbal component of anxiety is the last of the four components studied in this book to decrease in response to treatment. I have only noted the verbal component to be the first to decrease in response to treatment on one occasion. One commonly notes a decrease in the motor, affective, and autonomic components of anxiety with the pressure and content of speech remaining the same. On occasion one notes a decrease in the verbal component prior to the disappearance of secondary symptoms and signs. By this I mean that the secondary symptoms and signs are expressed or repreated more slowly. Occasionally the secondary symptoms and signs will all but disappear, but the patient may mouth fragments of these secondary symptoms and signs in a slow, rambling, monotonous fashion devoid of affect. The patient is often unaware that he is being repetitious.

The following cases illustrate some of these points.

Case Histories

1. A twenty-nine-year-old nurse had a long history of referential trends, intermittent alcoholism, and intermittent codeine addiction. At times her behavior was characterized by explosive outbursts of anger. She had been hospitalized on a number of occasions and had been treated by various techniques, all without avail. Psychosurgery was recommended. During the course of the craniotomy she was extremely anxious and alternately required amphetamines and barbiturates intravenously to maintain a relative level of calm.

At the moment the lobotomy was begun, the patient was extremely anxious. She demonstrated marked restlessness and marked increase in muscle tonus. Severe affective changes were demonstrated by facial grimacing and repetitive cries of "No, no, no!" The patient was terrified that she would lose contact with reality, this loss of contact representing a state of oblivion far more excruciating than any physical distress.

The sectioning of the lateral half of one frontal lobe resulted in a very slight decrease in muscle tension without any other change being noted. When the medial half of the same frontal lobe was sectioned the tension decreased to a greater degree and there was a decrease in the affective and autonomic components of anxiety. The patient continued to cry out "No, no, no!" and to relate that she was afraid of the impending oblivion.

However, these statements were now relatively denuded of the affect that had characterized them before.

After the medial of the other frontal lobe was sectioned, the patient continued to repeat "No, no, no!" However, now when she was asked how she felt, she stated "I feel fine." In response to whether the fear of oblivion was still present she answered in the negative. In response to questioning as to why she continued to say "No, no, no!" she laughed briefly and answered, "I don't know. It's silly." When this was brought to her attention, she stopped saying "No, no, no!"

2. A fifty-two-year-old housewife had a ten-year history of recurrent paranoid states in which the delusion that her husband was going to poison her dominated the clinical picture. She responded partially to repeated series of electroshock treatment given by a previous physician. She functioned at a relatively low intellectual level, and analytically oriented psychotherapy attempted by various competent psychiatrists ended in failure. The patient was seen by me in a state of extreme agitation associated with the delusion that she was in danger of being poisoned by her husband. She demanded to be hospitalized for her own protection. When she was admitted to the hospital she paced incessantly, pounded the walls, pulled her hair, and cried out repeatedly in an anguished fashion, "Don't let him kill me! Don't let him kill me!"

The patient was given 75 milligrams of chlorpromazine intravenously over a period of two minutes. Four minutes after the completion of the injection there was a noticeable lessening of her restlessness and muscle tension. Two minutes later it was noted that she continued to cry out, "Don't let him kill me! Don't let him kill me!" But now her facial expressions and quality of voice had changed to a considerable degree. At the same time she repeated these phrases, but more slowly. Four minutes later the repetitious remarks stopped. When she was asked, "How do you feel?" she stated, "I feel much better." In response to the question "Is someone going to kill you?" she answered, "I thought so, but it doesn't sound right to me now."

Experimentally, a patient who has already demonstrated a decrease in the verbal component at times can have this state reversed by just restricting him physically or demanding silence. This reversal in response to restriction, as noted before, is usually transient. In general, if effective therapy is maintained, there is a progressive amelioration of all components of anxiety.

Table 5.4 reveals the frequency with which the verbal component of anxiety appears to be the last of the components to decrease in response to various treatments. As I mentioned before, this phenomenon is usually quite striking and easy to perceive. This fact is reflected in the high frequency percentages that characterize the findings no matter what type of therapy was employed.

With regard to the use of electroshock some may maintain that the organic mental syndrome that develops secondary to this technique might confuse the evaluation. At this point I was not interested in the degree of confusion present. I was simply concerned as to whether the verbal phase of anxiety was the last of the four components to show signs of amelioration.

TABLE 5.4. Frequency with Which Verbal Component Anxiety Is the Last of the Components to Decrease

Types of Therapy	Number of Patients	Patients in Whom Verbal Component Was Last to Decrease	
		Number	Percent
Psychotherapy and drugs	267	229	85.8
Electroshock	224	189	84.4
Intravenous phenothiazines			
1. To block effects of hallucinogens	23	19	82.6
2. In agitated schizophrenic patients	79	73	92.4
Lobotomy under local anesthesia	29	26	89.7

PREFRONTAL LOBOTOMY AND THE AMELIORATION OF ANXIETY

Before ending this chapter I would like to summarize the pattern of anxiety amelioration observed as the result of lobotomy because this study is unique in all the psychiatric literature. Its uniqueness lies in the fact that all of the patients were fully conscious during the lobotomy, and accurate observations could be made during the process of sectioning the frontothalamic fibers. Following the completion of the lobotomy, continuous and direct recordings of the patient's behavior patterns were made from one and one-half to several hours. Then the patient was sent to a recovery room where he remained for at least seventy-two hours. During this period I visited the patient regularly and evaluated the patient's behavior on a systematic basis in which both quantitative and qualitative factors were recorded.

At this point I would like to describe the chronologic appearance of the initial evidences of a decrease in the intensity of the four components of anxiety in relationship to the fractional prefrontal lobotomy, in other words, in relationship to the amount of brain cut.

In order to understand the therapeutic technique some further technical explanation is necessary. For descriptive reasons we divided each frontal lobe into two halves, medial and lateral, making four quadrants that had to be sectioned. There was no routine pattern as to whether the left or right hemisphere or the medial or lateral quadrant was sectioned first. In fact, a constantly changing sequence of sectioning was carried out in an effort to determine whether unique changes in behavior might occur with particular sequences. It required approximately ten minutes to carefully complete a quadrantic leucotomy.

Perhaps the most striking observation I made was that *the amount or mass of frontal lobe tissue sectioned had a direct relationship to the qualitative and quantitative amelioration of anxiety.* In this regard the following patterns were noted:

1. After sectioning only one quadrant the initial decrease in the motor component of anxiety was recorded in sixteen patients. In only two patients were any of the other aspects of anxiety effected by the cutting of one quadrant.

2. After sectioning two quadrants eleven additional patients evidenced the additional decrease in the motor aspect anxiety. However, I now noted that eleven other patients demonstrated the initial decrease in the affective component. (In all but two patients the decrease in the motor aspect preceded a decrease in the affective component.) At this point in the leucotomy only one patient showed any change in the verbal component. Most of the patients who evidenced an initial decrease in the motor phase following the sectioning of a single quadrant showed a further improvement in the motor component following the sectioning of two quadrants.

3. When the third quadrant was cut eleven additional patients evidenced the initial amelioration in the affective aspect of anxiety. But now I also noted that eight patients demonstrated the initial decrease in the verbal component. Most of the patients who showed initial improvement in the motor and/or affective components during or following the sectioning of one or two quadrants had further improvement in these aspects.

4. Finally, with the sectioning of all four quadrants the other patients evidenced a decrease in the verbal component.

In essence then I noted that *it required less frontothalamic sectioning to produce the initial amelioration of the motor aspect of anxiety than it did to initiate a decrease in the affective component. In turn, it required less sectioning to ameliorate the affective component than was required to effect improvement in the verbal component.*

6

DECREASING ANXIETY
AND SYMPTOM AMELIORATION

As an introduction to this chapter, I would like to repeat that anxiety must be quantitatively decreased before a symptom or sign or a succession of symptoms or signs disappears.

Another cardinal point to be emphasized is the fact that a symptom or sign does not vanish until the affective component of anxiety is overtly decreased in intensity. This statement should be broadened to read *a symptom or sign does not disappear until both the affective and autonomic components are decreased*, because it appears that these two components of anxiety are ameliorated at approximately the same time in response to all types of therapy.

A patient manifesting a marked increase in all components of anxiety together with a number of secondary symptoms and signs prior to the introduction of some form of treatment might show a marked decrease in the motor aspect of anxiety without any decrease in the affective or autonomic components. In these instances there is no amelioration of the secondary symptoms and signs. Not until the affective component is decreased is there a disappearance in the secondary symptoms and signs. The reader is referred once again to Table 5.3, which indicates the frequency with which a decrease in the affective component of anxiety precedes the amelioration of secondary symptoms and signs in response to various types of therapy. *The number of symptoms and signs that disappear depends on the degree of amelioration of anxiety.*

A given symptom or sign does not seem to disappear completely until the degree of anxiety decreases below a certain threshold, which is unique for the individual patient. A transition period results in which a symptom

60

is relatively denuded of its original emotional impact prior to the complete clearing of the symptom. This transition period is usually very striking. It is not often so dramatically seen in patients treated with psychotherapy alone because the process of improvement is much more gradual.

The duration of the transition period of emotional denudation varies depending on the type of treatment used. When psychosurgery or intravenous phenothiazines were employed the denudation might last five to thirty minutes. With psychotherapy in combination with oral phenothiazines it might last for days. With psychotherapy alone, the denudation could last days or even weeks.

The same degree of anxiety decompression for all patients is not necessary to ameliorate a particular symptom, but varies from patient to patient. In a few patients I was able to observe the repeated appearance and disappearance of the same symptom before it disappeared entirely. This fluctuation in the overt status of the symptom is usually associated with a slow gradual decrease in its emotional impact as compared with that noted prior to therapy.

I could not differentiate with any consistency whether anxiety caused by current stress cleared before anxiety based on similar earlier real or apparent situations. Usually the stresses appeared fused as one force. In some patients, as therapy progressed the anxiety secondary to the more immediate situation appeared to lessen prior to any evidence of a decrease in the unconscious push. However, I noted other patients in whom the reverse was present.

The last symptom or sign to appear during the period for which anxiety is increasing is usually the first symptom to disappear as the level of anxiety is reduced. This finding should not be surprising because the last symptom to appear requires the greatest degree of anxiety, so to speak, to call it into play as a defense mechanism according to the quantum concept of anxiety in relationship to symptom appearance, which I proposed in an earlier chapter.

The type of treatment used did not determine which symptom was the first to be ameliorated. This statement was confirmed in patients who had received two or more types of therapy. Only the rate of symptom amelioration depended on the type of treatment.

Table 6.1 illustrates the frequency with which the last symptom or sign to appear was the first to be ameliorated following a decrease in the degree of anxiety secondary to different types of therapy. Those patients who were treated with psychotherapy plus drugs or electroshock therapy, in general, had been ill for a relatively brief time. This made it possible for me to determine rather accurately the exact pattern of symptom appear-

TABLE 6.1. Frequency with Which the Last Symptom or Sign to Appear
Is the First To Be Ameliorated in Response to Various Therapies

Types of Therapy	Number of Patients	Patients in Whom Last Symptom or Sign to Appear Is First To Be Ameliorated	
		Number	Percent
Psychotherapy and drugs	208	176	84.6
Electroschock	148	132	89.2
Intravenous phenothiazines			
1. To block hallucinogens	23	19	82.6
2. In agitated schizophrenic patients	79	73	92.4
Lobotomy under local anesthesia	28	26	92.8

ance and to compare how frequently the last symptom to appear was the
first to disappear.

An occasional exception to the rule was noted. Some patients with
psychosomatic problems in whom the psychosomatic disorder was the
last to appear in response to mounting anxiety did not demonstrate a
disappearance of the psychosomatic symptom as the initial response to a
decrease in anxiety if there were signs of organic tissue changes, as in some
patients with peptic ulcer, colitis, asthma, and hypertension.

*The general pattern of disappearance of symptoms and signs was the
reverse of the appearance of symptoms and signs.* This also did not depend
on the type of treatment utilized. The number of symptoms and signs to
be ameliorated appeared to depend on the intensity and duration of
treatment. Table 6.2 illustrates the frequency with which the general pattern of amelioration of symptoms and signs is the reverse of the sequence
of appearance of symptoms and signs for various types of psychiatric
therapy.

In a few severely agitated schizophrenic patients who were given
intravenous chlorpromazine I administered just enough of the drug to
ameliorate a given symptom and then withheld further medication. I could
observe the initial ameliorating effect of the drug wear off, and the symptom then would return within a few minutes. If a larger amount of
phenothiazine was then administered the reversal pattern would again
recur to the point that the symptom was blocked completely for the duration of the particular period of treatment.

I also studied patients who had two or more episodes in which they manifested severe psychiatric exacerbations on two or more occasions. It was

TABLE 6.2. Frequency with Which the General Pattern of Amelioration of Symptoms or Signs Is the Reverse of the Sequence of Appearance

Types of Therapy	Number of Patients	Patients in Whom General Pattern of Amelioration of Symptoms or Signs Is Reverse of Appearance	
		Number	Percent
Psychotherapy and drugs	208	167	80.3
Electroshock	148	124	83.8
Intravenous phenothiazines			
1. To block effect of hallucinogens	23	17	73.9
2. In agitated schizophrenic patients	79	71	89.9
Lobotomy under local anesthesia	28	26	92.8

noted that *patients demonstrate essentially the same pattern of amelioration of symptoms and signs in response to repeated therapeutic interventions.*

One hundred and forty-six patients, who were observed for more than one year, had two or more episodes in which they manifested severe anxiety with the return of symptoms and signs. One hundred and nine (74.7 percent) had essentially the same pattern of symptom amelioration in response to repeated therapy. Some of these patients were treated by psychotherapy alone; some received drug therapy in combination with psychotherapy.

Six very agitated schizophrenic patients had two or more periods of treatment in which intravenous phenothiazines were utilized. All six showed essentially the same pattern of symptom reversal.

I indicated in Table 4.1 that during the performance of craniotomies under local anesthesia many patients had two or more episodes in which they became very anxious. This afforded an excellent opportunity to study the amelioration of repeated bouts of anxiety. Many therapeutic techniques were used. A number of these therapeutic techniques will be described in detail in Chapter 12.

I would like to mention at this time that several techniques were employed, each of which depended on the type of clinical response noted in the patient. Some patients received small doses of intravenous barbiturates, usually Seconal (sodium secobarbital, Lilly). The barbiturates very temporarily alleviated anxieties produced by minor physical discomforts and the overwhelming reality of the operation.

These restricted doses of barbiturates, though initially successful in reducing anxiety, in some instances secondarily increased the level of anxiety by slightly reducing the patient's level of consciousness. In some schizophrenic patients this reduction resulted in distortions of ego boundaries, producing difficulties with reality contact, which in turn produced a degree of anxiety at times greater than that for which the barbiturate was originally given. In these situations I found that small amounts of amphetamine given intravenously would increase the level of consciousness sufficient to ameliorate the anxiety.

In still other patients, as described in Chapter 5, anxiety could be reduced and symptoms ameliorated by permitting the patient to attempt to hurt the therapist by squeezing his hand. On other occasions I deliberately squeezed the patient's hand to cause him pain, thereby diverting his focus of concentration away from the operation and at times producing a marked decrease in anxiety to the point at which symptom disappearance was effected.

The following is a clinical illustration.

Case History

The patient was a nurse in her mid-thirties. During the course of her craniotomy she had multiple episodes in which she repeatedly became extremely anxious, the anxiety being associated with the appearance of various secondary symptoms and signs. These bouts of anxiety responded very dramatically to a variety of treatments. On the basis of her presurgical studies I had predicted that she would probably have periods of catatonic excitement during the craniotomy. I predicted that this excitement would appear when the reality of the surgery itself became too marked and also if she became drowsy. This last prediction was based on her history of great difficulty with reality contact leading to episodes of panic in response to small preoperative test doses of barbiturates.

In the anestheia room, while she was being positioned on the operating table, and when various pieces of recording apparatus were being readied, the patient became extremely anxious in anticipation of the forthcoming surgery. (This patient was a nurse who had a great deal of operating room experience.)

She showed extreme muscle tension and repeatedly cried out anxiously. She became aware of slight tachycardia and became obsessed with the thought that she would have a heart attack. These thoughts developed into full-blown somatic delusions in which she claimed that her "heart had infarcted." At this point 0.2 gram of Seconal was slowly administered intravenously. In response to this she very rapidly demonstrated a decrease in tension followed by a decrease in affect paralleled by a slowing of her pulse. This was followed by the amelioration of the paranoid delusions, and, shortly thereafter, her hypochondriacal preoccupation with her heart cleared and she was again very cooperative.

During the injection of her scalp with a local anesthetic, the patient again became anxious and showed the same pattern as described above. This time she was given 20 milligrams of Demerol (meperidine hydrochloride, Winthrop) intravenously. This produced a reversal of the symptoms. However, five minutes following the completion of the injection of Demerol, the patient demonstrated a state of catatonic stupor with some cerea flexibilitas. After five more minutes she suddenly became very alert and extremely panicky with the return of the symptoms described above. She cried out repeatedly, "Is this real? Is this real?" She was given a great deal of positive reassurance and an additional 20 milligrams of Demerol intravenously. Once again the symptoms cleared.

These episodes recurred six times during the course of the craniotomy which took one and one-half hours. On two occasions sodium pentothal (5 cubic centimeters of a 2.5 percent solution) was given to control the periods of catatonic excitement.

When we were ready to perform the lobotomy proper the patient again was in a state of catatonic excitement with somatic delusions about her heart, with paranoid references to me and the hospital being very evident. When the medial half of the left frontal lobe was sectioned a marked decrease in the motor component of anxiety was noted. She continued to have difficulty with reality contact and repeatedly asked, "Is it real? Is it real?" When the medial half of the right lobe was sectioned there was a marked decrease in the affective component of anxiety together with a decrease in her pulse, which had been very rapid. The patient's paranoid behavior disappeared three minutes after the lateral half of the right frontal lobe was sectioned. By the time the lateral half of the left frontal lobe was sectioned her somatic delusions were also gone.

Some significant findings with regard to hallucinations are very pertinent. They will be described in detail in Chapter 8, but some mention of them is in order at this time. Six patients were actively hallucinating at the time the prefrontal lobotomies were begun. I noted that hallucinatory material did not disappear en masse in response to the lobotomy. This pattern was confirmed in a few patients who were actively hallucinating prior to the administration of intravenous phenothiazines. The more primitive aspects of the hallucinatory material disappeared first. For example, if the patient had olfactory or tactile hallucinations in addition to auditory and visual hallucinations the olfactory and tactile hallucinations disappeared first, leaving the visual and auditory hallucinations seemingly unchanged. Further therapy would relieve the visual and auditory hallucinations as the the degree of anxiety decreased further.

In subsequent chapters clinical examples illustrating many of the patterns of symptom amelioration will be presented. These patterns of clinical behavior were usually readily observed, particularly in the very ill patients seen in this series and especially when rapidly acting therapeutic techniques were employed.

7

DREAMS

In 1956 I initially reported the results of my studies on what was then a new psychotherapeutic technique, namely the use of psychoanalytically oriented psychotherapy in combination with the tranquilizing drugs (Lesse, 1956). This was the first detailed report dealing with this new technique to appear in the literature. Very early in my experience with the phenothiazine preparations I was struck by the spontaneous comments made by many patients that they were "dreaming much more than ever before." It appeared to me that this combined therapy technique might offer an excellent opportunity to observe just what happens phenomenologically and psychodyanamically to dreams when anxiety was rapidly decreased in intensity. This study enlarged into a broad investigation of the relationship of the intensity of anxiety and the various components of anxiety to dreams.

Before entering into a discussion of anxiety in relationship to dreams I would like to call to the reader's attention a great fault in all psychiatric research that is glossed over by most investigators. In general, patients try to please their therapists. If a therapist is interested in dreams the patients will recall dreams. If a therapist is interested in various types of dream symbols they will please the therapist by "thinking" in terms of certain symbols. If the therapist is interested in color dreams they will increase the frequency of their color dreams.

It is very difficult for an investigator to hide his special interest from a discerning patient. In these studies of anxiety I interrogated the patients very sharply with regard to the various components of anxiety. I am certain that many patients accommodated me, for they too became "experts" in the study of anxiety. These accommodations represent a type of placebo reaction that inescapably colors all therapy and research. This is discussed in great detail in Chapter 10, "The Placebo Phenomenon." All therapists, particularly therapists who are doing research investigation, create a type of conditioned response in a patient.

DREAMS AND MOUNTING ANXIETY

I gathered my material on dreams from patients who were treated by several techniques, namely: (1) reconstructive psychoanalytic techniques; (2) brief psychoanalytically oriented psychotherapy; and (3) brief psycho-analytically oriented psychotherapy in combination with various tranquilizers.

There was great opportunity to collect this material during the initial phases of treatment and during the course of therapy in which patients showed periods of exacerbation of anxiety in response to environmental stress and stress precipitated by psychotherapy itself.

For all practical purposes, my studies reflect on the frequency with which dreams are reported by the patient and only indirectly on the amount of dreaming that the patient actually does. There are a number of research projects in this country in which investigators stimulated by the original works of N. Kleitman and W. C. Dement are attempting to record the actual frequency of dreams by indirect measurement. Thus far there have been no significant reports by these researchers relating the intensity of anxiety to the frequency of dreams.

Between 1954 and 1962 I made an intensive attempt to correlate dreams with the degree of overt anxiety in almost 250 patients. I noted that with mounting anxiety some patients reported dreams with increasing frequency, whereas others reported dreams less frequently than they had during a state characterized by a lesser degree of overt anxiety. It must be appreciated that it is extremely difficult to obtain any accurate statistical data in this manner because of the placebo effects caused by the very process of my combined research-therapy, which made the patients much more aware of their dreams in response to my questioning. I can only repeat the general observation that some patients report fewer dreams in response to increased stress, whereas others report an increase in dreams.

Anxiety demonstrated in the manifest content of dreams is often the initial signal of mounting anxiety. Thus may precede by many days the other overt manifestations of an anxious response to stress. This observation has been reported by other men, particularly Gutheil (1951, pp. 26–39).

This anxiety primarily is related to the latent content of the dream and not always to the manifest content. For example, some patients as they become increasingly anxious will demonstrate a manifest dream content that belies the emotion behind the dream. Indeed, a paradoxic reaction may be seen in that the dream material during anxious states appeared to be more devoid of anxiety than dreams that had been reported during periods when the patient was actually less anxious. Some dreams appear to be lacking in emotion altogether in great contrast to the overt manifestations of anxiety noted when the patient was awake. These seeming paradoxic reactions between anxiety and dreams will be discussed further under the subheading "Anxiety Beyond Nightmares."

With mounting anxiety I noted in many instances that a patient consciously may appear to have a "flat" affect and demonstrate only through his dreams the anxiety-laden impact of his reaction to various stressful phenomena. Others, as described above, may show considerable overt anxiety during consciousness, and yet their dreams, at first glance, appear devoid of anxiety (as described according to the four components considered in this book).

Gutheil (1951) refers to these apparent paradoxic relationships between the patient's overt conscious behavior and the quality of the manifest dream as an example of an emotional economy performed by dreams or, to use his term, the "regulation of affect metabolism." Though his statements appear to have merit, the psychophysiologic mechanisms by which they occur are unknown. As I will describe later in this chapter the Law of Initial Value would appear to play a role and to a degree helps to explain some of these apparent paradoxes.

The vast bulk of the literature dealing with dreams has been preoccupied with the study of symbols. I have no quarrel with the concept that there are cultural similarities in symbol formation as has been elaborated on in the extensive writings of Jung and his group. Similarly, Freud and those of us who practice Freudian or neo-Freudian techniques have elaborated to an extreme degree on dream symbolism. However, arguments have developed ad nauseam with regard to the meaning of symbols. It is almost as though various therapists have implied that "My symbol is better than your symbol."

I have a vast body of evidence that patients who come from therapists with a particular philosophic leaning interpret their symbols in the fashion of their last therapist. I also am certain that after a period of therapy with me that symbols were interpreted in a different fashion, one that mimicked my particular concepts.

However, I was much more interested in the emotion expressed in dreams than in symbolization, and I repeatedly projected this idea to the patient. I am firmly in agreement with Gutheil's (1951) observation that the most reliable part of dream content is the emotion contained therein."

The common pattern noted in dreams as the degree of anxiety is increased is that the manifest content of the dreams will be associated with more motion. There is more activity on the part of the characters in the dream. This increased activity, which is an expression of the motor component of anxiety, is commonly overlooked by psychotherapists. In fact, I have found no reference to this phenomenon in the literature. Affective expression in dreams is also a manifestation of increasing anxiety. I could make no correlation with regard to an increase in the pressure of speech as a manifestation of overt anxiety in dreams.

If the patient remains under great stress, one can note a change in the manifest content of dreams, particularly in patients with schizoid personalities. The manifest content in such patients in response to increased anxiety may become more primitive and bizarre, at times a forewarning of an impending psychotic break. A failure to heed these warnings may result in a massive psychosis requiring long periods of therapy before psychic integration can be achieved.

Dreams and Decreasing Anxiety: Phenothiazines

As I mentioned before, I was struck very early in my experience with the phenothiazines that patients spontaneously stated, "I am dreaming more than ever before." In a previous report (Lesse, 1959), I stated that, during the first two weeks after patients were started on phenothiazines, eighty-seven (67.0 percent) of 130 patients reported that they were congizant of more dreams than they had been aware of prior to the onset of the phenothiazine therapy. These 130 patients were part of a group of more than 250 patients who were treated with phenothiazines in combination with psychoanalytically oriented psychotherapy. They reported dreams with sufficient frequency to permit me to observe dream mechanisms in relationship to the degree of anxiety. Sixty-one of these eighty-seven patients reported this experience spontaneously, whereas the other twenty-six revealed it during the course of direct questioning.

In all cases the change was very striking to the patient. The sudden awareness of these dreams was accompanied, in many instances, by an eagerness on the part of the patient to relate them to the therapist.

I found, after correlating this finding with various other clinical factors, that *the increase in dream awareness invariably occurred in those patients who manifested marked, overt anxiety and did not pertain to patients in whom the initial affect was relatively bland.* Furthermore, I have observed that *this greater awareness occurred only in those patients who showed rapid improvement on drug therapy*. By rapid, I mean definite improvement during the first two weeks of oral phenothiazine therapy. More specifically, those patients who failed to demonstrate a significant lessening of the level of anxiety did not manifest a marked increase in dream awareness.

On the basis of the above observation I deliberately gave chlorpromazine or promazine to a total of thirty-four patients for the sole purpose of increasing dream awareness during the course of psychotherapy. It proved to be a very successful stimulant to dream awareness in nineteen patients. I had not informed these patients that I expected greater dream awareness. However, I cannot guarantee that my expectation of a possible increase in dream recall may not have been transmitted to the patient and that this expectation may have acted as a placebo inducing dream recall.

Of the thirty-four original patients tested twenty-five manifested a marked degree of overt anxiety; the remaining nine had a very bland affect. Eighteen of the nineteen patients in whom I was able to enhance dream production were from the group of twenty-five very anxious patients, whereas only one was from the group that manifested relatively little overt anxiety.

The period of enhanced dream awareness corresponded roughly to the period of rapid anxiety decompression and to the rapid amelioration of other clinical symptoms. As soon as the general emotional tenor struck a plateau of relative calm in which there was greater psychic integration with greater ego strength the artificial abundance of dreams decreased. This decrease was usually very striking to the therapist and to the patient as well with the patient often spontaneously remarking, "I don't seem to be dreaming as much."

The most striking observation, aside from the fact that the dreams were being presented in greater numbers, was the finding that *a decrease in affect associated with the manifest content of the dream was the first change to be readily observed during successful phenothiazine therapy. This phenomenon was most clearly seen with nightmares and rage dreams*, but less often also in dreams of desire.

I can also state that if one is sharply aware of motor activity in the manifest content it can be observed that a decrease in the motor component at times appears to precede a decrease in the affect associated with the manifest content. (I believe that a decrease in the motor component of anxiety of dreams precedes a decrease in the other components just as it does in the conscious state. However, the psychotherapist has a scienfically untrained observer in the form of the patient, and it is from the patient that his reports about dreams are derived.)

For example, there are many patients who related nightmares or rage-filled dreams prior to the onset of drug therapy who after a brief but successful period of phenothiazine therapy related essentially the same dreams with the same or similar symbols but with the original affective impact considerably blunted. From the patient's standpoint the nightmares had lost their quality of terror, and the rage dreams were denuded of their anger. This change could occur in a matter of days if the patient was on phenothiazine therapy. The period of relative denudation of affect might last for days or even weeks if the patient was treated solely by psychotherapeutic means.

The same or similar dreams, detached from the original affective impact, commonly recurred for a number of days before the manifest content and finally the latent content would be changed. It seemed, when these observations were examined in the context of the complete psychiatric problem, that the general level of anxiety or rage was decreased initially to a degree that permitted the affective pressure behind the dream to decrease. There was, however, enough residual anxiety or rage, although not overtly expressed, to stimulate the production of the dream. It seemed that it was not until the level of anxiety was decreased below a certain threshold—unique for each patient—that the dream content changed.

To summarize then, with a decreasing level of anxiety secondary to therapy, there first was a decrease in the affect associated with the manifest content of the dream. The manifest content reappeared for a variable period of time relatively denuded of affect. Then, if the patient continued to improve, the manifest content changed. In some instances different symbols having similar meaning would appear. Finally, all symbols suggesting a common latent content disappeared.

The following are examples illustrative of this pattern.

Case Histories

1. The patient was a thirty-four-year-old, married security officer, the product of a broken home, raised in part by foster parents. He had always had marked feelings of inadequacy for which he had attempted to compensate by extremely aggressive, rigid, compulsive, intellectualized mechanisms. He was overwhelmingly obsessed with fears of failure. For a period of two months he had experienced increasing anxiety, insomnia, difficulty in the performance of his job, social seclusiveness, and referential trends toward his superiors. He appeared extremely anxious and agitated. The patient had feelings of dissociation and was plagued by the fear that his future was ruined.

The patient was started on chlorpromazine, fifty milligrams four times a day. The dose was raised by degrees so that by the end of one week he was receiving 500 milligrams per day. On the third day of therapy he stated that he was sleeping better, and, indeed, although he was still extremely anxious, he was able to remain seated in his chair during his interviews.

On the night of the second day of treatment, he had the following dream:

"I was my present age i⁻ the beginning. I gradually began to shrink in size and became younger. I was filled with helpless terror as I shrank into a shrieking, wiggling, mass of shapeless matter. I awakened drenched in perspiration."

This dream gave pictorial expression to his distorted schizophrenic feelings of dissociation and destruction the ultimate in terror and punishment.

On the fifth day of therapy, the patient appeared much less anxious. He sat quietly in my office, free of motor restlessness. However, he continued to speak too loudly and too fast. The feelings of dissociation and referential trends had disappeared, but he still complained of feeling very anxious. He had the following dream the previous night:

"I was in the office, when the Chief informed the group that a valuable document had been stolen from the files. Though I was innocent, I was sure he suspected me. I sat helpless in my chair, while he stared at me."

In this dream as in the first, a painful fate threatened the patient, but in this second dream the symbols were much better organized and there was much less terror and violent action than there had been in the first dream. This dream was relatively denuded of affect as compared to the first dream. The symbols, as I have already mentioned, were better organized, but were different from those contained in the first dream. However, the implied latent anxiety was great enough to result in a dream in which fear was expressed in the manifest content.

On the eighth day of treatment, the patient appeared claiming that he felt wonderful and was slightly annoyed when he was refused permission to return to work on the following day. He had had a dream the previous night:

"I was talking to a group of men from my district. They told me the Chief wanted to see me. I was curious but not frightened."

The patient then spontaneously stated that he had had many dreams such as this in the past, and they had always been associated with a feeling of terror. I would like to point out here that this is another example of a latent content similar to that associated with the first two dreams. However, now the manifest content is almost completely denuded of anxiety.

Three days later, the patient was back at work. He related a dream in which the manifest and latent content appeared to be definitely changed.

"I was bowling with a group of the fellows. I was having an unusually good night and my score was excellent."

Here we see not only a change in the manifest content but a change in the latent content.

This patient changed in a period of eleven days from a decompensated, terrified, vocationally and socially indigent psychotic to a functioning individual. He had gained as yet little or no insight into his illness. The third dream (the one in which his Chief wanted to see him) is illustrative of the fact that the general level of latent anxiety can be decreased to such a degree that it is not overtly expressed in the manifest aspect of the dream. However, the degree of anxiety was still sufficient in this instance to stimulate the production of a dream with manifest content similar to the previous dream (the second dream) which was characterized by marked anxiety. Not until the level of latent anxiety was decreased beyond a certain threshold did the manifest content change completely, as it did in the fourth dream, which dealt with bowling.

2. The patient was a thirty-four-year-old woman who had been divorced for nine months. She had considered herself to be a very happily married woman for eleven years. Approximately one year prior to her divorce her husband became very abusive and even brutal toward her. She learned from him that he had been having extramarital relations

with a woman she had always considered to be her close friend. After several chaotic months the patient sued for and obtained a divorce. Her husband married her ex-friend a short time afterward.

Following this, the patient became very frightened and was terrified to be alone. She was extremely phobic and depressed. For a period of two weeks prior to her initial visit, she manifested vertigo and difficulty in walking. These symptoms were terrifying to her. Neurologic studies were entirely within normal limits. The patient was started on chlorpromazine, and during the following week the daily dose was raised from 200 to 600 milligrams.

On the third day of therapy, the patient related the following dream:

"I was in a rage. I was sitting and kicking my ex-husband's new wife. I had the overwhelming desire to beat her to death, to mangle her."

The patient related that she had had similar dreams recurring nightly and even several times per night. In some of the dreams, the patient felt terrified following the beatings that she had envisioned that she was administering. She interpreted them as suggesting that in reality she might lose control and kill her ex-husband's new wife.

Eight days after the onset of therapy the patient first showed some clinical improvement. Her vertigo and unsteadiness disappeared. She was less agitated, and her phobic manifestations improved to a degree. She related the following dream:

"My ex-husband's new wife was acting very domesticated, a role that was in reality very unnatural and very unreal for her. I lectured her in a rather calm, cold, highly intellectualized fashion against such artificial behavior. It seemed strange to me that I felt so salm in the dream."

On the ninth day of treatment, the patient reported the following dream:

"I lost my pocketbook containing all my belongings including my fountain pen. Everything but the fountain pen was found."

The patient related that she was not frightened in this dream. It ended on the note that she would probably find another fountain pen. Though the symbolism was very striking, the lack of affect associated with the manifest content was very dramatic when compared to the first dream.

On the fourteenth day of therapy, the patient appeared quite composed. She was not disturbed by her phobias on that particular day. She related the following dream:

"I was decorating my new apartment. I was very pleased with the results I was obtaining." (In reality the patient was preoccupied with the decoration of her new apartment.)

Once again, one can see a rapid decrease in the affective push behind the dreams before the manifest and especially the latent content were changed. Also it is an example in which the latent content is denuded, as it were, of its affective push before it changed.

I think it of worth to reiterate that there may be a decrease in the motor activity paralleling or even preceding the decrease in the affective pressure in the dream. This lessening of the motor component, even in a nightmare or rage dream, may be the earliest prognostic sign of decreased anxiety. Expressing it in another fashion, the gradation of terror and violence in dreams must be weighted as prognostic signs during the course of therapy. Too often, I believe, all nightmares are considered as having equal weight, based purely on the fact that the patient is awakened by the dream.

I would like to point up a paradoxic reaction. Some patients with nightmares accompanied by very little motor activity may show an increase in motor activity associated with the manifest content as the initial sign of improvement. This is a very uncommon process. I will refer to this again in an example given below in connection with a clinical phenomenon I have designated as *anxiety beyond nightmares.*

ANXIETY BEYOND NIGHTMARES

I observed a group of patients who as they responded to the combined psychotherapy-drug therapy technique began to relate terrifying nightmares and rage-filled dreams, whereas they had no recollection of such dreams prior to the onset of the drug therapy. This stage rarely lasted for more than a few days, for, as the level of anxiety was decreased further, the emotional impact of the dream also became blunted and the manifest and then the latent content changed in the manner that I have described in detail above.

I stopped the medication in some of these patients very early in the course of treatment, shortly after the nightmares appeared. I found in some instances that as the degree of anxiety increased the nightmares disappeared. Then when the drugs were effectively reintroduced, the nightmares returned. I repeated this experiment a second time in three patients.

It appeared from my observations that there are some patients who are so terrified that they repress any conscious recollection of terror or rage dreams. Though this seems paradoxic, when we consider that one of the fundamental purposes of dreams is the protection of the integrity of the ego these findings are not so strange as they might appear on first examination. Also these paradoxic reactions are predictable on the basis of the Law of Initial Value described in detail in Chapter 11.

The following are examples of these patterns.

Case Histories

1. The patient was a thirty-one-year-old male junior executive, the product of a home in which his mother was an obsessive-compulsive, very sadistic, punitive personality. He came into therapy because he suffered with severe mucus colitis and multiple allergies. The patient had always been extremely mechanistic, meticulous, and self-righteous in his habits. He had difficulty performing vocationally, socially, and sexually. His wife was a rather dominant personality who made all of the emotional decisions in the home.

On the surface the patient was very calm. As he expressed it, "Most people think I'm a rock of Gibraltar." However, in addition to the very handicapping psychosomatic problems enumerated above, he felt a growing sense of inner anxiety. The patient denied recalling any dreams for many years prior to entering treatment. He was referred into treatment by his internist who had been unable to help his colitis and allergies by routine medical care.

During the period of the history-taking, the patient was very reserved and appeared to be superficially calm. Whenever he was questioned about his mother, he had to excuse himself and go to the bathroom to defecate. After one week, he was placed on chlorpromazine, 150 milligrams per day. This dosage was gradually increased to 400 milligrams per day.

Three days after the onset of chlorpromazine therapy, the patient reported the following dream:

"I was lying at the bottom of a lake floating peacefully in a very quiet fashion. I knew I was drowning. I then awakened. After I awakened, I felt very tense and itchy. I always feel itchy when I feel tense."

In this dream, one notes an example of a patient who had the recollection of a nightmare after the onset of drug therapy. He had been in therapy for ten days at that time. For seven days he had had no drug therapy. The dream is also of interest because it shows a rather paradoxic reaction. In this nightmare, there is little or no motor activity, even though the dream represents the fear of death and although he awakened as a defense mechanism.

On the sixth day of drug therapy, the patient stated that he was less restless at work and at home. His colitis had not yet improved but his pruritus was not so persistent. He related the following dream:

"I had a nightmare last night that awakened me. I was being chased by three huge women with knives and hatchets. I escaped them and awakened."

In this dream also there are nightmarish qualities. However, though the patient had shown slight clinical improvement, there was considerably more motor activity demonstrated in this dream. As I mentioned earlier in this chapter, this is quite an unusual pattern. It is much more common for the degree of motor activity associated with the nightmare to decrease as the patient shows clinical improvement.

Eight days after the onset of drug therapy the patient informed me that he was feeling less anxious and also was much less restless at his job and at home. Slight improvement was noted in the frequency of his bouts of diarrhea. He reported the following dream:

"I was being chased through the cars of a train. I don't know by whom. I was terrified. I felt itchy all over. In the race between the cars, I pulled a bolt that uncoupled the rear cars where my pursuers were. The part of the train in which I remained was attached to the engine, and as we pulled away from the stranded cars I felt much better and the itching subsided. I did not awaken from this dream."

This dream illustrates continued motor activity, and there was still an element of terror. The patient actively aided himself against the impending danger. His self-defense resulted in an improvement in his pruritus. The terror qualities of the dream were less than in the previous two dreams as illustrated by the fact that the patient did not awaken.

The clinical picture continued to improve, particularly with regard to his colitis. Two days later he reported the following dream:

"I had an argument with my secretary, who is really a very efficient but bossy person. I gave her hell for disputing my orders. I felt very good afterwards."

It will be noted that there is no nightmarish quality in this dream. Though in reality the patient had not displayed this kind of strength in everyday life, the dream implies that his anxiety was muted permitting his suppressed anger to manifest itself at least in a dream situation. One notes also that there is not much motor activity in this dream, but considerable affect is demonstrated.

Four days later, the patient showed an over-all clinical improvement of considerable proportions, although as yet there was little insight into the basic psychodynamics of his problems. His stools were better formed. There was no longer any mucus associated with defecation. Very little pruritus remained. He reported the following dream:

"Yesterday I went sailing with my friends. Last night I dreamt I was in a large sailboat with a group of these friends. The water was choppy but the wind was good, and I did not have great difficulty in controlling the ship. As the day progressed, there was a threat of a squall, and for a while I was quite anxious. However, the weather improved."

One notes here that the content of this dream is considerably different from the first three that were reported. There was no nightmarish quality to the dream. The change in the manifest content implying a change in the latent content paralleled the clinical improvement noted during the waking state.

At this point, the patient had been in treatment approximately three weeks. During two of these three weeks he had been on chlorpromazine. He objected to "being dependent on drugs." He insisted against advice that the drugs be discontinued. The chlorpromazine was discontinued.

For the next five days little or no change was noted in the clinical picture. Then the patient began to complain of gradually increasing pruritus and several bouts of diarrhea associated with a great deal of mucus.

About that time his mother accused him in a dramatic, tearful session of "hating her, after all she had done for him." After this scene, the patient was plagued with repeated bouts of mucus-covered diarrheal stools that continued without letup for almost eight hours. Toward the end of this period the stool was blood-tinged. He scratched his skin unmercifully although he took antihistamines and applied analgesic ointments to his skin.

At this point the patient had been off drugs for eight days. During this period he had no recollection of any nightmares. He pleaded to be placed on chlorpromazine again, and in view of the severity of his diarrhea he was started on 75 milligrams four times per day. This dose was increased to 400 milligrams per day after thiry-six hours. For the first four days of treatment no dreams were reported. I should mention that his pleadings for a return to drug therapy were made in a highly intellectualized fashion, at all times in a calm, controlled voice, although he said "I feel as though I am going to jump out of my skin." After the first four days of drug therapy, the patient stated that he felt slightly less anxious although his diarrhea and pruritus remained very severe. On the fourth night of treatment he had the following dream:

"I saw myself lying in a coffin in a large chapel. It was all very serene. I awakened and felt frightened and scratched my skin for a long time until it bled."

Once again, as he improved the patient began to have nightmares. The manifest content of his initial dream demonstrates, once again, literally no motor activity.

Two days later, the patient demonstrated definite signs of improvement. His pruritus was markedly improved, and his colitis showed evidence of lessening. He reported the following dream:

"A huge, monstrous female was preparing to attack me. I was terrified. I grabbed at a long sharp instrument and threw it at her. It struck her in the throat and she fell over dead. I awakened in a state of dreadful fright. Immediately, I went to the bathroom where I passed a copious stool."

In this dream, the patient demonstrated that as he improved clinically, his dreams, though retaining a nightmarish quality, were characterized by a great deal of motor activity and marked affect. In this dream, the patient's latent, murderous hostility toward his mother or maternal surrogates became evident.

During the week that followed, the patient continued to demonstrate further clinical improvement. He had dreams almost every night. On the fifth day following the last dream reported above he related this dream:

"I was in a very light, airy hospital room. My friends were with me and discussing the fact that I was to be discharged the following day. Two of them were going on vacation with me. I was secretly very delighted that I had discharged my nurse who had been a "battle ax."

Here it can be noted that the manifest and to a great extent the latent content of this dream had changed associated with a decrease in overt anxiety and a definite change in clinical symptoms.

2. This patient was a twenty-year-old, single, female university student who had been severely ill for less than two months. She came from a home in which both the mother and father had extremely high standards. "Perfection or nothing" was the rule of the home. The patient was an attractive, very intelligent young woman who literally had to be the "best student" in all of her classes or she became extremely uncomfortable. She was also very meticulous in her dressing habits and social behavior.

Three months prior to her initial visit, she became very attached to a senior student who was the campus hotshot. She began to come home late from her dates, and as a consequence her compulsive study habits were interrupted.

Her current difficulties began two months prior to her visit, when she was unable to complete a term paper on time. She became terrified that she would fail in the course and would lose face in her parents' eyes. The patient became very restless, had crying spells, insomnia, anorexia, and inability to concentrate on her work. She began to experience palpitations that panicked her. She was obsessed with the fear that she might die of a heart attack. When the palpitations recurred she screamed uncontrollably. Her parents were contacted by the college officials. Their repeated reassurances to the patient were of no avail. The patient, at the time of the initial interviews, denied having any recollection of dreams during the previous few years.

In view of her extreme anxiety and outbursts of screaming terror, the patient was started on 200 milligrams of chlorpromazine per day. This dose was increased during the week to 450 milligrams per day. By the second day of treatment there was a noticeable decrease in motor activity, and by the third day there was a definite decrease in affect. A marked tachycardia noted on the initial examination was ameliorated to a great extent.

On the third day, the patient related a dream she had had during the previous night:

"I was in the midst of an angry crowd of people who were taunting me and laughing at me. It appeared I was the town fool. I ran and turned to escape from them, but all exits were barred by the leering crowd. They began to close in on me. I awakened screaming. My screams alarmed the entire house."

One notes here that forty-eight hours after the onset of treatment, and after she had demonstrated some clinical improvement, the patient reported for the first time a nightmare. This was a usual type of nightmare in that it was associated with a great deal of motor activity.

On the fifth day of treatment, the patient related a dream that had occurred during the previous night:

"It was my wedding day. Everything went wrong. My mother did not like my intended husband. At the wedding the groom failed to show up. As the hours passed, the invited group began to snicker and then began to laugh out loud and taunt me. My mother repeated over and over again, 'I told you! I told you! I told you!' I felt my heart pounding. I was terrified that I was having a heart attack. At that moment, I awakened crying."

This dream had nightmarish qualities for this patient. It was not associated with the same degree of terror that characterized the previous dream. It will be noted that the motor activity and even to a degree the affective aspect was less in this dream than it had been in the first nightmare.

On the eighth day of treatment, the patient appeared to be considerably better. Her tachycardia had ceased and her preoccupations with her heart had lessened. She was able to sleep without medication, and she resumed some contact with her friends, whom she had avoided for almost two months. At this time she reported a dream:

"I was in class taking a test. I was not prepared up to my usual standards. I was concerned even though I knew most of the material. The instructor signaled the end of the test. I handed in my book with an uneasy feeling that while I had done moderately well, I would not have the top grade in the class. I wondered how my parents would take it."

The patient was not awakened by this dream. It did not have a nightmarish quality. The latent and manifest content of the dream showed a theme similar to that recorded in the first two dreams inasmuch as there was a relative feeling of failure and a threat of punishment. But the affective push associated with this dream was markedly ameliorated.

I saw this patient in early 1955 when chlorpromazine was a relatively new drug in America. Her mother's friend had been placed on the medication and had developed severe jaundice. Her mother became alarmed and refused to permit her daughter to continue on the drug. For all practical purposes, the mother took over therapy at this time. Her aggressive, perfectionist, critical habit pattern came to the fore once the patient had demonstrated definite improvement. About the same time her mother dictated that the drug should be stopped she began to push the patient to return to school and to admonish her; "with more effort she could again be the top person in the class." The patient very precipitously had a panic attack in which she was obsessed with the fear that she was dying of a coronary occlusion. She screamed uncontrollably. The mother, with a mixture of fear and hatred, forcefully slapped the patient in the face a number of times. This strong-armed technique was followed by the patient writhing about on the floor screaming. I was called by a desperate, terrified father.

Almost two weeks had passed since the drug had been discontinued. During the week that her mother had placed the patient under a great deal of pressure, the patient had no recollection of any dreams. After an initial intramuscular dose of chlorpromazine, she was started on 100 milligrams four times per day orally. Forty-eight hours after the reinstitution of drug therapy, she reported the following dream:

"I was in the university. I was called by the dean, and when I entered her office, it was my mother who was the dean. Though my mother is a little woman, in this dream she was considerably larger than she is in reality. She pointed a threatening finger at me and said, 'You are going to fail. I told you you would fail if you didn't concentrate on your studies!' She walked closer and closer to me and appeared extremely menacing. I screamed in the dream and ran out of the office. She chased me. I ran down a long corridor. I could tell by the shadows on the wall that she was gaining on me and that she was about to pounce on me. My heart was racing. I was enveloped by the shadow. I tripped and sprawled prone on the ground. At that moment, I awakened. I was sobbing and clutching at the sheets. My heart was racing, and I was in terror that it would burst. I cried out for my father over and over 'Daddy! Daddy!' "

Once again one notes the reappearance of a dream of nightmare proportions following the reinstitution of drug therapy. The dreams had not appeared for over a week while the patient was off drugs, even though she was in a state of great anxiety. As therapy progressed in this patient she demonstrated a very rapid decrease in the overt manifestations of anxiety and an amelioration of the hypochondriacal preoccupations with her heart. The nightmarish qualities of the dreams gradually ameliorated and finally disappeared.

The dream sequences of these two patients were reported in some detail here because both had been exposed to more than one episode of severe environmental stress early in therapy.

SUMMARY

It has not been my intention in this chapter to discuss the psycho-dynamics of dreams. I have focused upon the relationship between the intensity of anxiety and changes in the manifest and latent content of dreams. In addition I have stressed that nightmares may show qualitative variations in a given patient that are reflections of the intensity of anxiety present. These observations have important clinical significance that can be of considerable help to alert psychotherapists, because these qualitative changes in the manifest content of nightmares may be the earliest evidences of a serious impending crisis or the first implication of improvement. Last, I have indicated the fact that some patients may be so anxious that they will be amnesic for the recall of nightmares and that the initial suggestion of improvement, on occasion, may be the reporting of nightmares.

8

HALLUCINATIONS

Mounting Anxiety and Hallucinations

The pattern of the hallucinatory responses secondary to increasing anxiety follows the same phenomenologic rules of symptom formation described in Chapter 4. Hallucinations do not appear until there has been an increase in the level of overt anxiety and in the affective component. Characteristically, hallucinations usually appear last in the series of secondary symptoms and signs that occur in response to mounting anxiety.

It is extremely rare for hallucinations to occur as the initial response to mounting anxiety, and it is almost as rare to have them appear early in a series of secondary defense mechanisms. The only exception to this general rule appears to be in schizophrenic patients who are in a state of catatonic stupor. Patients in a catatonic stupor can manifest overt hallucinatory material early in the sequence of symptom formation. In all probability this does not mean that other symptoms and signs do not appear before the hallucinations, but that the hallucinations are the only means by which these patients can communicate.

I would like to remind the reader that, not uncommonly, patients in a state of catatonic stupor demonstrate an increase in the autonomic component of anxiety as the initial manifestation of increased anxiety. Though this may suggest a close relationship between autonomic functioning and hallucinations, in the absence of more conclusive documentation this point should be considered on the level of a supposition. When intensity of anxiety continues to increase after the initial appearance of auditory and visual hallucinations I noted the development of several different clinical phenomena, namely, (1) more primitive manifest content; (2) hallucinations referable to the other senses (that is, olfactory, tactile); (3)

combination of more primitive manifest content and olfactory and tactile aberrations; and (4) the state of psychic anarchy.

MORE PRIMITIVE MANIFEST CONTENT

If the level of anxiety continued to increase following the appearance of auditory or visual hallucinations the manifest symbolic content would commonly change. The motor activity reported was often increased. Most dramatic, however, was the nature of the manifest content in which the symbolization became more primitive. For example, expressions indicating conceptualizations of organ destruction and distortions of form, space, and time relationships became evident. These observations will be illustrated by clinical examples; the last vestiges of ego organization will be described later in this chapter. At this point, I simply would like to offer some quotes from several patients testifying to this type of change in manifest content: "I see my hands changing in shape." "Your face has no flesh." "I can only see his skull." "I don't hear her voice. It sounds like radio waves striking four per second." "Your lips cover your face. They look like slabs." A common pattern of regression in the manifest content of verbal hallucinations is the obsessive hearing of cursing, of references to feces, of repeated accusations of sexual distortions with the language becoming even more crude and repetitious.

HALLUCINATIONS REFERABLE TO OTHER SENSES

At times, if the level of anxiety is increased after auditory and/or visual hallucinations are already present, aberrations referable to other senses may be evoked. Olfactory and tactile hallucinations may appear without any significant regression in the manifest content of the auditory or visual symbolizations. It was rare for olfactory or tactile hallucinations to precede auditory or visual aberrations. Gustatory hallucinations were relatively uncommon.

These observations suggest, as one might logically expect from our knowledge of the hierarchical ordering of the central nervous system, that those senses associated with the neopallium (that is, auditory and visual senses) would be affected earliest in the distortion of ego boundaries. The more primitive senses, genotypically speaking, that are associated with the archipallium (that is, olfactory, tactile, and gustatory senses) are more resistant to distortion in the manifest content of hallucinations.

This order parallels the pathoanatomic and pathophysiologic phenomena in which the neopallium and visual and auditory senses are much more prone to destruction secondary to anoxemia than are the archipallium and the olfactory, tactile, and gustatory senses. Accordingly, the structures of the brain stem and spinal cord that carry the most primitive reflex arcs are the most resistant to oxygen deprivation.

MORE PRIMITIVE MANIFEST CONTENT AND OLFACTORY AND TACTILE ABERRATIONS

If the level of anxiety continues to mount one notes a combination of regressive patterns in which additional senses are involved and the manifest content of the hallucinations becomes more fragmented. The olfactory and tactile hallucinations, which usually appeared last, evidenced regression in manifest content as occurred in the auditory and visual aberrations.

I would like to reiterate very clearly that the degree of regression in manifest content and the number of senses involved depends on the intensity of anxiety secondary to a stressful situation and not on the nature of the stress. As I will illustrate, the changes that occur in hallucinations in response to mounting anxiety are similar in a given patient in response to different types of stress.

THE STATE OF PSYCHIC ANARCHY

If the level of anxiety continues to mount following the appearance of olfactory, tactile, or gustatory hallucinations and after the manifest content of the various type of hallucinations becomes more primitive, the ego boundaries become completely fragmented, a situation that I previously labeled "psychic anarchy." In this state the patient's verbal expressions become progressively more fractionated, and he finally lapses into periodic grunts, mumblings, or atonal cries. He may roll on the floor and lose sphincter control. This may be accompanied by sucking movements, a *Schnautzkrampf* reaction, athetoid posturing, and other fragmentary, extrapyramidal-like movements.

I am not implying that hallucinations have ceased at this point, but rather that the point has been reached at which the patient can no longer communicate the aberrations. This resembles the "wakeful state of unconsciousness" seen in patients who may become decorticated secondary to an organic brain lesion.

ADMINISTRATION OF MESCALINE OR LYSERGIC ACID

Fourteen of the twenty-five patients who received mescaline and/or lysergic acid developed hallucinations. All but three of the fourteen showed a marked increase in the motor and affective components of anxiety before other clinical symptoms and signs appeared. The hallucinations were not the first symptoms to appear in any of these fourteen patients. One or more other symptoms or signs, such as phobias, obsessive-compulsive states, hypochondriasis, and psychosomatic symptoms, appeared individually or in succession in response to mounting anxiety prior to the appearance of hallucinations.

The hallucinations came last in the succession of secondary defense mechanisms in all but three patients. These three were in catatonic stupor prior to the administration of the psychedelic agents. They showed an increase in the autonomic component prior to any motor or affective changes, and the hallucinations appeared very early in the scheme of developing symptoms.

Many papers have been written about the pattern of hallucinations that developed secondary to hallucinogenic agents. However, none have described in detail just what occurs in relationship to the amount of anxiety precipitated by the psychedelic preparations. Clinical examples will be presented at the end of this chapter.

HALLUCINATIONS DURING CRANIOTOMIES

A description of the process of mounting anxiety and secondary defense mechanism formation in response to this type of stress was described in Chapters 3 and 4. Twelve schizophrenic patients exposed to craniotomies performed under local anesthesia manifested hallucinations during the operations. In these instances, as in those following the administration of hallucinogens, the hallucinations appeared late in a succession of developing symptoms and signs. Also, as the patient's anxiety continued to mount after the hallucinations appeared the manifest content became more primitive, and on occasions the hallucinatory material was referred to the olfactory and tactile senses. At times the patients became overwhelmingly aware of the technique and discomfort of the operations per se, and the anxiety secondary to this awareness might precipitate a series of secondary defense mechanisms including hallucinations. On the other hand, some patients became increasingly anxious if they became even slightly drowsy, the soporific effects of the preoperative medications producing marked reality distortions. This extreme anxiety led to the formation of secondary defense mechanisms that in some instances included hallucinations, clinical examples of which will be described later in this chapter.

HALLUCINATIONS SECONDARY TO ENVIRONMENTAL STRESS

A similar process in which hallucinations appeared in response to increasing environmental stress was noted in many instances. In most cases the patients were treated before there was progressive regression of the symbolism of the manifest content and before olfactory or tactile hallucinations had developed. Once again, as noted in the more acute experiments in which the patients were exposed to the stress of a psychedelic drug or a craniotomy performed under local anesthesia, hallucinations were usually the last symptoms to appear. Only the rate of change differed in that it usually required days or even weeks for the necessary levels of regression to occur secondary to environmental stress, whereas the time required could be measured in minutes or hours when the patients were exposed to a hallucinogen or a craniotomy. Illustrative case material is presented later in this chapter.

DECREASING ANXIETY AND HALLUCINATIONS

In Chapter 6, "Decreasing Anxiety and Symptom Amelioration," I noted that the quantitative degree of anxiety must be decreased before a symptom or succession of symptoms disappears. I further noted that these symptoms and signs did not disappear until the degree of anxiety decreased below a certain threshold, which was unique for the individual patient. The transition period in which symptoms were relatively denuded of the original emotional impact prior to the complete disappearance of the symptom was clinically usually very striking. I also referred to my observation that the last symptom to appear during the period of mounting anxiety was usually the first symptom to disappear when the level of anxiety was reduced.

In response to treatment, after the motor and affective components of anxiety were reduced, I noted in hallucinatory patients that the hallucinations were almost always the first symptoms to be ameliorated. The most primitive aspects of the hallucinatory aberrations were ameliorated first, that is, the manifest content became less primitive before the hallucinations referable to a specific sense disappeared. Expressing it in a different fashion, the hallucinatory symbols became more mature or better organized prior to the amelioration of the aberrations referable to a specific sense.

Hallucinations involving the tactile, olfactory, or gustatory senses almost always were ameliorated before the visual and auditory aberrations. To state this in another manner, it appeared that the hallucinations involving what are in man the more sophisticated senses, namely the auditory and visual senses, were the last to disappear in response to treatment.

These observations with regard to the disappearance of the various hallucinatory aberrations are reaffirmations of the statement that the order of symptom amelioration in response to therapy is the reverse of the order of the appearance of symptoms and signs in response to increased anxiety.

Prior to the disappearance of any hallucination, there was a lessening of the emotional impact associated with the hallucination. These aberrations became relatively denuded of their original emotional charge before the manifest content changed. At times I could observe hallucinations that had become relatively denuded of affect in response to treatment, while other symptoms, such as obsessive-compulsive states, phobias, and hypochondriacal manifestations, remained charged with a marked degree of anxiety. The pattern of hallucination amelioration did not depend on the type of therapy used. Only the rate of improvement appeared to depend on the nature of treatment employed.

TREATMENT OF HALLUCINATIONS SECONDARY TO HALLUCINOGENS

Patients who had developed hallucinations in response to the administration of psychedelic drugs were treated either by a combination of sodium amytal plus amphetamines given intravenously or by intravenous chlorpromazine. A number of attempts were made using intravenous chlorpromazine to titrate the amelioration of various symptoms. By this I mean that a few patients were given small doses of chloropromazine intravenously in an attempt to reduce, or ameliorate, just one symptom. In this manner hallucinations could at times be ameliorated leaving other secondary symptoms and signs relatively untouched. I should point out that any improvement in one symptom obtained by this fractional intravenous administration of chlorpromazine was transient. I noted that after a very short period of time the patient's anxiety would mount and the hallucination would reappear. It did, however, illustrate how hallucinations could be removed without affecting other symptoms that had appeared earlier.

HALLUCINATIONS AND LOBOTOMIES

Six patients had lobotomies performed while they were actively hallucinating. In five the hallucinations either improved or disappeared entirely.

As I noted in Chapter 6, the degree of improvement appeared to depend on the amount of frontal lobe that was sectioned. The more primitive manifest content of the auditory and visual hallucinations improved before these types completely disappeared. Similarly when olfactory, tactile, or gustatory hallucinations appeared late in response to anxiety produced by the stress of craniotomy proper, they were ameliorated prior to the auditory and visual hallucinations.

The changes produced secondary to the leucotomy were extremely dramatic because a rapid amelioration of anxiety and secondary symptoms including hallucinations was accomplished in a matter of minutes.

INTRAVENOUS CHLORPROMAZINE

I administered chlorpromazine intravenously to thirty-four schizo-phrenic patients who were extremely disturbed and actively hallucinating. As a temporary therapeutic procedure it was extremely effective. If one administered this drug very rapidly all symptoms tended to disappear en masse. If one administered the drug slowly, it was often possible to dem-onstrate that the affective impact associated with the hallucinations was diluted before the manifest content changed or disappeared. Once again I was able to demonstrate with the use of intravenous chlorpromazine that olfactory, gustatory, and tactile hallucinations disappeared before auditory and visual hallucinations. Similarly, as I have described above in patients who were hallucinating in response to hallucinogens or anxiety secondary to craniotomy, the primitive manifest content changed before any hal-lucination disappeared.

ORAL PHENOTHIAZINES

When oral phenothiazines were administered in combination with psychoanalytically oriented psychotherapy, a process similar to that which I have described above several times was noted. However, the improvement noted with this type of therapy was much slower than that noted when intravenous phenothiazines or lobotomy were used. I have not used the combined oral phenothiazine-psychotherapy technique in patients who were as sick as those who were lobotomized or who required intravenous chlorpromazine. However, the combined oral phenothiazine-psychotherapy procedure afforded an excellent opportunity to observe the dilution of the affective impact associated with the manifest content of a hallucination before the hallucination completely disappeared. At times, as much as one week or more might pass in which hallucinations were reported, but during this period the patient also would report that "It doesn't bother me as much as before." When one such patient was asked, "Why doesn't it bother you?" he answered, "I don't know. I guess it should and it used to, but it just doesn't bother me as much now."

CLINICAL ILLUSTRATIONS

PSYCHEDELIC DRUGS

The psychedelic drugs mescaline and lysergic acid were employed as stress-producing agents and in some instances produced hallucinatory reactions in schizophrenic patients. Examples follow.

Case Histories

1. The patient was a twenty-six-year old, single, unemployed female secretary who had a history of impulsive, explosive temper outbursts beginning in childhood and severe hypochondriacal preoccupations with regard to her heart and head. In addition, she had intermitten severe claustrophobia and periodic agoraphobia that were completely incapacitating. Beginning at age twenty-two her work habits became very erratic. She lost many jobs owing to lateness and absenteeism. Her social relationships also became very chaotic, and, though she made friends very easily, these friendships were usually brief owing to her inconsistent and unpredictable behavior.

For a period of two years she was supported economically by a devoted older sister. Two years prior to her hospitalization her hypochondriacal preoccupations in which she felt she was having repeated heart attacks and strokes became more frequent. These preoccupations were associated with severe panic attacks. Her agoraphobic manifestations restricted her to her apartment. Even this did not relieve her terror, for on many occasions she was unable to close the kitchen or bathroom door as this limitation of space would cause her to feel that "the room was closing in on me." A growing referential trend directed toward her sister and other family members appeared and gradually became more marked. At times there were rage episodes in which she would destroy anything that came into her grasp. It was in this state that she was admitted to a psychiatric hospital.

In the hospital setting the patient's symptoms disappeared when she was placed on a regimen of oral phenothiazines and supportive psychotherapy. After all the symptoms had cleared and the patient was calm she was given intravenous mescaline. Five minutes after the injection of the mescaline she became noticeably more restless. Shortly thereafter, her face demonstrated signs of apprehension, and she began to whimper. Her pulse rate and blood pressure increased. The patient became very aware of the developing tachycardia and placed her hand over her heart. She cried out, "My heart! My heart!" A few minutes later she cried, "My head feels full! It feels as if it's going to explode!" About that time the patient exclaimed, "The room is closing in! I feel suffocated!" Feelings of body distortion were then manifested. She claimed that she could feel her "heart swelling and her brain throbbing."

The patient then exclaimed with marked anxiety, "The room is changing color. It's turning blue." Then in a terrifed fashion, "I'm dying! I'm dying! You're killing me!" The patient then screamed, "I heard you say that you're going to kill me!" This was repeated over and over again.

The patient paused briefly and then shouted, "I heard you tell the man in the other room to take my body and hide it!" She cried, "I'm dying! I'm dying!"

Then, her face a mask of terror, she screamed, "Your face! It's changing shape! My chest is shrinking." She tore at her clothes. "Look at my body. It's out of shape!" Following this the patient retched and screamed, "My body is rotting! I can smell myself, I feel bugs eating me! Please, please, get them off! My stomach burst! I stink from my bowels!"

At this point she was given 75 milligrams of chlorpromazine intravenously, and the symptomatic affects of the hallucinogen were ameliorated rapidly as I will describe presently.

Thus far this patient illustrates the appearance of a mounting level of anxiety prior to the onset of any secondary symptoms and signs. This case also illustrates the fact that hallucinations appeared late in the chain of secondary defense symptoms. The hallucinations when they first appeared were in the auditory and visual spheres. As the level of anxiety increased, the manifest content of the auditory and visual hallucinations showed regression in the nature of the symbolism used. Further ego decompensation was demonstrated by the appearance of olfactory and tactile hallucinations.

At this point 75 milligrams of chlorpromazine were administered intravenously over a seven-minute period. The hallucination remained unchanged for five minutes after the completion of the injection. Until this point there was no noticeable alteration in the motor or affective aspects of anxiety associated with the aberrations. The patient continued to cry out in terror as I have already described.

Seven minutes following the completion of the injection the patient stopped all references to the olfactory hallucinations. She no longer complained that she could smell her "rotting body." Shortly after that references to the tactile hallucinations and the visual hallucination in which she felt that the therapist's face was changing shape also ceased.

However, at this point she continued to repeat, "I heard you say you were going to kill me!" These references to the auditory hallucinations now had a decreased affective impact.

Five minutes after the disappearance of the olfactory hallucinations all hallucinatory aberrations cleared. The patient continued to complain about her head and heart and to refer to her claustrophobic difficulties. Fifteen minutes following the completion of the injection of chlorpromazine the patient sat quietly in her chair. At this point no spontaneous complaints were offered. She was asked, "How do you feel?" "I feel tired but okay. My heart and my head seem all right. The room isn't closing in on me anymore."

One can note that the pattern of disappearance of the hallucinatory aberrations was essentially the reverse of the pattern of appearance. In this clinical example the general rule that I described in the previous chapter to the effect that the last symptom to appear is the last symptom to disappear in response to treatment is borne out.

2. The patient was a twenty-five-year-old engineer who was always very quiet and shy. He came from a family in which his uncle and several siblings had periods in which they were actively schizophrenic. The patient was brought up in a milieu in which the parents fought physically on repeated occasions. He performed moderately well throughout high school and college. At age twenty-two, he complained of restlessness and difficulty with his powers of concentration. About the same time, he began to manifest band-like headaches and a throbbing, beating sensation over the occipital area of his head. Referential trends became prominent. He felt that the neighbors were accusing him of lacking religious feeling and of being against God.

Because of these symptoms, the patient was referred for treatment. The patient was admitted to a private psychiatric hospital. While there, he became less anxious, and the presenting symptoms began to ameliorate spontaneously. After a period of two weeks the patient stated that he felt much better, and he superficially appeared free of all symptoms.

At that time, the patient was given 150 micrograms of lysergic acid (LSD-25) orally. Approximately forty minutes after he took this medication he became increasingly restless and began to pace about the room. Ten minutes later he appeared very alarmed and his facial muscles became drawn. Fifty-five minutes after taking LSD he began to complain about a throbbing sensation over the back of his head. He was afraid that he was having a stroke. A severe band-like headache developed that became progressively worse. The patient became terrified that his head would be "crushed." He then exclaimed, "The neighbors are behind this. I heard them talking about me."

When asked what they were saying, he replied, "I am anti-Christ! They are saying that I killed Christ!" "I see God. He is in this room. He came to see me, and He looks very angry. He is an angry old man."

The patient continued to complain about his head. His symptoms became progressively more delusional. "My brains are being squeezed! They feel like they will be squeezed through my nose and my eyes!" He then began to shout, "I'm losing my brains! I'll die! My whole head is out of shape and my face—my face—my nose is rotting away!"

In view of the rapid deterioration of the patient's ego defenses, the effects of the LSD-25 were rapidly terminated by the use of intravenous chlorpromazine. Before this aspect of the experiment is discussed, however, it should be pointed out that this patient demonstrated a process of increasing anxiety, calling into play secondary defense mechanisms, with hallucinations appearing late in a sequence of secondary symptoms and signs. One can clearly note here that, after hallucinations once appear, if the level of anxiety is increased further, hallucinations referable to other senses are brought into play and the manifest content of hallucinations takes on a progressively more primitive quality.

As mentioned above, this patient was given intravenous chlorpromazine in an attempt to reverse the rapidly regressive pattern stimulated by the lysergic acid. Seventy-five milligrams of chlorpromazine were given intravenously over a seven-minute period. Three minutes following the completion and ten minutes after the beginning of the intravenous injection the patient, who had been pacing and thrashing about and screaming in association with his terrifying hallucinations, appeared slightly less agitated. He gradually demonstrated less motor activity.

After a few minutes of silence, he was asked, "What are you thinking about?" He answered, "I am talking to God. He is with me. I am explaining to Him that I am not anti-Christ and I'm not anti-God."

The patient was then asked, "How are your face and your brains? Are they still deteriorating? Aren't they oozing through your nose and eyes?" "No", replied the patient. "Were they, a few minutes ago?" "Yes, they were," replied the patient. "But they appear to be all right now. Please let me be! I can't hear God with you talking so much to me!"

The patient lapsed into silence, but there were changes in his facial expression. "What are you thinking about?" "I'm still talking to God." The patient was rubbing his head. When asked what was wrong he said, "My head hurts! My head hurts!"

Fourteen minutes after the onset of the injection and seven minutes following the completion of the injection, the patient appeared to be more alert. He was still very restless and complained incessantly about his throbbing headaches. He was then asked, "Are you still talking to God?" "No." "Well, weren't you talking to Him before?" "Yes, I was." "Why aren't you talking to Him now?" "I don't know, may be it really wasn't God. Maybe it was a trick of the neighbors. I can hear one woman accusing me of being anti-Christ."

It should be noted that this was all said with great affect. Three minutes later—seventeen minutes after the onset of the injection and ten minutes following its completion—the patient was clutching his head and saying, "This headache is killing me." He was asked, "Are the neighbors bothering you now?" "No, they're not. I just feel extremely tense as if my head is going to blow up." "Weren't the neighbors bothering you before?" "It seemed that way, but I don't think so now. If I could only get rid of this headache. I'm scared."

Two minutes later, the patient appeared to be in less distress. When he was asked whether his head bothered him, he said, "It hurts a little bit, but certainly not as bad as it did before." The patient appeared to be much less restless.

Two minutes later—twenty-one minutes after the onset of the injection and fourteen minutes following its completion—the patient sat quietly in his chair. He was asked, "How do you feel?" "I feel all right. I'm extremely tired. That was a terrible nightmare

I went through. It reminds me of some of the experiences that I had before I came into the hospital, only this was much worse. It's unreal. It seems impossible that I have said the things and talked about the things that I did just a while ago. How long have I been here?" When told that he had been in the laboratory for about an hour, he said, "It seems like I have been here for an eternity."

In this case, as in the first, the general pattern of simple amelioration was the reverse of that noted in response to increasing levels of anxiety.

LOBOTOMY

Craniotomies performed under local anesthesia were extremely stressful to a number of schizophrenic patients and resulted in hallucinatory aberrations in twelve. We were then able to observe the effect of lobotomy in the amelioration of the hallucinations.

Case Histories

1. The patient was a twenty-two-year-old, female college student who was born in Vienna and came to the United States at age nine to escape Nazi persecution. She adjusted poorly in this country, for she felt extremely lonely and discriminated against as a foreigner. At age eighteen she had a fantasied loved affair with one of her employers. She began to imagine that people were attacking her with their eyes. All people, particularly Blacks, were communicating with her through "signals." "All persons stare at me because I'm a foreigner."

She received psychiatric help at age eighteen and apparently obtained a complete remission after a long series of electroshock treatments. At age nineteen she entered college but did poorly there because she was unable to concentrate on her studies. She became very preoccupied with her body functions.

At age twenty she had a frustrating love affair following which she became very apathetic. The patient began to imagine that her psychology teacher could read her mind and was plotting against her. Once again, she received electroshock therapy, this time without significant benefit. Psychoanalytically oriented psychotherapy also was very unsuccessful, and she was admitted to a city hospital from which she was transferred to a state hospital.

There she received insulin and electroshock therapy. No benefits were obtained from these regimens and psychosurgery was recommended (this was in 1952). At the time of her operation her diagnosis was schizophrenia, chronic, mixed type. The patient was intermittently flat as to affect, but on occasion became very agitated. Her behavior was often characterized by spontaneous episodes of crying or laughing and giggling associated with her hallucinations. She was dominated by the delusions that Christians and Jews were persecuting her. They controlled her body and mind. The patient was obsessed with the fear that her brain was disintegrating from cancer. "Sometimes by brain cells go on thinking by themselves." She was preoccupied by auditory hallucinations as well.

During the early phases of the craniotomy the patient appeared relatively calm. She was actively hallucinating, and she described the aberrations with great clarity. During the drilling and sawing of the calvarium the patient demonstrated a marked increase in the motor aspect of anxiety followed by changes in facial expression and quality of voice.

She became extremely hostile toward me when I questioned her because "You are interfering with the voices that are communicating with me." At times the voices cursed her and used obscenities "because I am a foreigner." In some instances there were visual hallucinations associated with the auditory aberrations. As she became increasingly anxious she described that she could no longer hear the voices distinctly.

She cried out, "The cancer in my brain is spreading. It's pouring out of my mouth as I talk. It's flowing down my neck. Mop up my brains. I can smell my brain cells. They smell like vomit." The patient continued, "The brain cells are irritating my skin. They feel slimy like worms."

During this period the patient was extremely restless and her voice denoted terror. She talked incessantly. As the calvarium and dura were reflected the manifest content of the patient's hallucinations became progressively more primitive. Her speech finally became halting and fragmented. Neologisms were used. During periods of silence she pursed her lips and made sucking movements. At this point she ceased communicating verbally or by any other means. At this moment the lobotomy was begun.

This patient, who had a history of hallucinations prior to the operation, demonstrated under severe stress how the manifest content becomes more primitive as the level of anxiety is increased, and how olfactory and tactile hallucinations appear very late in the sequence of symptom formation. Finally in response to continued pressure all capacity to communicate was lost and the patient became completely mute.

The lateral half of the left frontal lobe was sectioned first. This resulted in a slight decrease in the motor component of anxiety in that the patient was slightly less restless. No changes were noted in any of the other clinical symptoms. The medial half of the left frontal lobe was the next portion of the brain to be sectioned. This produced a greater decrease in the motor component of anxiety, and the sucking movement disappeared. The patient began to speak again, but now made no reference to smelling her "decomposing brain." In response to direct questioning she stated that she heard people talking about her critically and that some young men were trying to talk her into sexual activity.

During the cutting of the medial half of the right frontal lobe the affective impact associated with the auditory hallucination was sharply decreased. At this time, when the patient was asked whether the voices were bothering her, she answered, "They're talking to me but they don't bother me." Ten minutes after the completion of the lobotomy all hallucinations disappeared. She also denied any difficulties with her brain. Her paranoid delusion had cleared. The patient appeared very relaxed physically and answered all questions calmly.

One could observe during the course of the lobotomy how this patient shifted from a noncommunicative state to a gradual amelioration of her various hallucinatory manifestations. The more primitive hallucinatory patterns were ameliorated first, as I repeatedly noted with all types of therapy.

2. Another female patient, age thirty-five, had a history of recurrent hallucinations of several years duration. She had a long history of hypochondriacal manifestations beginning in adolescence. During her twenties the hypochondriacal pattern at times became distorted and took on the quality of somatic delusions. These symptoms responded only partially to psychotherapy, insulin coma, and electroshock treatments. Her auditory hallucinations had a strong sexual content in which the voices accused her of sexual perversion. More recently she was distressed by aberrations in which "a ray that was projected from Brooklyn 5000 miles away was irritating her vagina." This pattern began as a "sputtering" or "hissing" sound that became fused with the auditory hallucinations in which she was being accused of sexual perversions. The hissing sound was then associated with "a ray," whose purpose was to irritate her vagina.

In late 1952 the patient was prepared for a lobotomy. During the preoperative preparations and also during the craniotomy proper the patient was only slightly restless and the level of overt anxiety was relatively less than that seen with most other patients. During the earliest portion of the operation, while the scalp was being incised, she denied any hallucinations. However, when the burrholes were being drilled and when the calvarium was being sawed the patient complained about auditory hallucinations that were similar to those that had been present for a number of years. The auditory hallucinations persisted for almost twenty minutes before she complained about "the ray originating in Brooklyn 5000 miles away that irritated her vagina." The patient demanded that her arms be released so that she could scratch the vulva area.

In this patient the medial half of the right frontal lobe was the first portion of the brain to be leucotomized. This resulted in a definite decrease in muscle tonus and the disappearance of all restlessness. At this point the patient continued to complain about her various hallucinations. However, following the sectioning of the lateral half of the right frontal lobe the tactile aberrations disappeared completely. She continued to complain that she heard voices, but there was less affect associated with these residual hallucinations at this particular point. All the hallucinations disappeared following the cutting of the medial portion of the left frontal lobe.

This patient demonstrated how, under the stress of a craniotomy, hallucinatory patterns similar to those that occurred secondary to environmental stress could be reproduced. During the course of the lobotomy one noted that the tactile hallucinations disappeared prior to the disappearance of the auditory hallucinations.

ELECTROSHOCK THERAPY

As part of my study I treated many actively hallucinating schizophrenic patients with a series of electroshock treatments.

Case History

1. The patient was a thirty-two-year-old, single, female schoolteacher who had demonstrated difficulty in social situations since adolescence. It should be mentioned that her father had two siblings who were confined in mental institutions. The mother was a very rigid, dominant, rejecting personality who displayed considerable sadism at times. The patient was in constant conflict with her.

In high school, the patient had difficulty socializing; this continued in college and in graduate school. She obtained a job teaching grammar school, but always functioned at a very marginal level. Hypochondriacal trends manifested themselves whenever she was exposed to stressful situations, even those of minor proportions. At times, they progressed to the point that they took on the characteristics of somatic delusions. She was frequently referential toward her colleagues.

Approximately two years prior to the onset of psychiatric care, her performance in school deteriorated further, and she became very restless. She often awakened her family at night complaining about her heart or head. Any menstrual irregularity terrified her. In response to psychotherapy in combination with oral phenothiazines she demonstrated a moderate degree of improvement and then withdrew from treatment.

The patient returned to her job, but it soon became an overwhelming task. She again became very restless and paced incessantly. This was always the first indication of increasing anxiety in this patient. During the next few days she appeared very anxious, developed marked logorrhea, and incessantly argued with her mother. The patient became preoccupied with her heart. She then was afraid that she had some terrible blood disease and was obsessed with the fear that she was dying. Associated with some slight menstrual irregularity, she became convinced that she was pregnant although she had never had any sexual contacts.

In this state, she was admitted to a private psychiatric hospital. In the hospital, she became increasingly anxious. Shortly after admission she expressed ideas that the attendants were plotting to kill her under my direction and that her parents were involved in the plot. The patient felt that the room was tapped and that whatever she said or thought was being recorded. She had visual hallucinations to the effect that I had entered the room during the night to observe her. (No one entered her room.) She accused me of taking blood from her during the night as part of the plot to gradually debilitate her, a debilitation that was calculated to surreptitiously cause her death.

The patient refused food for fear that it was poisoned. After seventy-two hours in the hospital she awakened in terror, complaining that gas was being released into the room. "The gas smelled like rotten eggs and it was cyanide." She complained the following morning that she could taste poison in her saliva.

Twenty-four hours later, when the therapist entered her room, she cried out, "I'm dead. You've finally killed me. I will kill you with my poison." With that she touched her lips with her finger and then touched the therapist's hand. "You are now dead. Your face is decaying, just like mine." She then began to scream, "Don't touch me! Don't touch me!" Following that, she cried out in terror, "My hands, you've taken my hands! They're just stumps." Within five more minutes, the patient was unable to communicate verbally. She tore at her clothes, urinated on the floor, and lay down in her urine and rolled about moaning and shouting incomprehensibly.

Thus far the patient had demonstrated the development and appearance of a series of secondary defense mechanisms. She developed auditory and then visual hallucinations. As the level of anxiety continued to increase the manifest content of these hallucinations became more primitive. The patient also manifested olfactory hallucinations. Finally she manifested the psychic anarchy state in which she lost all capacity to communicate and was dominated by primitive nonpurposeful behavior patterns.

On the same day, she was started on electroshock treatment. The only change noted after the first two treatments was that verbal communication was reestablished with the patient, who was again able to verbalize her hallucinations. She continued to have tactile, olfactory, visual, and auditory hallucinations. The patient remained extremely paranoid toward the entire staff.

Following the third treatment, the tactile and olfactory hallucinations disappeared. She no longer complained that her hands were stumps, and she no longer claimed that her room was filled with cyanide. The delusion that she was dead also cleared at this point. However, she continued to have visual and auditory hallucinations and remained very referential toward the entire staff. The patient still maintained that staff members came into her room at night for the purpose of killing her and that there was a grand plot between the staff and her parents.

Following the fifth treatment the patient seemed slightly less agitated. Although the patient paced the floor less frequently, she continued to scream at the staff on frequent occasions. Following the tenth treatment, there was far less affect related to her hypochondriacal manifestations. After the eleventh treatment, all complaints with regard to any of her organ systems cleared. She was much calmer and was very cooperative and cheerful in her relationships with other patients and with the hospital staff. There was surprisingly little organic mental deficit as a result of the eleven treatments.

This patient too dramatically demonstrates that which occurs as the intensity of anxiety rapidly increases. It is particularly illuminating as to the process through which hallucinations proceed as a patient becomes progressively more anxious, in that additional senses become involved while the manifest content of the hallucinations becomes increasingly primitive.

After electroshock treatment was instituted, it was noted that the last symptom to appear during the phase of exacerbation was the first to disappear. With reference to hallucinations, the more primitive ideation and the aberrations referring to phylogenetically more primitive senses cleared before the visual or auditory hallucinations disappeared. I have noted consistently that, even after the more primitive types of hallucinations appeared (olfactory, tactile), if the patient became increasingly anxious a point was finally reached when there was complete disintegration of the patient's ego, until he or she literally would crawl about in the fashion of an animal of a low phylogenetic order.

9

PSYCHOSOMATIC DISORDERS

The psychiatric literature dealing with psychosomatic disorders is a mass of confusion. Nowhere is this more evident than in the psychoanalytic literature in which specific psychodynamic patterns have been attributed to disorders associated with different organs or organ systems. The literature is also replete with poorly controlled experiments in which a multitude of mechanical recording devices have been offered as a substitute for good experimental design. Only a sprinkling of papers, most of them found in the European literature, have taken into consideration Wilder's Law of Initial Value (Wilder, 1931, 1956). There is no branch of psychiatry in which a recording of the prestimulus or pretherapeutic level of functioning is more important than in the study of psychosomatic disorders. In the absence of such knowledge research reports have comparatively little validity.

In this chapter I will report on my observations of the relationship between the quantitative degree of anxiety and the appearance and amelioration of psychosomatic symptoms. A study of psychosomatic disorders provides an excellent opportunity to study the autonomic component of anxiety. This is so because psychosomatic disorders represent, in great measure, an extension or prolongation or objectification of the autonomic component of anxiety.

In all my studies I could not elicit any valid information as to why one specific organ system became abnormally involved in response to stress. Indeed, as I will discuss later in this chapter, my studies indicated that the basic psychodynamic mechanisms for all psychosomatic disorders were very similar. The retrospective type of analysis, on which much of the psychiatric literature dealing with psychosomatic illnesses is based, unfortunately reflects more the philosophic prejudices of the authors than a dispassionate capacity for observation.

In all, a total of 151 patients who had psychosomatic manifestations as part of their over-all psychiatric illnesses are included in this study. This diagnostic spectrum in this group is very broad. All the patients treated by intensive psychoanalysis could best be characterized as having psychoneuroses in combination with social and sexual maladaptation. Most of the patients treated by brief psychoanalytically oriented psychotherapy alone also fell into this diagnostic category. Some were categorized as having schizophrenia, pseudoneurotic type. Those patients treated with brief psychoanalytically oriented psychotherapy in combination with psychotropic drugs included individuals with schizoid personalities in various degrees of decompensation, patients with involutional depressions, and patients with severe psychoneuroses. Those who required electroshock therapy were either severely decompensated schizophrenic patients or individuals with very severe agitated depressions. As I have enumerated in other chapters, those who received hallucinogenic drugs, in all but a few instances, were severely decompensated schizophrenics.

The patients who had psychosomatic illnesses as part of their clinical psychiatric syndromes represent almost one quarter of all the patients included in this book. This point may be accounted for by my being on the neurologic staff of a large, integrated medical center and very frequently called in consultation by members of various other departments, my being board certified in both psychiatry and neurology and in addition being an analyst, and my having had a special interest in psychosomatic problems. The following types of psychosomatic illnesses were studied in 151 patients:

Illnesses	*Patients*
1. Autonomic faciocephalalgia (cluster headaches)	45
2. Migraine headache	20
3. Essential hypertension	19
4. Colitis	13
5. Peptic ulcer	13
6. Vertigo (no objective organic deficits)	12
7. Asthma	10
8. Urinary dysfunction	8
9. Neurodermatitis	5
10. Diabetes mellitus	4
11. Angioneurotic edema	2
Total	151

A number of patients had psychosexual problems, such as impotency, frigidity, and dyspareunia, in addition to the problems listed above. I have not included psychosexual disorders in this chapter.

There are some readers who may disagree with the inclusion of vertigo and diabetes mellitus as psychosomatic illnesses. As far as the first of these ailments is concerned, I have seen far more patients with a clear history of vertigo who after intensive laboratory studies have demonstrated no organic deficit than those for whom organic deficits have been documented. Those patients who experience vertigo secondary to emotional stress do not have associated nystagmus. In listing diabetes mellitus I am not negating the proven anatomic and endocrinologic abnormalities that clearly have been demonstrated as a definite cause of this ailment. To the contrary, I merely mean to stress the close relationship between diabetes mellitus and psychic disturbance in some patients.

MOUNTING ANXIETY AND PSYCHOSOMATIC SYNDROMES

As I have noted in earlier chapters, an increase in the motor component of anxiety (tension) heralds mounting anxiety in the vast majority of patients. Also, the various psychiatric symptoms and signs begin to appear only after there is a definite increase in the affective component. Of great importance in this chapter is my observation that an increase in the autonomic aspect of anxiety usually parallels an increase in the affective component.

SOCIOENVIRONMENTAL STRESS

I was able to obtain very detailed accounts of the development of a variety of clinical psychiatric symptoms and signs in relation to environmental stress for 126 of the 151 patients who had psychosomatic syndromes.

I found convincing data for 109 (86.5 percent) of these 126 patients indicating an increased degree of anxiety prior to the onset of any clinical symptoms and signs. For eighty-eight (80.8 percent) of this group of 109 patients an increase in the motor aspect of anxiety signaled the appearance of an emotional disturbance. Ninety-nine (90.9 percent) of these same 109 patients demonstrated an increase in the affective component of anxiety prior to the appearance of well-defined psychosomatic disturbances.

Psychosomatic disorders rarely exist as an isolated clinical psychiatric entity. They are usually seen as part of the mosaic of clinical psychiatric symptoms and signs that occur as a result of stress. Further, it is uncommon for the clinical manifestations of a psychosomatic disorder to be first in the parade of symptoms and signs that make up the fully developed clinical psychiatric picture.

Symptoms such as phobias, hypochondriasis, obsessions, and compulsions usually were noted prior to the appearance of psychosomatic problems.

For 116 (92.1 percent) of the 126 patients whose histories were considered adequate for reliable evaluation as to the appearance of secondary defense mechanisms, there was no particular predilection for a specific symptom or group of symptoms to precede a given psychosomatic disorder if the study group was considered as a whole. It should be pointed out, however, that it is very rare (one patient) for bizarre aberrations such as delusions, illusions, and hallucinations to antedate the overt appearance of a psychosomatic disorder.

In Chapter 4 I indicated that there is a definite pattern in which symptoms and signs appear secondary to increasing anxiety. Psychosomatic disorders, in a given patient, have their specific position in the order in which clinical symptoms and signs appear. This observation was substantiated in a study of eighty-four patients who were followed for more than one year and who, during this period, had two or more exacerbations of their psychosomatic disorders in response to repeated bouts of severe stress. Seventy-one (84.4 percent) of these eight-four patients demonstrated that the psychosomatic symptoms had a similar position in the sequence of symptom appearance on more than one occasion in response to repeated bouts of marked anxiety secondary to recurrent periods of stress.

The following case history illustrates some of these points.

Case History

1. The patient, a forty-two-year-old, unmarried, female executive assistant had always been a very conscientious, hard-working individual. She was devoted to her family. When she was age eighteen her mother became handicapped by rheumatoid arthritis and diabetes mellitus. The patient took it upon herself to be her mother's nurse, her father's housekeeper, and, at the same time, to care for her younger brother who was severely crippled. These obligations were in addition to her job as an executive secretary. In the management of all her activities she was meticulous. Her mother died when the patient was twenty-five. Though the patient was socially active with female friends, she rarely went out with men. She continued to care for her father and to "mother" her brother.

When she was aged thirty her father died suddenly. It was about that time that she had the one romance of her life. Although marriage was discussed, she terminated the relationship with the rationalization that "my brother needs me most." During this period she developed a severe, spasmodic torticollis, which lasted about eight months and then cleared spontaneously without any formal psychiatric help.

Ten months prior to her first psychiatric visit, her brother married a young woman who was also crippled. Prior to her brother's marriage but following his engagement her fellow employees and friends noted that she was "very restless and fidgety." Before they called this to her attention she was totally unaware of these symptoms. Prior to the wedding she became more restless and even tremulous at times.

Her friends and colleagues commented that she "appeared worried," was often irritable, and frequently shouted in response to questions or when giving an order. Immediately prior to the wedding her work, which had always been exemplary, was characterized by unnecessary compulsiveness that severely limited her efficiency. She became obsessed with infinitesimal details and incessantly checked and rechecked her work. Shortly after her brother's marriage, an elevator in which she was a passenger was caught briefly between two floors. She was very frightened by the episode and thereafter was very apprehensive and phobic in anticipation of riding any elevators. She later became extremely disturbed in anticipation of entering subways or airplanes or riding through tunnels in an automobile.

One month following her brother's wedding, which was nine months prior to her first visit, her new sister-in-law informed the patient that she and the brother were planning to move to a Southern city. At that point the patient experienced a burning pain over the right maxillary area that rapidly became excruciating and radiated to her right eye and over the right side of the bridge of the nose. The right eye began to lacrimate and the conjunctiva showed vascular engorgement. The nasal mucosa and the hard and soft palate on the right side became swollen. This entire episode lasted approximately forty minutes and left the patient feeling exhausted.

For approximately two months she had recurrences of these painful episodes every three to seven days, each episode appearing approximately one to one and one-half hours after she fell asleep. Seven months prior to her neuropsychiatric consultations these episodes of autonomic faciocephalalgia spontaneously remitted. About the same time her friends commented that she appeared to have accepted her brother's departure. She became less tense and restless, and her phobic problems cleared. Her work patterns improved also in that her obsessive-compulsive behavior was vastly improved.

Three months, later, following an extended period of work under great pressure, she again showed signs of increasing anxiety initiated by restlessness and tremors. The obsessive-compulsive work habits reappeared, and shortly after this she again became claustrophobic in elevators. Five days following the exacerbation of the claustrophobic symptoms the very painful cluster headaches returned. These excruciating paroxysms of pain came on approximately two or three times per week. After visits to several physicians she was referred for neuropsychiatric evaluation at which time I recorded the preceding history from the patient and two of her colleagues and friends.

This then was a patient who had two similar episodes of symptom appearance in response to environmental stress. One can note that on each occasion, in response to mounting anxiety, the patient first developed obsessive-compulsive problems which in reailty were extensions of her rigid personality matrix. On each occasion these in turn were followed by phobic manifestations and finally by severe psychosomatic symptoms. The characterization of autonomic faciocephalalgia in this case history as being severe is an understatement; it represents one of the most excruciating types of pain known to neurologists.

HALLUCINOGENIC AGENTS

Five of the severely ill patients who received hallucinogenic agents had psychosomatic disorders as part of their clinical syndromes. Diagnostically these patients could be categorized as follows:

1. Two patients had severe agitated depressions. One also had autonomic faciocephalalgia. The other had migraine headaches.

2. Three patients were diagnosed as being schizophrenic. One had colitis. A second had vertigo associated with nausea and, at times, vomiting. A third had angioneurotic edema.

In Chapter 3 I described the relationship of the various components of anxiety in relationship to one another secondary to hallucinogenic agents. In Chapter 4 the relationship of symptoms and signs secondary to mounting anxiety was described. In those patients who received hallucinogenic agents vital signs were recorded at two-minute intervals. In addition, continuous psychogalvanometric recordings were made in some patients. Three case histories follow.

Case Histories

1. The patient was a forty-five-year-old housewife who had a recurrent history characterized by compulsions and severe agitated depressions. She had a long history of psychiatric treatment including more than six years of psychoanalytic psychotherapy and several series of electroshock treatments. The electroshock treatments produced transient improvement. The patient also had a history of migraine headaches beginning during early adolescence. These could be precipitated during periods of frustrated anger and during the premenstrual phase of her menstrual cycle. In 1954, during a severe exacerbation of an agitated depressed state associated with marked suicidal preoccupations, she was admitted to a psychiatric hospital.

The patient was a very aggressive, dogmatic perfectionist who dominated her home and the social life of the small community in which she lived. Her father was a passive, dependent man completely dominated by an obsessive-compulsive, hypochondriacal wife. The patient's mother was a martyr in her own eyes and never failed to inform the patient of "how much she had done for her." The patient, an only child, was in constant conflict with her mother and at age eighteen "escaped" into a marriage to a very passive, dependent man whom she dominated completely.

In the hospital the patient very rapidly improved symptomatically without specific therapy. On the seventh day of hospitalization she was given mescaline intravenously. Prior to the injection she appeared relatively relaxed and cheerful. Eight minutes following the injection she became restless and bagan to fidget with her clothes. At this point, when asked how she felt, she replied that she felt quite well. The restlesness increased in degree, and the patient began to tremble.

Twelve minutes following the injection the patient's face became very taut and she cried out and repeated in a crescendo fashion, "No! Stop! Let me alone!" When questioned she related with great animation the recurrent obsessive thought that "I struck my mother with a sharp instrument and wounded her gravely." Immediately after relating this story the patient complained of flashing, jagged lines in her right eye. Accompanying this she became very nauseated. Two minutes later she complained of intense, throbbing, right-sided headaches associated with nausea and vomiting. The entire episode was aborted after ten minutes by an intravenous injection of 75 milligrams of chlorpromazine.

This patient demonstrated in rapid fashion marked motor restlessness followed by an increase in the affective aspect of anxiety. I then noted obsessive phenomena followed by migraine prodromata and finally the development of a severe migraine headache.

2. A forty-two-year-old housewife had a three-year history of intermittent episodes characterized by a unilateral facial pain usually occurring one to two hours after she fell asleep. The pains were described as "burning, boring or tearing sensations" beginning over the inner canthus of the right eye, spreading over the right maxillary and the temporomandibular regions. These areas all became exquisitely tender to touch. The conjunctiva of the right eye became engorged and there was profuse ipsilateral lacrimation. The nasal mucosa and the hard palate on the same side swelled greatly. If the patient did not receive parenteral treatment these agonizing episodes lasted from thirty to ninety minutes. If at the very onset of the episode the patient received ergotamine tartrate intramuscularly, the pains could be aborted in ten to fifteen minutes.

The patient was a very active, capable woman who assumed the emotional responsibilities of her siblings and her elderly parents in addition to those of her husband and three children. She was meticulous in all her activities and anything that interfered with her routine household chores was extremely disturbing to her. Four years prior to her initial psychiatric consultation, following the death of her father, she assumed even greater responsibilities by taking her mother into her home. Two months later the patient was noted to be restless and complained of fatigue and insomnia. At night she often awakened complaining of severe dyspnea and palpitations. She became terrified that she was dying of a heart attack. Repeated investigations by several cardiologists revealed no cardiac deficit.

During the next few years, associated with periods of increased family problems, she had similar panic attacks. Three months prior to her first visit to my office her mother died. This precipitated a severe agitated depression characterized by overwhelming suicidal drives that finally led to her hospitalization.

In the protective surroundings of the hospital her agitated depression subsided to a considerable degree without specific treatment. She then was given intravenous mescaline. Ten minutes following the injection she became very restless, then tremulous. Two minutes later her face became contorted and she appeared terrified. Fifteen minutes after the injection she began to moan and clutch her chest. She cried out in terror that she was having a heart attack. At this point a moderate tachycardia and slight decrease in both systolic and diastolic blood pressures were noted.

The patient began to weep and beg forgiveness for the fact that she had wished her mother's death and for the many arguments she had had with her siblings and husband. In this setting she began to complain about a dull, throbbing pain around and in the right eye. This rapidly increased in severity and was then described as being agonizing in degree and boring and burning in quality. The pain spread to involve the fronto-temporal and maxillary regions, nose, and hard palate all on the right side. Marked conjunctival vascular engorgement was noted together with unilateral lacrimation and severe edema of the right nares and hard palate. The episode was terminated by the intravenous administration of 75 milligrams of chlorpromazine.

One again, in response to the use of an hallucinogenic agent this patient demonstrated the rapid development of the motor component and then the affective aspects of anxiety followed by hypochondriacal manifestations. Next, expressions of excessive guilt mechanisms were noted. Lastly, the patient developed a full-blown autonomic facio-cephalalgic syndrome.

Neither of these two patients developed aberrations such as illusions or hallucinations.

3. The patient was a twenty-two-year-old, single musician who was described as having been "an outstanding student but rather shy as a child." He was extremely conscientious and very courteous. However, though he was very demanding of attention he was also very cold in his family relationships. He was meticulous with his possessions and in his study habits. As an adolescent he was a top student, but socially he was always very seclusive.

Most of his time was spent alone either reading or practicing the saxophone. His compulsive behavior became more pronounced, and, if his room was disturbed by a member of the family, violent temper tantrums occurred. To the outside world he remained a very courteous, intelligent adolescent. During this period he had repeated fantasies and dreams in which his mother had a penis. He masturbated several times per day, particularly if he anticipated taking an examination. The masturbatory fantasies always consisted of his suckling the breasts of and practicing fellatio on a large-breasted, middle-aged woman who had a huge organ that protruded from her vagina.

Following his graduation from high school he entered college, where he majored in music. He had difficulty adjusting to the new surroundings. Though his grades were average he was noted to be more restless. By the end of his freshman year he was unusually apprehensive about his examinations. He was constantly worried and on occasion had crying spells. Sometimes he had severe temper outbursts directed especially toward his very agressive mother. Following each of these aggressive episodes he was consumed with guilt.

He was also obsessed with the fear that he had cancer associated with a nonspecific, transient enlargement of his inguinal lymph nodes. This cancer phobia continued even though the lymphadenopathy cleared. In addition to this he became preoccupied with fears that he might make mistakes in his homework, and be began to compulsively check and recheck everything he did.

Shortly before his first examination he became very vertiginous. Associated with this he had profuse nausea and vomiting. A thorough neurologic examination including laboratory testings revealed no organic deficits. Though he passed his courses, he dropped out of the university for eighteen months. During this period his symptoms continued. Whenever he was exposed to situations that were in any way stressful he developed marked vertigo associated with nausea and vomiting. At no time was nystagmus observed.

When he returned to college he was unable to perform effectively. His compulsiveness increased in severity and his bouts of vertigo became more frequent and severe. He developed referential trends toward his teachers and then toward a specific neighbor. One night before dinner he pounced on his mother when she asked him to wash his hands. After shouting at her and striking her a few times he began to scream uncontrollably. A local physician was called, and the patient was sedated. He was referred to a psychoanalyst and intensive therapy was begun. In spite of this treatment he became progressively worse. Auditory hallucinations associated with frank, paranoid delusions developed.

After almost two years of treatment he was seen by me in consultation. At that time he was actively psychotic and was diagnosed as having schizophrenia, mixed type. He was extremely agitated, and hospitalization was advised.

During the first few weeks in the hospital with simple supportive psychotherapy he appeared calmer and his hallucinations subsided. The obsessive-compulsive patterns were less marked and the vertigo cleared. In this setting he was given 125 micrograms of oral lysergic acid.

Approximately one hour after the drug was administered he became very tense and restless. When asked whether he was frightened he answered, "No!" After another forty-five minutes had passed he appeared overtly frightened and began to cry. His pulse rate and respiratory rate increased, and there was a moderate rise in systolic blood pressure. He became terrified that he was going to die. He was afraid that either I or the hospital attendant was going to hurt him. The patient began to scream. Following this he complained of a throbbing in his head and then severe vertigo associated with nausea and retching. No nystagmus was noted. The vertigo persisted for fifteen minutes.

The patient then complained of terrifying visual and then olfactory hallucinations all related to the idea that his head and genitals were becoming deformed. He began to babble wildly and incoherently. At this point intravenous chlorpromazine was administered and the psychotic episode was terminated.

This very sick schizophrenic patient demonstrated, in response to LSD-25, increased anxiety followed by hypochondriacal manifestations. These, in turn, were followed by psychosomatic difficulties. Last, hallucinations appeared.

CRANIOTOMIES

Of the forty-three chronically ill schizophrenic patients exposed to the stress of a large craniotomy under local anesthesia only four had definite psychosomatic problems as part of their illnesses. All four were diagnosed as having schizophrenia, pseudoneurotic type.

The following are some examples of these patients' responses to the stress of the operation:

Case Histories

1. The patient was a thirty-seven-year-old, unmarried secretary who had a twelve-year history of pananxiety and panphobic states. She had a proven duodenal ulcer that was relatively inactive as measured by the lack of clinical complaints. The patient had many years of intensive exposure to psychoanalytic treatment and various organic therapies prior to her hospitalization in 1951, at which time a leucotomy was recommended. In addition to frequent panic attacks and her panphobic states, which had rendered her completely indigent vocationally and socially for many years, there were periods associated with marked anxiety during which time there were clear-cut difficulties with reality contact.

At the onset of the craniotomy the patient appeared relatively calm. Even when her scalp was being injected and incised she demonstrated very little increase in anxiety. However, as the burr holes were being drilled she began to clench her fists, and there was a marked increase in muscle tension in all limbs. At this time there was no change in affect.

As the calvarium was being sawed she began to grimace and her voice denoted marked apprehension in response to my questions. Simultaneously the pulse and respiratory rate increased, and there was a dramatic increase in systolic blood pressure. Concomitantly a decrease in electrical flow was recorded psychogalvanometrically. At this point the patient cried out in terror, "Something terrible is happening! I think I'm going to lose my mind!" Fears of dying reminiscent of the terror she had repeatedly experienced since adolescence were expressed. "I'm going to have a stroke. I'll die! I'll die!" Shortly thereafter claustrophobic symptoms, similar to those that plagued her in everyday life, became prominent. "I'm smothering. Untie my wrists. The room is hot It seems like the walls are closing in."

Following this she began to complain of a constant, severe burning and gnawing sensation in her epigastric region. "Damn it! Damn it! There go my ulcer pains again!" The epigastric pains continued during the remainder of the craniotomy. They were finally ameliorated by the lobotomy.

In summary, this patient demonstrated an increase in the motor component of anxiety followed by the simultaneous change in the affective and autonomic phases of anxiety. Shortly thereafter hypochondriacal and then phobic symptoms appeared Psychosomatic manifestations followed in turn.

2. This patient was a nineteen-year-old unemployed male who had been psychiatrically ill since childhood. His adolescence was characterized by extreme sociopathic behavior in which he was involved in gang wars and acts of stealing. Marked emotional lability and a very low threshold to any stressful phenomena characterized his difficulties. In addition, the patient had a very severe neurodermatitis involving his face. Despite active treatment by many dermatologists his face was a mass of scar tissue interspaced by infected, weeping wounds that were aggravated by compulsive picking and scratching. The patient had several years of intensive psychotherapy followed by repeated exposures to electroshock and insulin coma without any significant benefits. In 1951 he was finally referred for psychosurgical help.

Very early during the craniotomy the patient showed a marked increase in muscle tonus followed by severe restlessness. During the scalp incision his face began to contort, and he cried out in alarm, "I'm going to die! I'm going to die! Don't let me die!" There was a marked increase in pulse rate and a moderate rise in blood pressure.

At this point he began to complain of marked facial pruritus. He pleaded and then demanded that someone scratch his face hard. Though I rubbed his face with a wet cloth it afforded no relief. His agitation and his struggling with his wrist and ankle restraints and his agonizing preoccupation with his face became so pronounced that it was necessary to administer a general anesthetic, and the remainder of the craniotomy and subsequent lobotomy were performed while he was anesthetized.

The patient, in summary, was a severely ill, decompensated schizophrenic with marked sociopathic overtones. As he became increasingly anxious during the craniotomy, despite vigorous attempts at adequate preoperative sedation (this antedated the introduction of the tranquilizers), his psychosomatic complaints exacerbated following an increase in the motor and the affective and autonomic phases of anxiety. In this patient the psychosomatic symptoms were the initial secondary defense mechanisms.

This pattern was observed in a few patients in whom sociopathic behavior was a prominent part of the clinical picture. In this patient the persistent and usually destructive process of acting out, which had been his prime means of anxiety decompression, was inhibited on the operating table. The only other secondary defense mechanism that had become a conditioned response in this patient, in response to rapidly mounting anxiety, was the psychosomatic process.

STRESS ASSOCIATED WITH PSYCHOTHERAPY

As all psychotherapists know too well, the very process of psychotherapy, whether intensive reconstructive psychoanalysis, the briefer psychoanalytically oriented type of psychotherapy, or even supportive psychotherapy, may in itself be the source of increased stress that at times may be of pronounced proportions. This adverse response appearing secondary to the psychotherapeutic procedure per se affords the psychiatrist an excellent opportunity to study the relationship between anxiety and other clinical symptoms and signs even though the psychophysiologic changes that occur in this setting are usually not so rapid and intense as those induced by biochemical or neurosurgical means.

I treated 125 patients who had psychosomatic problems by various psychotherapeutic techniques. Fifteen were treated by intensive psychoanalysis, twenty-four by psychoanalytically oriented psychotherapy alone, and eighty-six by psychoanalytically oriented psychotherapy combined with various psychotropic drugs.

In some of these patients I frequently observed recurrent exacerbations of their psychosomatic complaints in response to pressures that were directly attributable to the psychotherapeutic process. Some exacerbations were due to miscalculations on my part; some were unavoidable; others were deliberately caused by me as part of the study.

I would like to point out that, with all types of psychotherapy where an exacerbation of symptoms occurs in response to the stress of therapy or to a persistent environmental stress, the exacerbation of clinical psychiatric symptoms and signs paralleled the sequence noted in the patient's history. The instances in which the psychosomatic difficulties appeared as the initial symptoms in response to increased anxiety were in those patients in whom the psychosomatic problem was "fixed," that is, patients in whom the psychosomatic processes had produced definitive anatomic lesions. Examples of this were noted in patients with essential hypertension in whom there was severe cardiac enlargement; patients with chronic peptic ulcers associated with heavily scarred craters; patients with colitis associated with a chronic history of bleeding; patients with asthma associated with definite emphysema.

DECREASING ANXIETY AND PSYCHOSOMATIC SYNDROMES

As I recorded in Chapters 5 and 6, the degree of anxiety must first be decreased before a symptom disappears. These observations were seen with great consistency with all types of therapy and were confirmed in my study of patients with psychosomatic symptoms.

INTENSIVE RECONSTRUCTIVE PSYCHOANALYSIS

As I mentioned before, fifteen patients with psychosomatic illnesses, all within the framework of a psychoneurotic process, were treated psychoanalytically. They had the following psychosomatic illnesses:

Illness	*Patients*
1. Peptic ulcer	3
2. Autonomic faciocephalalgia	3
3. Migraine headaches	3
4. Essential hypertension	3
5. Colitis	2
6. Diabetes mellitus	1
	—
Total	15

As one might expect, the amelioration of the presenting signs was not so dramatic or rapid when psychoanalytic psychotherapy was used alone as compared with the results obtained with various organic therapies. However, if the psychoanalyst is keenly aware of the relationship between anxiety and other clinical manifestations, and if he records this relationship as therapy progresses, he will see a very dramatic biodynamic scene unfold before him.

I found that thirteen of the fifteen patients in this group demonstrated a decrease in the motor aspect of anxiety heralding any improvement. Improvement in the affective component usually followed in from one day to one week. As related in earlier chapters, improvement in the clinical symptoms and signs followed the decrease in the affective component. The relative denudation of the affect associated with the various symptoms was noted. As I noted in Chapter 6, the last symptom to appear was usually the first symptom to be ameliorated. This rule, in general, also pertained to psychosomatic disorders. The exceptions that did occur were in those patients in whom there was very severe anatomic change associated with a chronic psychosomatic disorder.

An illustrative case follows.

Case History

The patient was a twenty-five-year-old, married, female secretary who was an identical monozygotic twin She had been a very anxious person since early childhood. The patient disliked being a twin and felt that she was always "on display." She was in constant competition with her twin sister, whom she considered to be more attractive than she and who she felt was their parents' favorite.

The patient attempted to gain attention through intellectual pursuits and was meticulous in all her behavior patterns. During childhood she exhibited varied hypochondriacal patterns, particularly the persistent fear of hurting herself physically. Intermittently since childhood she had bouts of mucous colitis.

During midadolescence she became "extremely embarrassed for other people if they made fools of themselves. This made me feel physically ill." By this she meant that she would become nauseated and have episodes of diarrhea. In these situations, which could take place even if she was looking at a television program, she would become panicky and dash from the room. Similar behavior patterns occurred whenever she was the center of attention. During her midadolescent period the patient also developed marked claustrophobic problems and band-like tension headaches.

At age nineteen she married a very passive, dependent person. From the very beginning there were general discord and severe sexual problems. Approximately one year later the patient developed severe epigastric distress, and a duodenal ulcer was diagnosed roentgenologically. Three years later, because of the persistence of these symptoms, she began psychotherapy.

During the first few months of treatment the patient demonstrated marked anxiety that prevailed in her psychotherapeutic sessions as well as her everyday performance. The first signs of improvement were evidenced by a decrease in movement in the manifest content of her dreams. Several weeks later I noted the patient was much less restless during her sessions, and I was informed that she had ceased pacing and fidgeting in the waiting room. However, she still was overtly anxious as expressed by her facial expressions and tone of voice. Over the next two weeks the patient's affect improved. However, her psychosomatic problems, phobias, and obsessive thinking continued even in this relatively calm atmosphere.

The patient went through many stressful situations during her three years of psychoanalytic psychotherapy and there were repeated remissions and exacerbations of symptoms and signs. However, the pattern of symptom appearance and exacerbation was repeated essentially without change on each occasion. The number of symptoms that appeared or remitted depended on the intensity of the increase or the degree of amelioration of anxiety respectively. It was interesting to note that as the patient became more anxious the mucous colitis, chronologically by far the oldest of the psychosomatic problems, always presented itself before the epigastric distress associated with her peptic ulcer. However, in keeping with the general rule that the last symptom to appear is usually the first to clear, as the patient became less anxious the epigastric distress improved before the bouts of colitis subsided.

PSYCHOANALYTICALLY ORIENTED PSYCHOTHERAPY IN COMBINATION WITH PSYCHOTROPIC DRUGS

The eighty-six patients treated with this combined therapy were diagnosed as having (1) schizophrenia, pseudoneurotic type, (2) severe agitated depressions, or (3) severe psychoneuroses. In all instances they were extremely anxious at the onset of treatment. I noted a decrease in the motor component of anxiety heralding the earliest improvement in seventy-two of the eighty-six patients. It was rare for the improvement in affect to precede or even parallel the improvement in the motor component.

The process of the reduction of the degree of anxiety and the rate of amelioration of other symptoms and signs including the psychosomatic symptoms was much more rapid when phenothiazines were used in combination with psychotherapy than when psychotherapy was used alone.

The following is a rather typical example.

Case History

The patient was a thirty-eight-year-old, married, business executive who was a driving, aggressive, meticulous person whose vocational life occupied almost all of his waking hours He was extremely successful in his chosen field. As a husband, father, and social being he was a failure. He was dominated by feelings of inadequacy, which were just below the level of consciousness. His life was spent compensating for these feelings. Six months prior to his first visit, following a long period of financial pressure, he had a panic attack during which he was obsessed by the belief that he was dying of a heart attack. Subsequently he had many similar attacks, especially when he was in a light state of sleep.

Shortly after the first panic attack, the patient began to develop a pananxiety state and a succession of phobias. He was intermittently agoraphobic. At times he had claustrophobic manifestations. Elevators became a problem. He substituted taxis for buses and subways. His fears began to limit his abilities to perform vocationally, a fact that enhanced his feelings of inadequacy.

Three months following the first panic attack the patient began to complain of epigastric distress. One month later, a duodenal ulcer was diagnosed following an upper gastrointestinal X-ray series. In spite of active medical treatment his abdominal complaints continued.

The patient became increasingly anxious. He developed the delusion that his children did not resemble him and were not really his. About the same time, he became obsessed with the thought that his wife might die. In a very compulsive fashion, he became overprotective to the point that she became a virtual prisoner in one room of their home.

When first seen, the patient was extremely agitated. He was unable to sit for more than a few minutes and paced the floor incessantly. He cried and pleaded for help. Marked logorrhea was present. A diagnosis of schizophrenia, pseudoneurotic, was made. He was placed on chlorpromazine, 300 milligrams per day. This was increased to 600 milligrams per day by the end of the first week.

After two days of treatment his restlessness was considerably reduced, but he continued to be just as terrified. On the fifth day of treatment he no longer cried and, in general, appeared more calm. However, his logorrhea continued. His wife reported that he appeared calmer at home but that he continued to have the same phobias, epigastric distress, obsessions, and referential trends that were noted above.

By the eighth day of treatment most of his compulsive overprotectiveness of his wife ceased and his delusions with regard to his children disappeared. However, his epigastric symptoms and phobias continued. His gastrointestinal difficulties and phobic phenomena remained unchanged for one more week. On the fifteenth day of treatment the patient stated that his abdominal difficulties had improved greatly. In spite of this improvement, his phobia relative to coming up in the elevator remained unchanged. This last symptom was gradually ameliorated during the following two weeks.

This particular patient demonstrated how the secondary defense symptoms disappeared in an organized fashion. He demonstrated also the manner in which the last symptom, namely the referential trends and delusions, were ameliorated prior to a remission of the psychosomatic difficulties.

INTRAVENOUS CHLORPROMAZINE

Earlier in this chapter I described the events that transpired when a patient with a history of migraine headaches was given intravenous mescaline. I also described the reaction of a patient with autonomic faciocephalalgia in response to psychedelic agents.

I was able to abort these episodes very quickly by the use of intravenous chlorpromazine. In the case of the patient with autonomic faciocephalalgia

I repeated the mescaline experiment on two different occasions. In the first experiment the autonomic facial pain developed to its maximum intensity before the phenothiazine was administered. When the patient was given the drug on the second occasion the only discomfort was a warning pain over the right eye, and I immediately administered chlorpromazine intravenously. Though the pain became slightly more severe and the ipsilateral conjunctive became slightly injected, I was able to abort the pains before they spread to the remainder of the face, and to prevent the swelling of the nasal mucosa and the soft palate that would have occurred if the process had taken its usual course. This is an excellent example of what can occur if the emotional trigger that is behind the autonomic dysfunction is blocked.

Once again, the patterns of symptom amelioration in patients receiving hallucinogenic agents and subsequently receiving intravenous phenothiazines is similar to that already described for other types of therapies. The last symptom to appear is usually the first symptom to disappear as the level of anxiety is reduced.

ELECTROSHOCK THERAPY

Twenty-nine of the patients who received electroshock therapy had psychosomatic problems. These patients were either very anxious schizophrenics or had severe agitated depressions. The pattern of anxiety amelioration and symptom remission has been described in Chapters 5 and 6. I reported then that it required approximately three to five electroshock treatments to effect a definite lessening of the motor component and that the affective component usually changed after an additional two or more treatments. The amelioration of psychosomatic symptoms during the course of electroshock therapy can readily be demonstrated. The following is an example.

Case History

The patient was a sixty-two-year-old married painter who had always had a very rigid, compulsive personality. For a period of several years he had been preoccupied with his "hearing." In truth, he had slight presbycusis associated with intermittent tinnitus. Three months prior to his consultation he became very restless. Soon after this insomnia and anorexia were noted. His local doctor recorded a marked increase in systolic blood pressure that had not been noted four months previously. The patient had difficulty in performance and became extremely depressed, this depression being associated with suicidal preoccupations. Several weeks prior to his psychiatric consultation be became quite paranoid toward his wife, accusing her of infidelity.

Because of the progressive paranoid symptoms and the suicidal preoccupations the patient was given electroshock treatments.

Following the fourth electroshock treatment the patient was mush less restless and muscle tonus was reduced. Following the seventh treatment he appeared less anxious and his paranoid delusions with regard to his wife were lessened. The delusions disappeared after the eighth treatment. Also, after the eight treatment a decrease in blood pressure was recorded. About this time his depressed affect changed. However, he continued to complain about tinnitus. Following the tenth treatment he did not spontaneously refer to the tinnitus. On questioning he would state that it was present but that it did not bother him.

This is a rather typical pattern of symptom amelioration in response to electroshock therapy. As one can note it is very similar to the pattern of therapeutic remission noted with other types of treatment.

SUMMARY

In this chapter I have presented a number of case histories in an effort to illustrate certain recurrent clinical patterns. I have not concerned myself with theory, for it is my belief that in clinical medicine theory should be a natural extension of observation.

Psychosomatic medicine is struggling in a quagmire of theory based on theory treated as fact. As such I believe a few additional observations based on my study of 151 patients with psychosomatic ailments is in order.

It has been asserted for many decades that there are specific psychodynamic mechanisms for specific psychosomatic syndromes. Others have claimed that various emotions have their concomitant psychosomatic expression. Based on these concepts, elaborate, retrospective psychodynamic patterns have evolved.

In psychoanalytic psychotherapy these mechanistic structures are obsessively presented to the patient until the patient has memorized the specific jargon. Any improvement in the patient's psychosomatic disorder is attributed to the insights the patient has gained from his therapist. In reality patients improve despite the nature of the specific insight that is the semantic stock and trade of a given school.

I would like to state uncategorically that, although I attempted to delineate specific psychodynamic patterns that could be related to a specific psychosomatic disorder, in all the 151 patients that made up this study I was unable to do so. Having been trained in the psychodynamic concepts of psychosomatic problems I found it easy, "if I let myself go," to pigeonhole patients into a given dynamic pattern. However, the truth of the matter is that the psychodynamic profiles of patients with various psychosomatic problems are very similar. In many ways they resemble the psychodynamic patterns seen in depressed patients. In part, perhaps, this accounts for the fact that a history of psychosomatic disorders is obtained in a very large number of patients who finally have agitated depressions.

The personality profiles, ontologic development, and parental background of patients with obsessive-compulsive difficulties, agitated depressions, and psychosomatic difficulties are quite similar. Almost all have rigid, mechanistic, compulsive personality profiles. Life is seen in a polar fashion, black versus white without many shades of gray interposed. One can find in almost every history a dominant, rigid, obsessive-compulsive, often rejecting, even sadistic parent (in our culture, this parent is usually the mother). In this parental environment the child has a negative image of himself, feels inadequate, and is self-derogatory.

There is often a history of childhood temper tantrums in which the child has attempted to coerce the dominant parent into recognizing him. If the temper tantrums have been met with overwhelming, crushing punishment the patient's capacity for compensatory anger and even his drive to compensate for feelings of inadequacy may be crushed for life. The usual mechanism, however, is that the patient, in a very mechanistic, rigid fashion, attempts to compensate for his feeling of inadequacy and to develop an image of self with which he can live and to prove to the dominant parent that he is deserving of recognition and love. The patient thus drives himself through life. The routine obligations of life commonly are seen as urgencies or emergencies even when these do not exist. If the patient obtains some degree of higher education the mechanistic manner of handling daily pursuits is often blended with a pattern of overintellectualization.

It should be noted that these psychodynamic patterns are accompanied by either overt or covert hostility, particularly if the patient is frustrated in his daily pursuits for self-recognition. During adolescence and early adult life most patients with obsessive-compulsive defense mechanisms can compensate for the daily environmental stresses. It is for this reason that psychosomatic disorders are most commonly seen in the later part of the second, third, fourth, fifth, and sixth decades. When the patient can no longer readily compensate for daily environmental stresses in a rigid, mechanistic fashion one sees evidence of increasing anxiety with the development of various secondary defense mechanisms. Some of these patients also become hypochondriacal and may manifest severe depressive reactions. Others may develop psychosomatic difficulties; still others may show paranoid defense mechanisms. Finally, some of these patients will demonstrate combinations of these secondary defense mechanisms. I should mention that phobic phenomena may also be a part of this mosaic of symptoms.

At the present time, although I have minutely dissected the vast material that I have collected for sixteen years, I have not been able to determine which patient will develop obsessive-compulsive problems alone, psychosomatic problems alone, hypochondriasis alone, or depression alone. I do not believe that this answer will come solely through a knowledge of psychodynamics. Whether hereditary or congenital factors reinforced by environmental conditioning lead to development of a vegetative stigmatization (often designated as a locus minorus resistentiae) account for the development of a specific psychosomatic disorder is an unanswered question. However, it appears to have great merit.

With theorization such as this one must enter into the realms of neurophysiology and neurobiochemistry. In these fields there is not much specific data on which one might draw in an attempt to confirm the theories just proposed. The neurophysiologic and neurobiochemical literature is just as contraversial as the clinical psychiatric literature. Much of the confusion is owing to the fact that the Law of Initial Value and a consideration of possible placebo effects have not been taken into account in the planning of research models.

The school of conditioned reflexology, particularly its Russian branch, has made notable contributions to our knowledge of psychosomatic and somatopsychic interrelationships. Its work on the "second signal system" has close correlations with the development of psychosomatic disorders.

All psychiatrists who have extensive experience with psychosomatic disorders have noted, on occasion, that some patients with psychosomatic problems, if they become psychotic, may demonstrate an improvement in the psychosomatic ailment. Conversely, in some patients, as their psychosis improves, there may be an exacerbation of the psychosomatic problem. I have also noted, on rare occasions, in patients who have more than one psychosomatic problem that, as one psychosomatic difficulty improves, the other may exacerbate for a variable period of time.

One can only speculate at this time as to the reasons for this inverse relationship between psychosis and psychosomatic disorders. Wilder, in his early studies of the Law of Initial Value (1931, 1956) demonstrated that with more extreme high or low prestimulus or pretherapeutic levels there is a progressive tendency to "no response" or to "paradoxic reactions." Further studies into paradoxic studies may contribute to our understanding of the phenomenology of this inverse relationship between psychosis and psychosomatic disorders.

I do not believe that the final answers to these problems will be obtained until the teaching of medicine becomes synonymous with the teaching of the interrelationship among physiodynamics, psychodynamics, and sociodynamics. Our fragmented studies in which the experimental models are concerned with one or another of the three dimensions can only continue to lead to glorious inaccuracies.

10

THE PLACEBO PHENOMENON

In the first nine chapters of this book I have attempted to describe in detail, first, just what happens as patients respond with progressively increasing levels of anxiety to various types of stress and, second, the step-by-step observations of what takes place psychopathologically as patients with marked anxiety respond to different treatments. The six chapters that follow deal in detail with the therapeutic guidelines, and some of the techniques that I have utilized during the past eighteen years in the treatment of severely ill psychiatric patients in whom marked anxiety has been a prominent feature.

At the very outset of this portion of the book, devoted as it is to therapeutic modalities that have proven to be effective in the management of a very large number of severely anxious individuals, I would like to emphasize that a multitude of factors, intended and unintended, intrude with varying intensity into the therapeutic scene, each determining to some degree the final outcome of both short- and long-term treatment.

There has been a very slow but gradually increasing awareness in the various branches of medical science that many factors enter into a therapeutic response of a given patient that are independent or only slightly related to the specific reaction of a procedure or a drug. This awareness is very keen among a few investigators interested in setting up experimental models, but not among most investigators engaged in both animal and clinical research. The reliability of the results of most research is open to serious doubt owing to this basic omission. In general, we who practice psychiatry, a field in which one is concerned in great measure with very subtle, subjective complaints of patients, have not shown sufficient interest in or awareness of the nonspecific effects related to the various tools that are a part of our therapeutic armamentarium. The lack of appreciation of these nonspecific reactions ranges in degree from slight oversights to massive clinical blindness.

This criticism pertains to all branches of psychiatry, those primarily concerned with organic treatment and those dealing with the psychotherapies. There have been relatively few serious attempts to measure the relative efficacy of the various psychiatric techniques. Very often we have been guilty of immodest, dogmatic claims of clinical findings or pronouncements of theoretic formulations based on insufficient or no realistic documentation. If one takes the time and trouble to trace some of the alleged observations or theroretic constructs back to the original articles, very often one will find that the original reports were not founded on sound clinical techniques.

These reports are in part responsible for the development of rigidly held doctrines or cult-like schools of thought ranging from unimaginative, mechanistic, clumsy, purely organic concepts to a type of metaphysical mysticism that is pawned off as psychotherapy.

The current psychiatric scene has been characterized by bitter, factional battles between these various schools with would-be apostles, in child-like fashion, quoting the dogma of deceased masters.

If psychiatry is to be recognized as a mature biopsychosociologic science we must carefully reevaluate our observations, our techniques, and our theories. This self-observation should include an awareness that many factors enter into the therapeutic response demonstrated by a given patient. Some arc specific or intended phenomena, whereas others are either independent or only slightly related to the actions of a given procedure or drug. We who practice psychiatry are no less derelict than those practicing in the other clinical branches of medicine, but the repetition of an error does not justify its existence.

Any significant self-evaluation must include an investigation of the quality, frequency, and intensity of the nonspecific or unintended effects that play a role in our various psychiatric techniques. The vast literature dealing with psychiatry has considered the changes in a given patient that take place during the course of treatment to be secondary to the intended efforts of the therapist. This is particularly true of positive or beneficial reactions, whereas negative or deleterious effects are often as not implied as occurring secondary to unintended reactions. As a result of these naive concepts there are very few instances in which the changes that do occur as a result of psychiatric care can be documented as to whether they are the result of (1) intended specific phenomena or (2) unintended nonspecific phenomena.

All studies, whether alleged research investigations or therapeutic trials, must be evaluated by the reader as to how much specific versus nonspecific factors determined or may have determined the results obtained by the particular author. To accept results without such evaluation is to be a pseudoscientific pawn, an intellectual automaton.

In this chapter I would like to focus sharply on the therapeutic importance of those nonspecific reactions that have been haphazardly labeled as *placebo effects* with particular reference to the method by which they influence the treatment of patients manifesting marked anxiety.

DEFINITION OF PLACEBO REACTION

The placebo must be considered from a broad perspective as pertaining to procedures as well as drugs. This broadened concept of placebo is in keeping with the accurate definition of the term. The popular concept of limiting the term to drugs is simply owing to tradition. The term *placebo*, derived from the Latin word *placere*, means "I shall please." In general, a *placebo* refers to something intended to soothe, conciliate, or gratify.

My definition of a placebo effect is an extension of a description by Shapiro (1959), namely that a placebo is "the psychologic, physiologic or psychophysiologic effect of any medication or procedure given with therapeutic intent, which is independent of, or minimally related to the pharmacologic effects of the medication, or to the specific effects of a procedure, and which operates through a psychologic mechanism." I have expanded this definition to include the observation that the relative or complete remission or exacerbation of any symptom, sign, or syndrome as the result of the administration of any drug or the application of any technique cannot be ascribed to the specific effect of the drug or technique unless it can be demonstrated that the improvement or worsening is not due to this nonspecific placebo effect (Lesse, 1962).

CLASSIFICATION OF PLACEBO REACTIONS

At the outset, to avoid confusion, one must distinguish between the *placebo* (the drug or procedure) and the *placebo effect* (the reaction). This distinction is necessary because different parameters must be used for the measurement of the intensity and quality of each, even though they are indivisibly related as to cause and effect. Placebos may be classified in different manners. These are summarized in Table 10.1.

TABLE 10.1. A Classification of Placebos

Pure Versus Impure Placebos

Pure: Chemicals or procedures that are, in themselves, psychobiologically inert or inactive

Impure: Chemicals or procedures that have psychobiologically active elements that have no direct effect on the patient's symptoms or signs

Planned Versus Unplanned Placebos

Planned: A pure or impure placebo that is intentionally used, the therapist being fully aware that the chemical or procedure is a placebo

Unplanned: A pure or impure placebo that is believed by the therapist to produce a specific physical or psychologic effect in a given patient, but that in reality has no such specific effect (usually impure placebos producing nonspecific reactions falsely interpreted as being specific effects)

Positive Versus Negative Placebos

Positive: A pure or impure, planned or unplanned placebo that produces beneficial effects

Negative: A pure or impure, planned or unplanned placebo that produces deleterious effects

---

A *pure placebo* is one that is an inactive or inert chemical or procedure in itself psychobiologically inactive. On the other hand, an *impure placebo* is one in which there are biologically or psychobiologically active elements that do not directly affect the patient's symptoms or signs.

If a placebo is given intentionally this is called a *planned*, or *intentional*, *placebo*. These planned placebos may either be pure or impure in type. Often a physician will employ a drug or procedure that he is certain will produce a specific physiologic or psychologic reaction in a given patient but that, in reality, has no such specific effect. This then would be an *unplanned*, or *unintended*, *placebo*. These unplanned, or unintentional, placebos may be pure or impure in nature. They are usually impure placebos that cause only nonspecific physiologic or psychologic reactions.

Placebos may also be classified with regard to their beneficial or harmful effect. A *positive placebo* is one that produces a beneficial effect, whereas a *negative placebo* produces adverse effects. These may be pure or impure, intentional or unintentional placebos.

The unfortunate aspect of unintended placebos is that the expectant physician usually falsely interprets the results as being specific reactions. These false interpretations may develop into convictions and may appear in the literature where some of the inaccuracies hopefully may be detected and corrected. At times, however, these inaccuracies assume the mantle of dogma. These references to unintentional or unplanned placebos apply to some of the reports in recent literature dealing with psychopharmacologic agents in the management of anxious neurotic and psychotic patients. They apply equally well to much that has been written and taught about various psychotherapeutic techniques.

Placebo responses are not infrequent; indeed, there are some reports that suggest that these reactions may rival in degree of effectiveness some of the so-called specific therapies. Beecher (1955) in a study of more than 1000 patients, reported that placebos produced significant responses in approximately one third of the group. Kurland (1957), in a partial review of the literature, observed that various papers reported that from 4 to 52 percent of the patients studied had placebo reactions. A growing number of articles in the literature testify to the fact that placebo reactions noted in the treatment of diverse symptoms, signs, and syndromes are of a magnitude that rivals in degree the effectiveness of some of the so-called specific therapies. Negative placebo reactions are often prominent and very uncomfortable to the patient (Beecher, 1955; Fischer and Dlin, 1956; Dichl, 1933; Wolf and Pensky, 1954).

Specific therapies also have some degree of placebo reaction. It is often quite difficult to differentiate between the specific and nonspecific placebo effects of a given therapy. At present it is even more difficult, indeed usually impossible, to evaluate to what degree one reaction is present as compared with the other. The impact of the placebo reaction may seriously modify the value of various experimental tools, for example, the use of the double- or even triple-blind techniques. It is important to recognize that placebo reactions may enhance or negate a specific positive or negative therapeutic procedure and also that placebo reactions even may enhance or negate the effects of various placebos. At first this may sound complicated but, examples in this and the next section illustrate these various possibilities, which are summarized in Table 10.2. I believe these examples to be important in evaluating the results of any therapy. These various possibilities must be considered before attributing any change in the patient to the specific reactions of a particular therapy.

TABLE 10.2. The Possible Effects of Placebos on Therapies with Specific Actions and on Other Placebos

---

Therapies with Specific Action

Positive placebo effects:

1. Will enhance or magnify the beneficial effects of a positive specific drug or procedure beyond that produced by a specific effect of the drug or procedure. It may mask the dangers of the drug or procedure

2. Will dilute or cancel the deleterious effects of a contraindicated specific drug or procedure

(Continued)

TABLE 10.2. continued

Negative placebo effects:
1. Will dilute or cancel the beneficial effects of a positive specific drug or procedure
2. Will enhance or magnify the deleterious effects of a drug or procedure having specific action and make them appear worse than they really are

Therapies That Operate Through Placebo Effects

Positive placebo effects:
1. Will enhance the positive beneficial effect of a positive placebo (that the patient believes to be a specific drug or procedure)
2. Will dilute or cancel the apparent deleterious effects of a negative placebo (a drug or procedure that the patient originally believed to be detrimental)

Negative placebo effects:
1. Will dilute or cancel the beneficial effects of a positive placebo (which the patient initially had believed to have specific positive effects)
2. Will enhance the apparent deleterious effects of a negative placebo (this would occur only in an experimental setting)

THE POSSIBLE PLACEBO EFFECT ON THERAPIES WITH SPECIFIC ACTION

POSITIVE PLACEBO EFFECTS

1. *Magnification of a positive specific drug or procedure—a drug or procedure with a positive specific effect may have this effect magnified beyond that actually produced by the specific effect of the drug or procedure.* Examples of this process are very common. In the days when chlorpromazine was first available in the treatment of very anxious patients the positive or specific effects of the drug were greatly enhanced by the positive expectations from this new "magic medication." These expectations, stimulated by mass publicity, greatly enhanced the impact of the drug in many patients. Similarly, the task of the psychotherapist in America is enhanced by the conviction, held by some groups, that psychotherapy is the treatment of choice in the care of emotional illnesses. This expectation is stimulated by dramatic accounts of psychotherapeutic successes in the movies, on television, and radio, in books written by those who have been psychoanalyzed, as well as in the enthusiastic accounts of therapy by former patients.

2. *Dilution or cancellation of deleterious effects of contraindicated drugs or procedures—a positive placebo effect may dilute or even cancel the adverse effects of a contraindicated drug or procedure.* For example, I treated a very anxious, neurotic, slightly hyperthyroid patient who unwisely had been given desiccated thyroid by her local physician. This drug had further elevated her thyroid function, producing tachycardia, heightened anxiety, and diarrhea. However, she had been told by the physician,

who had treated her since she was a child, that the drug would be beneficial. The patient interpreted the adverse signs of hyperthyroidism as evidence of improvement and initially she vigorously protested any cancellation of the drug. Her attachment to the physician who had administered the thyroid produced a strong positive placebo reaction.

NEGATIVE PLACEBO EFFECTS

1. *Dilution or cancellation of beneficial effects of a positive specific drug or procedure—a negative placebo effect may dilute or cancel the beneficial effects of a positive specific drug or procedure.* When a negative placebo effect occurs the physician is usually unaware of the process and blames the failure on the drug or procedure itself. I noted a very dramatic example of this phenomenon in a patient who was diagnosed as having schizophrenia, chronic, pseudoneurotic in type. As part of his ailment he demonstrated a severe pan-anxiety state and marked hypochondriasis. I administered chlorpromazine orally and the initial reaction was that the level of anxiety subsided and the hypochondriacal symptoms were greatly reduced in severity. This was the positive effect of the drug. Very quickly, however, the patient had difficulty with reality contact associated with a nonspecific soporific side effect of the chlorpromazine. The patient became extremely anxious, indeed terrified, to the degree that the drug had to be discontinued. The patient's reaction to the nonspecific soporific side effect of the chlorpromazine was the negative placebo reaction that cancelled the positive specific effect of the drug.

2. *Enhancement or magnification of the deleterious or adverse effects of a drug or procedure—a negative placebo effect may enhance or magnify the deleterious effects of a drug or procedure having specific action to make them appear worse than they really are.* For example, I was consulted by a patient who had a severe depression, characterized by a marked decrease in psychomotor activity and a multitude of hypochondriacal symptoms. She had been ill-advisedly placed on reserpine by her local physician. This medication had exaggerated her fatigue and lethargy and therefore may be considered as having a negative specific effect. About that time reports of extrapyramidal-like side effects due to reserpine were widely circulated in the press. After reading these reports the patient began to manifest a glissando-like increase in overt anxiety that expressed itself by mimicking the Parkinsonian-like symptoms about which she had read; she carried this mimicry to the point where she lay in bed with her body rigid. This rigidity cleared entirely as soon as one dose of reserpine was omitted. In this case her identification with the negative reports represented a negative placebo effect that exaggerated a negative specific reaction of the drug.

PLACEBO REACTIONS AND THERAPIES THAT OPERATE THROUGH PLACEBO
EFFECTS

Placebos themselves may be aided or counteracted by placebo effects from various sources. Various possibilities in this regard are listed below.

POSITIVE PLACEBO EFFECTS

1. *Enhancement of the positive beneficial effects of a positive placebo—a positive placebo effect coming through mass media may enhance the beneficial effect of a positive placebo (a procedure or drug that the patient believes to be a specific drug or procedure).* An example of this is a very anxious patient who came requesting therapy with chlorpromazine from which she expected to be greatly helped. She was given a chlorpromazine placebo. Her improvement was moderate until she read an article in the newspaper exploiting the "miraculous benefits of this drug." Following this her symptomatic improvement was most dramatic and the patient had a complete remission of her symptoms. In this instance, the greatly exaggerated article about the benefits of chlorpromazine acted as a positive placebo effect enhancing the positive placebo that she was given.

2. *Dilution or cancellation of the apparent deleterious effects of a negative placebo—a positive placebo effect may dilute or cancel the apparent deleterious effects of a negative placebo (a drug or procedure that the patient originally believed to be detrimental).* The author was consulted by an elderly, moderately depressed woman who had a long history of recurrent agitated depressions. She was skeptical of all psychiatrists and treatments and was very loathe to take the "antidepressant drug" that was prescribed (in reality this was a placebo). During the first few days in treatment she complained about all manner of adverse effects and claimed that her illness was worse. About that time the author appeared on a television program. She was very impressed by the fact that "her doctor was a radio celebrity." From that point on her clinical status improved very dramatically.

In this patient the drug that was given her acted as a negative placebo because she felt it to be detrimental to her though, in reality, it was not. The author's appearance on a television program had a positive placebo effect that counteracted the original negative placebo.

NEGATIVE PLACEBO EFFECTS

1. *Dilution or cancellation of beneficial effects of a positive placebo—a negative placebo effect may dilute or cancel the beneficial effect of a positive placebo (that which the patient believes is a specific drug or procedure).* An

example of this reaction was seen in an anxious, hypochondriacal, moderately depressed patient who requested iproniazid (Marsalid, Roche) when it was first written up in glowing terms in the press. He was given a placebo and demonstrated rapid improvement until he read that some patients had developed severe liver damage as a result of the drug. The patient began to complain about abdominal pains, jaundiced skin, light stools (all imaginary), and he became depressed once again. His pseudo-hepatic difficulties cleared in twenty-four hours after the placebo was discontinued.

In this patient the iproniazid placebo initially had a positive placebo effect. The adverse reactions of which he had read produced a negative placebo reaction counteracting the original benefits of the positive placebo.

2. *Enhancement of the apparent deleterious effects of a negative placebo— the apparent deleterious effects of a negative placebo could be enhanced by a negative placebo effect.* I do not have a personal experience with the particular combination of reactions, but I could devise an experiment that would prove this. The experiment would run in this fashion—a placebo would be deliberately administered to a patient by a very unenthusiastic physician. This drug then would have a negative placebo effect. After taking this placebo, artifical news of very adverse results could be circulated and attributed to the placebo that the patient was taking and that he felt was a potent drug. This would most likely accentuate the original negative placebo effect. Though I know of no such specific experiment, I believe it has occurred accidentally in many situations.

RECOGNITION OF THE PLACEBO EFFECT

I anticipate that this entire discussion of unintended or placebo effects will make many readers very uncomfortable. The concept of the placebo effect is extremely repugnant to many psychiatrists, organicists, and psychotherapists alike. The common reaction is one of hostility toward such articles and their authors.

I can sympathize with this reaction because I went through similar reactions prior to my initial interest in placebo research, which began eleven years ago. Though I am no longer adverse to the concept of placebo effects, it has significantly complicated my attempts to evaluate my own therapeutic results and the results reported by others. Though I do not argue with any beneficial results seen in my patients, I find myself repeatedly attempting to evaluate just how much of a given patient's improvement resulted from the procedures or drugs that I deliberately administered and that I assumed to have positive specific effects and how much of the improvement resulted from intended and unintended placebo reactions.

I have found that the concept of the placebo effect is completely alien to those whose practices are limited to the use of psychotherapy of various types. Most psychotherapists associate the time-honored concept of the *placebo* with drugs and drugs alone. Its application to psychotherapy is exquisitely painful to them. The term *unintended effects* produces less emotional and intellectual aversion.

I would like to continue for a moment with the subject of psychotherapy and psychotherapists. There are relatively few significant studies in which the results of the various psychotherapeutic techniques have been compared. Evaluations by some suggest that there is little or no significant difference in the final long-range results produced by one or another of these techniques (Eysenck, 1952; Appel, Lhamon, Meyers, and Harvey, 1953; Frank, Gliedman, Imber, Stone, and Nash, 1959). (In fairness I should state that all these authors are not necessarily sympathetic to the concept of psychotherapy per se.)

Further, psychotherapists have implied that the psychodynamic mechanisms of improvement gained through psychotherapy are different from those gained through other therapies. In this book and in a series of papers dealing with various types of organic treatments and psychotherapies, I have pointed out that the psychodynamic patterns of reintegration and improvement appear to vary only in the rate of change with the various therapies. This does not necessarily mean that one psychotherapeutic technique is not in reality more efficacious than another in the treatment of a specific problem. It does mean, however, that it has not been proven so as yet. The forces that determine the presence of a placebo reaction play a role in determining the final results in all psychotherapeutic procedures. Indeed, the similarity in these background qualities has led some observers to postulate that the placebo effect may account for the great similarity in these improvement rates (Eysenck, 1952).

FACTORS INFLUENCING THE PLACEBO REACTION

The placebo or unintended effect of any therapeutic procedure depends on one or more factors, which pertain primarily to the milieu, the therapist, the patient, or a combination of all. Various factors will be more prominent than others depending on the procedure used. The material that I will present is relevant primarily to the various psychotherapies, because it is the relationship between the placebo reaction and psychotherapy that I have been most interested in during the past few years. However, these factors do pertain to all types of psychiatric treatment.

THE THERAPEUTIC ENVIRONMENT

The term *therapeutic environment* pertains equally to the broad cultural milieu and the more immediate setting of the therapist's office.

At various periods in our history different therapeutic procedures have been popularly endowed with extensive curative powers, particularly as they pertain to the amelioration of marked anxiety. These cultural expectancies in themselves set the mood for positive results. In ancient Egypt the use of various amulets was believed to have therapeutic benefits. In medieval Italy the playing of the tarantella to calm wild, exhausting gyrations of St. Vitus Dance (tarantism) had therapeutic value. Throughout the centuries various spas have been frequented by thousands of persons with magical expectations about the healing powers of certain waters. To this day, primitive man's belief in the restorative powers of water is held in high repute in certain quarters.

The implied promise of magic cures from mass, high-powered, hard-sell advertising techniques has produced a positive mood for various drugs and machines. This "cultural hypnotism" by mass advertising has a short-lived but important effect. Similarly, the psychotherapist's task in America is enhanced by the conviction held by some groups that psychotherapy is the treatment of choice in the care of emotional illnesses. More specifically, dramatic portrayals of successful, even miraculous psychotherapeutic scenes in the movies, television, radio, theater, books, and enthusiastic verbal accounts by former patients has created an expectant population. In many instances the therapist's task is aided before the patient enters his office.

The therapist's office setting is important. If the office is in a large, nationally known clinic or hospital, the prestige of the environmental setting accrues to the therapist. This in itself may initially enhance the therapist's image in the patient's eyes. In connection with this I should point out that I treated many patients in an internationally prominent hospital setting. Indeed, some of the patients were referred to me by the hospital.

The psychosurgical procedures in this study and some of the studies with hallucinogenic drugs were performed in a nationally prominent psychiatric research hospital. Initially, the therapist-experimenter "borrows" the prestige of the hospital. The positive benefits of this borrowed prestige is transient and must be supplemented by a strong, positive relationship between the patient and therapist.

The decoration and illumination of the psychiatrist's office may have some effect on the patient. Some recent papers have pointed out that the type and amount of illumination may be very relevant to psychological activities and movement in group psychotherapy (Tibbetts and Hawkins,

1956). The psychotherapeutic climate in group psychotherapy may be related to the time at which the group meets and even to the relationship of the meeting time to mealtime. The presence or absence of mirrors or the color of the walls may affect some patients (Feldman, 1957).

The therapist's image is also enhanced at times by the referring source. I mentioned above an instance where a large hospital was the referring source. If the referring source is a prominent, respected physician the therapist is initially his psychotherapeutic surrogate until a direct positive transference develops.

I have mentioned but a few of the unintended factors pertaining to the therapeutic environment. I could list many more, and a far greater number of influences of which I have not been cognizant could be listed by others.

THE THERAPIST

The greatest number of positive placebo effects and the most enduring are obtained, in general, by optimistic, enthusiastic therapists who have very strong convictions as to the response they expect to receive from a specific drug or procedure (Tibbetts and Hawkins, 1956; Feldman, 1957; Goldstein, 1960). Indeed, the psychotherapist's expectations of patient improvement had a greater influence on the patient's personality change than did the patient's own expectations (Tibbetts and Hawkins, 1956). This correlation holds true for psychologic and somatic therapies alike. The intensity of the patient's positive reaction to the therapist affects the therapist's estimate of the degree of improvement that will take place in the patient (Heller and Goldstein, 1961). In other words, the patient's enthusiasm enhances the therapist's enthusiasm. The actual duration of therapy is also positively affected by the therapist's early prognostication as to the length of treatment (Frank, 1959). This undoubtedly contributes to the efficacy of brief therapy.

In connection with the therapist's expectations one might postulate that the positive placebo reaction obtained by an eclectic psychotherapist would be less than that obtained by one who employs only one sharply defined technique. This is so for several reasons. First, the therapist who utilizes one technique for all patients is completely dependent on this technique for his results, his pride and pleasure, his positive self-image, and his economic security. For these reasons alone a very strong positive expectancy might be anticipated. One would not anticipate the same enthusiasm by an eclecticist for any one therapy unless he is very certain as to his ability to select and apply that technique "ideal" for a given patient.

Apathetic, unenthusiastic, passive, or hostile therapists produce fewer positive placebo reactions and a greater number of negative responses. The therapist's behavior is connected intimately with the patient's reactions to the extent that one cannot fully comprehend the latter's behavior without a definite knowledge of the behavior of the former. This concept may be best summarized by the statement that "the personality of the therapist is a prime factor in psychotherapeutic results," an opinion held by many observers.

Such factors as the therapist's ability to empathize and communicate with the patient, whether on a verbal or nonverbal level, are important in influencing the placebo effect. In some instances the therapist's facial expressions, tone of voice, handshake, the way he walks or shuts a door, and so on, may have as much impact on the patient and influence the results of therapy as that which is said. There is a universal adage that a parent cannot hide his true feelings from a child. This statement is equally true of the therapist-patient relationship. The degree to which a therapist is able to empathize with the patient and his capacities for "warmth" have great influence on the placebo reaction and cannot be readily disguised from the patient.

The problem of reinforcement or conditioning has been little appreciated in the various types of psychiatric treatment, particularly in psychotherapy. Whether directive or nondirective the therapist's behavior acts to reinforce his expectations (Greenspan, 1955; Salzinger and Pisoni, 1958).

In a very interesting experiment, Pilowsky and Speer (1964) demonstrated that two therapists in the same environmental setting, asking only one question, "Would you tell me about the way you feel?" elicited significantly different responses from a series of patients.

A conditioned pattern also may be established depending on the intensity and frequency of the reinforcement of the therapist's expectations. This can be accomplished, for example, when the therapist repeatedly gives active approval of the patient's actions or statements (Frank, 1959). A true conditioned reflex of the "second signal system" type may be established in this fashion.

Other factors may also play a role in the intensity of the placebo reaction. For example, the professional prominence of a therapist, particularly one who has found favor in the public eye through popular writings, radio or television programs, court appearances, and the like, may produce a halo effect that enhances the patient's positive expectancy. This glow of public prominence and acceptance has a magnetic therapeutic effect on the average patient. A single utterance from a modern therapeutic oracle may temporarily carry more weight than days or weeks of ardent treatment by a lesser soul.

The age of the therapist may have a positive or negative effect for different reasons. Some patients associate wisdom with age; some associate progress with youth.

Another nonspecific factor to be considered is the therapist's emotional maturity and his personal adaptation to his culture. It determines in great measure the goals that will be presented to the patient and the degree of avoidance of countertransference mechanisms.

Recently attention has been drawn to the fact that in America, at least, the therapist expects to dominate and the patient expects to be dominated (Storrow and Spanner, 1962; Balint, 1957). The therapist is often unaware of his desire to dominate and may strongly suppress or repress this drive because it runs counter to the popular concepts of an ideal patient-therapist relationship. In an opposite vein, authoritarian therapists are commonly very moralistic and rejecting. These patterns tend to produce negative placebo reactions. There is also an indirect relationship between the degree of the therapist's anxiety and his results (Librosky, 1952), some of which may be accounted for by weak positive or strong negative placebo reactions.

Finally, a positive placebo effect of great proportions may result from the enthusiastic expectancy of a young, inexperienced therapist in the treatment of a patient with a very difficult psychiatric problem because "he did not know that he was supposed to fail with this particular type of patient." An older and wiser therapist, because of a negative expectancy toward a particular type of patient, based on long-term personal experience and an awareness of the literature, might cause a negative placebo effect.

THE PATIENT

A positive placebo effect in psychiatric treatment, and this applies to all therapies, is dependent, in great measure on the patient's desire snd expectancy that therapy, especially a particular kind of therapy, will relieve his symptoms and in general correct his problems (Rosenthal and Frank, 1956; Goldstein, 1962; Kelly, 1955; Lipkin, 1964).

Unsophisticated, uneducated, superstitious patients, indeed all suggestible patients, are prone to develop positive placebo effects (Lasagna et al., 1954). Mass communication techniques, as I mentioned before, have primed a large segment of our population to be suggestible.

Patients with histories of long, unremitting illnesses and those with severe hysterical conversion syndromes do not commonly develop positive placebo effects (Kurland, 1958; Cartwright and Cartwright, 1958). This is in contrast to patients who manifest marked overt anxiety. Anxious, hypochondriacal patients, though initially prone to develop positive placebo reactions, may shift rapidly to a negative placebo reaction if there is an adverse side effect to therapy. Positive placebo reactions in schizophrenic patients are subject to rapid unpredictable fluctuations. Sociopaths do not commonly develop strong positive placebo responses; negative reactions are far more frequent with them.

The patient's expectancies will depend in part on his previous experiences with physicians and his image of them (Frank, 1959). In a broader vein, the patient's experiences with authoritative persons in general color his anticipation as to what his relationship with the therapist will be (Snyder and Snyder, 1961).

One study (Friedman, 1963) indicated that patients who obtain marked relief from their discomforts tended to have high levels of expectancy from psychotherapy. A reduction in reported symptom intensity occurred significantly more often when a reduction was anticipated by the patient than when it was not anticipated. The expectancy of help through psychotherapy appears to be activated during the first patient-therapist contact, and this is an important determinant of symptom reduction.

This question of the patient's expectancy in psychotherapy was investigated by the Cartwrights (1958) who delineated four types of patient expectancy: (1) expectancy of certain resultant effect; (2) expectancy that the therapist will be the greatest source of help; (3) expectancy that the technique will be the greatest source of help; (4) expectancy that the patient will be the main source of help. The authors felt that only the last type of expectancy was correlated with subsequent improvement.

Another aspect of patient expectancy is the patient-prognostication expectancy, which greatly influences the placebo reaction. If the initial level of aspiration is very high there will be a very strong positive placebo reaction. This initial reaction is seen commonly among patients with hypochondriacal defense mechanisms. As mentioned before, hypochondriacal patients with extremely high levels of aspiration may demonstrate rapid improvement. If they do not maintain this improvement a rapid shift to a negative placebo response may be expected.

The patient's conceptualization of psychotherapy determines in part the role he will assume and the role he expects the therapist to assume in treatment (Kelly, 1955). If there is harmony between the patient's and therapist's expectations of their respective roles a positive placebo effect can be expected. However, if they are at odds a negative placebo reaction, at times of marked proportion, is likely to occur.

The patient's motivation for psychotherapy, indeed all therapies, is a special phase of expectancy. It can be very discriminant with the patient being motivated for a particular type of therapy. Some authors (Cartwright and Cartwright, 1958) have expressed the opinion that those who put their faith in a technique per se as the main source of help rather than in themselves may be expected to have a poorer prognosis. A stronger, positive unintended reaction will occur when the patient believes in his own capacities aided by a specific technique. The entire question of motivation for psychotherapy in relation to the results requires further study. Based on level of aspiration studies it has been said (Chance, 1960) that there is a curvilinear relationship between goal setting and goal attainment. There is some question, however, whether the level of aspiration is an accurate measure of motivation (Kansler, 1959).

TRANSFERENCE, COUNTERTRANSFERENCE, AND THE PLACEBO REACTION

Transference phenomena occur with all types of therapy whether they are organic or nonorganic, directive or nondirective. In psychoanalytic psychotherapy, although a transference relationship is expected to occur as part of the free association technique, it is not directly planned or directed process. More specifically, it may be said to be an expected but unplanned process. It may be considered as a placebo effect of psychotherapy in that the formation of a transference relationship depends on all the unintended factors that determine a placebo reaction.

The transference phenomenon depends, in great measure, on the patient's expectation that the therapist will assume a certain role. The patient's initial conceptualization strongly affects his therapeutic behavior, particularly in the early interviews. In general, the more immature and the more suggestible the patient, the more marked the positive transference reaction.

Apfelbaum (1958), as part of a detailed investigation of transference reactions, studied the patient's expectancies in relation to the personality and behavior of prospective psychotherapists and then compared the therapeutic results with these expectations. He divided his study group into three expectancy types: (1) Nurturant—patients with infantile expectancies for which the therapist would be a complete parental substitute. (2) Model—patients expecting a mature, diplomatic, neutral listener. (3) Critic—patients expecting the therapist to be a critical and analytic individual who would demand that the patient assume many responsibilities. In correlating these types of transference with the therapeutic results he found that the patients with nurturant expectancies had the greatest degrees of psychopathology, as one might expect, whereas the model expectancy patient had the least degree of psychopathology. The patients with nurturant expectancies, those who expected guiding, protecting, and supporting therapists, obtained the best results as measured by MMPI and therapist ratings. This, at first glance, appears surprising from a clinical prognostic sense. However, the results are in keeping with the expectation of the Law of Initial Value. Studies of this nature are of extreme importance and should be repeated by many investigators of placebo factors.

Very strong positive transferences that threaten to destroy the therapeutic relationship are most certainly unintended placebo effects, as are all negative transference reactions.

The mutuality of the expectations as to role playing by both the patient and therapist is a strong factor in the transference phenomena. Where there is reciprocity between the patient's role expectancy of the therapist and the therapist's expectancy of the patient, strong transference phenomena can be anticipated (some may feel that in all instances the therapist's role expectancy of the patient is an aspect of countertransference). Lack of congruence between the role expectancies by patient and therapist of one another will lead to negative transference relationships (Leonard and Bernstein, 1960).

All transference reactions are not placebo effects. If the therapist deliberately plans to encourage a positive or negative transference reaction this should not be considered primarily as a placebo reaction (although, as I mentioned in the beginning of this chapter, all specific therapies have placebo effects). For example, with acting-out adolescents who have been unable to identify positively with a parent (particularly in cases where the parents were immature or rejecting), I have intentionally set about to foster a situation, during the initial phases of psychotherapy, in which the youth consciously views me as a strong, kind, but fair father substitute. This cannot be considered as a placebo reaction because it is deliberate. (I anticipate that many will consider any such suggestion as being reflective of infantile countertransference on the part of the therapist.)

The so-called transference cure is a fascinating subject that has been considered in too few papers (Goldstein, 1962; Kolb and Montomery, 1958; Alexander, 1956). Many of the factors that determine a transference cure are the same as those (enumerated in this chapter) determining a placebo reaction. Contrary to popular conceptions placebo effects and transference cures, which are placebo effects, can be very lasting. I believe it is safe to say that many assumed intended therapeutic cures are really unintended transference cures.

All instances of countertransference, because they are unintended, unplanned reactions, must be considered as placebo effects. The countertransference reaction, whether it is positive or negative in nature, usually reflects on the therapist's emotional immaturities. A negative countertransference may result if the therapist's role expectancy of the patient is strongly fulfilled by a hostile patient. In situations in which the role and behavior expectancies of the patient and therapist are dissimilar the therapeutic relationship is placed under great stress and a negative transference and countertransference may result.

THE LAW OF INITIAL VALUE

A prime factor effecting some placebo reactions is explained by Wilder's Law of Initial Value. The factor is of such great and all-pervading importance that Chapter 11 has been set aside for a detailed discussion of this principle, especially its relationship to anxiety. At this point I only would like to introduce this factor by stating that the immediate pretreatment psychologic or biologic state of the patient directly affects the course of the treatment, whether the treatment is specific or placebo in nature. This fact, for the most part, has been ignored in medicine in general and psychiatry in particular.

The Law of Initial Value as proposed by Joseph Wilder (1931, 1956) gives insight into this relationship. It states simply that "the change in any function of an organism due to a stimulus depends to a large degree on the pre-stimulus level of that function. This applies not only to the intensity (i.e., extent and duration) of response, but also to its direction. The higher the pre-stimulus level (the initial value), the less the tendency to rise in response to function-raising stimuli. With more extreme high and low levels, there is a progressive tendency to no response or to a paradoxic reaction (i.e., rise instead of fall and vice versa)."

This statement helps to explain many placebo reactions. These will be discussed in detail in Chapter 11.

SPONTANEOUS RHYTHMS

Rhythms or cyclic fluctuations characterizing phenomena in thirty-six separate disciplines have been alluded to by more than 2500 scientists (Dewey, 1961). Rhythmic or cyclic fluctuations refer to those variations in size, number, or quantity that recur with reasonable regularity, or with a beat. For example, the tides are rhythmic, as are the seasons, numbers of certain animals, variation in sun spots, and so forth. Many reports alluding to rhythmic fluctuations have assumed that the rhythms referred to were significant, that is, have a nonchance basis. At times this assumption cannot be validated. However, rhythms are regular and so persistent that chance alone is not considered to be an adequate explanation of them.

Members of various sciences have tended to assume a specific cause within a given discipline to account for rhythms. The biologist expresses a biologic cause; the geologist, a geologic cause; the climatologist, a climatologic cause; and so on. However, when the results of the research of various scientists are tabulated, there are instances where a rhythm discovered in the data of one discipline appears to have a wave length equal to the wave length of a rhythm noted in data pertaining to another discipline. This observation has led some scientists to suggest a common cause for many rhythms.

The entire subject of biologic rhythms has been neglected by most of the health sciences. Relatively few papers have appeared in medicine. There have been none, to my knowledge, in psychiatry except for a few inconclusive studies dealing with manic-depressive psychoses. The rhythms that have been studied in medicine have dealt with liver function, temperature curves, peptic ulcer, glycogen levels, cancer, genetics, and so forth. These studies have included endogenous as well as external rhythms and their interrelationships.

Rhythms can be described in different ways. They may be described according to the time element of the cycles. For example, a *circadian rhythm* is one that occurs every twenty-four hours, as is noted in body temperature. Some cycles may last as long as several days. Some may be *near-rhythms*, meaning that they occur every few hours. This has been reported for several body functions such as blood sugar levels, blood microfilaria, and electroencephalographs. Recent studies have suggested that there may be spontaneous rhythmic changes in adrenal cortical functions, leucocyte levels, blood pressure, and peripheral circulation. In current systems designed for space operation man's usefulness may depend in great measure on the modifiability of his biologic rhythms.

Though workers in psychotherapy have not written specifically about spontaneous rhythms as such, there has been comment about spontaneous remissions. D. S. Cartwright (1955) pointed out that those writers who have questioned the efficacy of psychotherapy as a technique have raised the issue of spontaneous remission. Some (Goldstein, 1962; Lesse, 1966) have considered that the so-called spontaneous remission of symptoms is in fact unspontaneous and a function of identifiable, causative factors. This is an important point, because the concept of spontaneous remission hangs on whether an explanation of the causative factors can be elicited. This does not, however, rule out the possibility that rhythmic or cyclic patterns may exist.

Goldstein (1962) has reviewed the literature in which the various arguments against the concept of spontaneous remission have been enumerated. These arguments include factors such as experimental design and control and many points that I have listed as determining the placebo reaction. If cycles or spontaneous rhythms do exist in psychiatry and psychotherapy they should be considered as specialized factors contributing to unintended reactions.

In all probability the qualifying *spontaneous* should be dropped before such terms as *rhythms, remissions,* and *exacerbations.* Perhaps such terms as *psychobiologic rhythms, nonspecific remissions,* and *nonspecific exacerbations* would be an improvement because the word *spontaneous* is basically an indication of a limitation in our current knowledge rather than a true scientific phenomenon. It should be emphasized, however, that whatever semantic mantle one would like to place on this problem, true maturity in our ability to evaluate therapeutic and research results will not occur until the question of psychobiologic rhythms or cycles is answered. This type of investigation poses problems of tremendous proportions even from the standpoint of the elaboration of a basic research methodology.

We, as practicing psychiatrists and psychotherapists, should not feel self-conscious in relation to those practicing in the sister branches of medicine or, indeed, to those representing other biologic sciences. It is the grand exception when unintended phenomena, such as placebo effects or rhythms, are taken into consideration.

Summary

I would like to stress the opinion that direct recordings made using one's senses may be far more reliable and valid if the various placebo factors are taken into consideration than are recordings made utilizing complicated batteries of equipment in which placebo factors are neglected.

This observation is nowhere more dramatically true than in the evaluation of the results of the treatment of patients in whom anxiety is a permanent feature. A striking example of this statement may be seen in the apparent contradictions and confusing results that can be found in the recent psychopharmacologic literature (Lesse, 1966; *Psychopharmacological Service Center Bulletin,* 1964).

Though the reasons for the apparent contradictory results are manifold, some researchers, myself included, have expressed the opinion that one of the most crucial factors in the assessment of anxious patients taking tranquilizers is a placebo phenomenon, namely, the nature of the verbal and nonverbal transaction taking place between the patient and psychiatrist. This interaction often causes a feedback that strongly influences the treatment outcome. If this patient-psychiatrist relationship, which is psychotherapeutic in nature, is not taken into consideration, the various rating scales are of little avail as far as the evaluation of reliability of treatment results are concerned. This is true whether or not computers, polygraphic equipment, or double- or triple-blind techniques are utilized.

It would be well to emphasize to those investigating the results of treatment in patients manifesting marked anxiety that there is considerable confusion in the minds of some between *statistical significance* and *clinical significance*. Not all instances of statistically significant differences can be considered clinically significant. The level of statistical significance may not reflect the true degree of difference between treatments. It may just reflect the size and homogeneity of the sample.

For all of us currently engaged in psychiatric research in this era of expanding automation and increasing reliance on computerized statistical programs, it is worthwhile to take note of the sobering motto of the mature cyberneticist, namely, that "if one feeds garbage to a computer, garbage will come out."

11

THE LAW OF INITIAL VALUE

The concept of the Law of Initial Value (LIV) is the result of the pioneering investigations of Joseph Wilder (1931, 1956), and it represents one of the outstanding contributions to our understanding of the biologic and psychologic sciences to be made in this century. As I noted in Chapter 10 it is a prime phenomenon in the consideration of placebo reactions. I consider it to be of significant moment to justify the presentation of a more detailed discussion of this principle, especially in its relationship to anxiety, as a separate chapter. Wilder's Law of Initial Value has to do with the prestimulus or pretherapeutic state of a patient or subject and its relationship to the results that are obtained in an experiment or as the result of treatment.

Wilder's law states simply that "the change in any function of an organism due to a stimulus depends to a large degree on the pre-stimulis level of that function. This applies not only to the intensity (i.e., extent and duration) of response, but also to its direction. The higher the pre-stimulus level (the initial value), the less the tendency to rise in response to function-raising stimuli. With more extreme high and low levels, there is a progressive tendency to no response or to a paradoxic reaction (i.e., rise instead of fall and vice versa)" (Wilder, 1956). Basimetry, which means the measuring of the base line, is the study and application of the Law of Initial Value.

I first became aware of the Law of Initial Value in 1956, when I was invited to address the Association for the Advancement of Psychotherapy. Dr. Joseph Wilder, who is one of the founders of this organization, was vice-president at the time and chairman of the meeting. I spoke on the use of tranquilizers in combination with psychotherapy, and as part of the talk I presented the results of my studies of chlorpormazine in which I had found that those patients who were most anxious responded most dramatically to this tranquilizer. I also had found that the converse was true, namely, that patients who manifested a very low level of anxiety prior to the introduction of the phenothiazines did relatively poorly.

These findings were a confirmation of the Law of Initial Value. In 1960 I summarized my findings pertaining to the relationship between the Law of Initial Value and anxiety at the Second International Conference for the Study of Biologic Rhythms, which was held in Siena, Italy.

In order to fully comprehend the findings presented in this chapter it is necessary to understand my method of evaluating the results of treatment.

EVALUATING THE LEVEL OF IMPROVEMENT

Subjective and objective factors were considered. I attempted to quantitate these factors wherever possible. It will be noted that the criteria used stress the patient's adaptation to routine responsibilities of everyday life in addition to the degree of symptomatic improvement. Also the degree of pride and pleasure gained from successful performance was considered.

PERFORMANCE

Vocational performance was evaluated as follows:

Key

1. Excellent: full-time employment; functioning efficiently without strain; deriving great pride and pleasure from achievements.
2. Good: full-time employment; greater effort required than was necessary prior to illness; moderate pride and pleasure in achievements.
3. Fair: works intermittently with considerable difficulty; frequent absences; faulty performance at times; lack of pride and pleasure in achievements.
4. Poor: unable to perform at all.

Social performance, that is, individual and group interpersonal relationships, were evaluated as follows:

Key

1. Excellent: active and comfortable; high level of pride and pleasure in achievements.
2. Good: active but with slight to moderate difficulty at times; limited pleasure capacity.
3. Fair: socializes with great difficulty; becomes anxious readily; lack of pride and very limited and infrequent pleasure.
4. Poor: seclusiveness or chaotic relations.

AMELIORATION OF ANXIETY

Anxiety is defined for our purposes here in its broadest aspect. We will consider it synonymous with *fear* whether this fear is generated by unconscious conflict or actual environmental difficulties. I attempted to quantitate anxiety according to a four-point scale after breaking down these psychophysiological phenomena into several components: the (1) motor component, (2) affectual component, and (3) verbal component.

Key

  1. Calm: no restlessness; overt expression of fear, when it occurs, is appropriate to the severity of the actual stress.
  2. Slight: slight restlessness; slight affectual expression of fear; slight pressure of speech.
  3. Moderate: marked restlessness, pacing; marked overt affectual expression of fear; often severe pressure of speech.
  4. Panic.

AMELIORATION OF INITIAL SYMPTOMS

We attempted to quantitate this on a four-point scale.

Key

  1. Excellent: all symptoms completely gone.
  2. Good: symptoms markedly reduced in intensity and frequency; patient able to cope.
  3. Fair: slight improvement only, with symptoms continuing to plague patient most of the time and with marked impact.
  4. Poor: symptoms unchanged or worse.

DREAMS

Whenever possible, dreams were sought out and studied in an attempt to gain additional information. Disappearance of nightmares, decrease in the frequency of rage dreams, and an increase in the frequency of pleasant dreams were points that were evaluated.

FINAL IMPROVEMENT RATING

The final improvement rating was indicated on a four-point scale that took into account all of the factors described above.

Key

  1. Excellent: full-time employment; active and comfortable in social performance; marked pride and pleasure in vocational and social performance.
  2. Good: full-time employment but requiring slightly greater effort than usual; active socially but with slight to moderate difficulties at times; slight residual anxiety; symptoms markedly reduced in intensity and frequency; slightly limited pride and pleasure in performance.

3. Fair: working but with considerable difficulties; frequent absences; socializing with great difficulty; moderate to marked residual anxiety; slight improvement, if any, in symptoms; minimal pride and pleasure in performance.

4. Poor: unable to perform vocationally or socially; anxiety level severe and unchanged; symptoms unchanged or worse; absence of pride or pleasure in performance.

ANXIETY AND THE LAW OF INITIAL VALUE

ORAL PHENOTHIAZINES

As I noted above I early found in my work with chlorpromazine that there was a direct relationship between a quantitative degree of anxiety and the degree of improvement following the oral administration of the drug. This relationship was reconfirmed in my studies of promazine hydrochloride and prochlorperazine.

In a study of 199 patients having a broad spectrum of psychiatric illnesses treated with chlorpromazine between 1954 and 1956, my colleagues and I found that forty-eight (24 percent) had excellent or good responses (final improvement ratings 1 and 2). I further noted that seventy-one patients (36 percent) showed slight improvement (final improvement rating 3), whereas the remaining eighty (40 percent) were not significantly helped (final improvement rating 4).

These figures suggest that chlorpromazine is a help in a large percentage of patients with psychiatric illnesses. They do not indicate the type of patient in which the drug is most effective. Studies of age, sex, and type of diagnosis did not shed any light on this question either. However, when the pretreatment level of overt anxiety is studied in relationship to the improvement rating, an important factor is discovered (see Figures 11.1 and 11.2). One notes that the greater the degree of overt anxiety, the better the results. Of the forty-eight patients having final improvement ratings 1 and 2 (excellent and good), forty-five (94 percent) manifested a marked degree of pretreatment anxiety.

DEGREE OF ANXIETY	IMPROVEMENT RATINGS 1	2	3	4
1	0	0	4	14
2	0	3	16	29
3	7	25	35	31
4	0	13	16	6
TOTALS	7	41	71	80

FIGURE 11.1. Anxiety as a factor effecting degree of improvement.

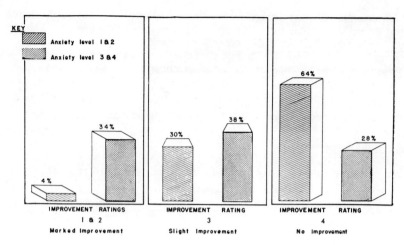

FIGURE 11.2. Degree of anxiety as a factor in improvement.

Expressed in another way, only three (4 percent) of sixty-six patients whose initial anxiety was nil or only slight (anxiety levels 1 and 2) had excellent and good improvement ratings. This was in striking contrast to the fact that forty-five (34 percent) of the 133 patients whose initial anxiety levels were severe or very severe (anxiety levels 3 and 4) attained excellent or very good improvement ratings.

At the other end of the improvement scale, I found that forty-three (64 percent) of the sixty-six patients with only slight or negligable expressions of overt anxiety were unimproved, whereas only thirty-seven (28 percent) of the 133 patients whose initial anxiety level was severe demonstrated a lack of improvement. My results were quite similar when promazine hydrochloride was used as a therapeutic agent. Therefore, chlorpromazine and promazine hydrochloride are in terms of the Law of Initial Value, function-inhibiting agents having their greatest effect when the initial value of anxiety is high.

Paradoxic reactions were seen with the use of the oral phenothiazines, but they were uncommon. For example, eight (6 percent) of the 133 patients manifesting a marked degree of anxiety prior to treatment demonstrated a paradoxic reaction in that they became more anxious when chlorpromazine was administered. My investigations of these paradoxic responses revealed that these eight patients were all schizophrenics in whom the unexpected paradoxic increase in anxiety appeared to result from difficulties with reality control occurring secondary to the soporific side effect that is often associated with the administration of chlorpromazine.

In another study I observed sixteen patients who manifested little or no overt anxiety (anxiety level 1) prior to the onset of therapy, who later developed panic reactions (anxiety level 4) as the result of the administration of chlorpromazine. In retrospect, these were all patients with either conversion phenomena or obsessive-compulsive states occurring in response to slowly developing environmental stress. These patients had strong unconscious feelings of inadequacy which they could not admit to themselves. They were in a perpetual struggle against the arousal into consciousness of fears of real or imaginary responsibilities with which they were unable to cope. The panic reactions seemed to occur when these feelings of inadequacy threatened to become conscious following the administration of chlorpromazine. It appeared that the drug had decreased the patient's capacity to repress and suppress these painful unconscious conflicts.

INTRAVENOUS PHENOTHIAZINES

I found that intravenous chlorpromazine was very effective in ameliorating wild panic reactions (anxiety level 4) observed in fifty-five (90 percent) of sixty-one very disturbed schizophrenic patients. As could be predicted, it was of no avail in eight patients in whom there was little or no pretherapeutic or overt anxiety (anxiety level 1).

Paradoxic reactions were noted following the administration of intravenous chlorpromazine when it was given to three schizophrenic patients who were in catatonic stupor. In response to intravenous chlorpromazine all three explosively developed catatonic excitement, which had to be controlled by electroshock therapy. I first noted this paradoxic reaction in early 1955, when I gave this drug with therapeutic intent to a patient in a catatonic stupor. The drug was given to the other two patients on an experimental basis.

The intravenous phenothiazines were found to be effective in directly reducing the level of anxiety in nineteen (76 percent) of twenty-five patients in whom marked anxiety (anxiety levels 3 and 4) resulted from the experimental administration of mescaline or lysergic acid.

SCHIZOPHRENIC PATIENTS DURING CRANIOTOMIES AND PSYCHOSURGERY

As I have noted in previous chapters the psychosurgical procedures performed as part of these studies took place between 1952 and 1954. The patients under went surgery under local anesthetia. Only a few of the patients who were finally lobotomized received test doses of chlorpromazine because this drug was not available in this country until 1954.

All but four of the forty-three schizophrenic patients who had craniotomies performed under local anesthesia manifested a marked degree of anxiety (anxiety levels 3 or 4) during the presurgical studies.

Very anxious patients were chosen for this procedure because long experience had indicated that those patients who demonstrated a low level of overt anxiety as part of the clinical syndrome did extremely poorly with psychosurgery. These procedures were performed in the department of the late Dr. Paul Hoch. Dr. Hoch had noted after many years of investigation that the best results obtained following leucotomy were to be found in schizophrenic patients who manifested marked overt anxiety without any signs of emotional and intellectual deterioration. The poor results that were reported by many psychiatric hospitals following the performance of lobotomies occurred mainly with chronic schizophrenic patients who had been living on the back wards of large state institutions for many, many years and who had long since demonstrated very marked emotional and intellectual deterioration. Most patients in this group were so-called burned out schizophrenics.

As I noted before thirty-four of the forty-three patients (79 percent) in the psychosurgery study were able to tolerate the craniotomies while under local anesthesia. A number of striking observations were possible with regard to the relationship between the intensity of anxiety and the Law of Initial Value. Paradoxically, several patients with previous histories of periods of uncontrolled catatonic excitement underwent the craniotomies in a state of relative calm.

Seven patients who received small doses of intravenous Seconal (sodium secobarbital, Lilly) manifested a paradoxic increase in anxiety. This increase in anxiety appeared to be related to difficulties with reality control associated with the slight depression of consciousness that was secondary to the barbiturate administration. The increase in the level of anxiety in these patients was ameliorated by the intravenous administration of amphetamines. Five other patients, who had difficulties with reality control during various phases of the craniotomies resulting in near panic reactions, became calmer when intravenous amphetamines were administered.

Paradoxic reactions associated with barbiturates or amphetamines have been reported many times in the psychiatric literature. For example, it is not rare for elderly patients to become hyperactive following the administration of barbiturates. Oral amphetamines have been used extensively in the management of hyperactive children, and this is a widely accepted and highly effective therapeutic technique. It may well be that the Law of Initial Value accounts for the apparent tranquil that occurs in these hyperactive children as a result of the use of these stimulants.

ANXIETY, DREAMS, AND DREAM-LIKE STATES

In Chapter 7 I reported the observation that many patients spontaneously noted that they dreamed more when they were taking phenothiazine drugs, particularly chlorpromazine. This increased dream awareness occurred only in those patients who had a high initial level of anxiety. I noted that they recalled more dreams when the initially high level of anxiety was rapidly ameliorated by the phenothiazines. I found that, in a study of dreams in 145 patients, ninety-five (66 percent) reported that they were cognizant of many more dreams than they had been prior to the administration of the phenothiazines. The period of enhanced dream awareness corresponded roughly to the period of rapid anxiety decompression that was approximately two to three weeks in duration on the average. The artifically produced abundance of dreams then tapered off.

The Law of Initial Value appears to play a role in that group of patients who manifested anxiety beyond nightmares. As I described in Chapter 7 these patients, as they responded to combined therapy, related terrifying nightmares,whereas they had no recollection of such dreams prior to the onset of drug therapy. This stage lasted only a few days and then, as the general level of anxiety was further decreased, the emotional impact of the dreams also became blunted. In this seeming paradoxic reaction it appeared that some patients were so frightened that they repressed or suppressed any conscious recollection of terror or rage dreams, and it was not until the level of anxiety was reduced in intensity that recollection of the nightmares or rage dreams was possible.

PSYCHOTHERAPY AND THE LAW OF INITIAL VALUE

It has long been recognized by experienced psychotherapists that patients who manifest a marked degree of overt anxiety associated with presenting symptoms respond to therapeutic measures much more dramatically than do patients who have a very flat affect. This could be logically anticipated in terms of the Law of Initial Value because psychotherapy, when it is properly utilized, is an anxiety-reducing procedure.

This does not mean that all anxious patients respond well to the various psychotherapies. I have found that there is a communication zone, namely, a level of anxiety at which the patient optically is able to communicate with the psychotherapist. If the level of anxiety is more extreme than is characteristic for a given patient's communication zone the relationship between the patient and therapist will be less than adequate. On the other hand, if the patient's symptoms are not associated with any overt anxiety there may be very little motivation for a meaningful relationship with the therapist. The quantitative degree of anxiety that one finds in the communication zone is unique for each individual patient, and it is dependent on many fluctuating factors that may be biophysical, psychologic, or sociologic in nature.

In keeping with this observation patients manifesting marked anxiety prior to the onset of therapy are more likely to develop a positive placebo response. Conversely, patients manifesting very little overt anxiety prior to the onset of treatment rarely are positive placebo reactors and, indeed, are prone to develop negative placebo effects.

PRETHERAPEUTIC REMISSIONS AND EXACERBATIONS

Basimetry, which is the application of the Law of Initial Value to experimental studies, was originally related to experiments with a steady experimental or pretherapeutic basal level. I believe it would be fair to state that many of the instances in which the Law of Initial Value is now being utilized by various enlightened clinicians and experimenters have to do with a relatively steady preexperimental or pretherapeutic basal level. However, this view and application of the Law of Initial Value is misleading, for in the biologic sciences the prestimulus or pretherapeutic levels in animals and humans are rarely steady.

I have attempted to study the pretherapeutic functioning of psychiatric patients in relation to a moving base line in which time is also a factor. More specifically I have investigated the results of therapy with regard to whether the patients were remitting, exacerbating, or in a plateau state with regard to their clinical status. The important aspect of this study was the fact that I was interested in studying the effects of a changing base line.

On first impression it would appear obvious that a patient who is remitting prior to the application of a specific treatment would have a better result than a patient who is exacerbating prior to the onset of treatment. In reality there are few studies in the literature in which the question of pretreatment remission or exacerbation is considered.

The study of pretherapeutic patterns of remission or exacerbation represents in reality a succession of initial values projected over a period of time. It is an active changing process and includes the study of (1) direction of change (improvement versus worsening); (2) relative intensity of illness (range); and (3) rate of change (rate of improvement or exacerbation).

If one takes but one recording of a patient's pretherapeutic status, then one cannot accurately state whether or not a given patient is actively remitting or exacerbating. However, a number of pretherapeutic recordings taken over a period of time would indicate the all important question of whether the patient is indeed improving or exacerbating.

I attempted to study this concept by means of some clinical evaluations. In this study the results of treatment were correlated with the treatment status of 200 patients who had received various psychotropic drugs. One hundred had been treated with chlorpromazine. All in this group had marked overt anxiety in common. A second group, consisting of 100 severely depressed patients, was treated with tranylcypromine in combination with trifluoperazine or imipramine hydrochloride. Each patient was studied intensively for a period of two to three weeks prior to the onset of treatment. Each patient was seen for a minimum of four visits during this interval. The patients and their families were screened carefully to determine the day-by-day functioning of the patients with regard to whether they were improving or exacerbating prior to and at the onset of treatment.

The method of evaluation used with those patients receiving chlorpromazine is similar to that described earlier in this chapter. This technique includes a quantitative evaluation of the patient's vocational, social, and sexual performance. It also quantitatively measures the level of anxiety. In addition this system of evaluation considers the appearance and intensity of various psychiatric symptoms. Finally, it includes a qualitative and quantitative analysis of dreams.

The technique for the evaluation of patients receiving antidepressant drugs is one that I have reported on in many papers during the past ten years (Lesse, 1962, 1966). It is described in detail in Chapter 15. It includes all those factors enumerated under the evaluation of patients receiving chlorpromazine, but in addition it evaluates mood and psychomotor activity much more intensively, because these are cardinal symptoms in depression.

As to the results, of fifty patients who were remitting prior to the onset of therapy thirty-eight (76 percent) showed a marked improvement within two weeks after receiving chlorpromazine. In the group of fifty patients who were exacerbating prior to the onset of therapy only nineteen (38 percent) showed a marked improvement in a two-week period after receiving chlorpromazine. This is a striking difference, when one considers that these patients were all very ill. It should be pointed out that the initial value of anxiety was high in all patients so that the placebo effect that was dependent on the initial value was quite constant.

The results of the studies with depressed patients were equally striking. Of the fifty patients who were remitting prior to instituting treatment, forty-six (92 percent) showed a marked improvement within a two-week period. In contrast to this only twenty-seven (54 percent) of the fifty patients who were exacerbating during the pretherapy period obtained marked improvement in a two-week period.

It would appear that the direction of change in the patient's pretreatment clinical status is of great moment in determining the final effect of therapy. This principle applies equally well to all types of biologic treatment and experimentation. It also has very definite implications for psychotherapeutic treatment.

The concept of rate of pretherapeutic clinical change as a factor influencing therapeutic results has not anywhere been evaluated adequately. In the studies presented above the patients were studied over a two-week period prior to the onset of treatment. My methods of evaluation were too crude to determine whether the rate of change was steady or whether it occurred in spurts. Various parameters must be devised by means of which rate of change can be related to psychologic phenomena.

I believe it is entirely appropriate to state that, unless the factors of pretherapeutic remission and exacerbation are considered, the validity of the reported results of any treatment procedure should be challenged. Also, it is literally impossible to compare the results of any given treatment, reported by different observers, unless the patient populations are comparable with regard to these phenomena.

Finally, from a research standpoint, only patients who are actively exacerbating prior to the institution of treatment should be used in the evaluation of the results of any given therapy. Even if this general rule would be agreed on by all researchers the problem would remain complicated, because the elements of rate and range of remission or exacerbation still would have to be standardized. But such a step would represent progress in the maturation of the psychologic, biologic, and social sciences.

12

THE STUDY AND MANAGEMENT
OF CATASTROPHIC ANXIETY

In planning this book I was hesitant to include my experiences in the preparation of extremely anxious schizophrenic patients to undergo craniotomies and lobotomies under local anesthesia. The reasons for this are several. First, lobotomy is currently a technique that is very rarely utilized in this country. The psychotropic drugs have eliminated, in the vast majority of instances, the need for leucotomies, and psychotherapy in combination with tranquilizers and antidepressant drugs, in general, has produced superior results. I am not deprecating the fact that there are some patients who obtained excellent results with psychosurgery, particularly those who were not extremely deteriorated, backward, state hospital patients.

Second, the research plan for the management of these very anxious, schizophrenic patients was devised eighteen years ago. The over-all plan reflected my basic background in pathology, neuropathology, neurophysiology, and neurology. Some of the more subtle points of observation that could have been suggested by my subsequent training and experiences in psychoanalysis and other types of psychotherapy were not reflected in this early planning. Third, the methods of evaluating patient responses were quite gross by my present standards. Similarly, polygraphic tracings in which motor and autonomic phenomena could be recorded were not employed owing to the lack of sufficient research funds and the fact that polygraphic devices were comparatively primitive at that time. Since then research funds have become plentiful, so plentiful that today some experimenters are literally drowning in money, money that is too often poorly utilized.

However, I finally decided to include this material because this particular phase of my research dealt with patients who, for the most part, were in a state of catastrophic anxiety. They were to be exposed to an extensive operative procedure, namely a craniotomy, under local anesthesia. As if that were not enough, their brains were to be cut. Surgery of this nature, even in patients with brain tumors, where at times it offers a chance for survival, may produce paralyzing anxiety. The patients included in this research program literally could not tolerate the stress associated with opening their eyes to face the new day.

In my survey of many hundreds of articles dealing directly or indirectly with anxiety, this particular research remains unique. I was faced with the problem of how to prepare patients, who were overwhelmingly terrified by the pressures of everyday life and by types of threats that were beyond the ken of so-called normal men, to face a two- to four-hour surgical procedure while fully conscious, not in a passive fashion but rather as an actively participating member of a highly integrated research team. This last point is important because the patients were required to report on their sensations during the phase of cortical and subcortical stimulation.

The methods that were successfully evolved for the preparation of schizophrenic patients, who were unpredictable and could not tolerate the stress of everyday living, to endure the stresses of a craniotomy, cortical stimulation, and finally a lobotomy, all under local anesthesia, has direct application to various psychiatric and nonpsychiatric situations. Among the nonpsychiatric situations in which this pretherapeutic preparation could be of extreme benefit is in the preoperative preparation of patients who are scheduled to undergo surgery, particularly those having only local anesthesia.

Though there have been great improvements in the technical aspects of surgical anesthesia, the psychologic preparation of patients for operations is in a primitive stage. In part this is due to the fact that the average anesthetist and surgeon have little comprehension and therefore are afraid and often intolerant of the psychologic problems that are concomitant to any surgical procedure.

The techniques that will be explained also have application in the preparation of patients who are to undergo very traumatic diagnostic procedures, such as pneumoencephalography, arteriography, gastroscopy, and bronchoscopy, to name but a few. Even very minor procedures, such as a lumbar puncture, are fraught with terror in the minds of some patients.

However, it is in psychiatric research that these special pretherapeutic or preexperimental preparations have their most sophisticated applications. The vast majority of studies dealing with anxiety have dealt with patients who have been only slightly or moderately anxious. In these settings unintended placebo factors can influence the changes in the patients as much as the stimuli or treatments employed. It is only by studying anxiety in extremely severe states, states in which there is no question as to the initial values, that reliable data can be collected.

I am firmly convinced that, if psychiatrists or psychologists interested in clinical or laboratory research can apply the techniques employed in this chapter, then patients with high initial values routinely could be used as research subjects.

TECHNIQUE OF PREPARATION

Without a special preoperative preparation it would be impossible to operate on a schizophrenic patient under local anesthesia. Prior to undergoing these special preparations, the patients were evaluated and reevaluated by a highly integrated staff of a psychiatric research department, through one or more anemneses and the daily reports of nurses, attendants, social workers, and occupational therapists, supplemented by the detailed appraisals of the entire medical staff. This degree of initimacy was possible, in part, because there were rarely more than ten patients on the research ward at any one time.

In addition to the appraisals made by the members of the staff, the patients were studied by me after amytal and amphetamines were administered intravenously. Finally, they were exposed to hallucinogenic preparations, such as mescaline or oral lysergic acid. These last two drugs exposed underlying psychic abnormalities and offered me an opportunity to observe the response of an already extremely anxious patient to tremendous stress. This permitted me to see what type of secondary defense mechanisms automatically were employed by the patient to combat mounting anxiety and how effective they were. A knowledge of the degree of impairment of ego boundaries produced by mounting anxiety and the further supplemental increase in the anxiety level, secondary to any reality distortions, was of particular importance. Finally, the normalizing effects of intravenous sodium amytal, intravenous amphetamine, and, in a few instances, intravenous chlorpromazine were analyzed.[1]

These preliminary studies gave me a graphic knowledge as to the types of drugs that could be used during the operative procedures should difficulties arise. It also aided in the determination of the types of preoperative medications that should be administered. The knowledge gained through the use of the hallucinogenic agents also suggested psychothera-

---

[1] These experiments were begun in 1952. Intravenous chlorpromazine was not available until the latter part of 1954.

peutic techniques that might be profitable in the management of mounting anxiety during the operation. I attempted to determine each patient's threshold of anxiety beyond which various secondary defense mechanisms would be invoked automatically as protective devices. A knowledge of this modus operandi was very important, for I often used these very secondary defense mechanisms to control the patient's anxiety during the operation.

A clear appreciation of the threshold of anxiety beyond which the patient experienced difficulties with reality control was of equal moment, because difficulty with reality control precipitated by rapidly increasing anxiety could be the prelude to wild, uncontrolled panic on the operating table.

To organize these data qualitatively and quantitatively I found it necessary to analyze anxiety into four components in the manner described in detail in Chapter 2. In a similar fashion I attempted to quantitate any trend toward reality distortion secondary to increasing anxiety in a given patient. This was tabulated on an ascending four-point scale in which number 1 was represented as indicating no feelings of unreality, even under extreme anxiety, and number 4 represented great difficulties with reality control. (In level 4 reality distortions were present even when the patient was not under extreme overt anxiety as measured according to the four components of anxiety employed in these studies.)

In addition to this I evaluated the patients' fears of loss of reality control. Various patients react differently when the borderlines of reality become hazy. For most schizophrenic individuals it was the most excruciatingly terrifying phenomenon that they ever had experienced. It was interpreted by most as being "like an impending doom," "like impending death from some unknown, unseen, horrible, torturing fashion," or "a feeling of impending desolation." Many panicked when these feelings became intense. Many were afraid that they would lose complete control. This fear of loss of reality control was also measured on a four-point scale ranging from 1, which represented lack of fear, to 4, which represented panic. Other factors, such as intellectual organization, desire and ability to aid the therapist, and ability to verbalize and free associate were also evaluated.

Table 12.1 is a summary of the quantitative evaluations of the various factors indicated above. This was a master chart from which the individual patient's reaction to the stress of the surgery could be anticipated. From this table one can discern that all but five of the patients were severely and even extremely anxious. Approximately one half of the patients had moderate or extreme difficulties with reality control. To go further, two thirds of the subjects lived in abject terror of losing contact with reality.

Intellectual integration was very satisfactory in all but a few patients. Approximately two thirds of the patients in this series were able to express themselves clearly and free associate very readily.

PRESURGICAL PREPARATION

After considerable thought and probing it was decided that a direct, repetitive, and minutely detailed explanation of factors specifically related to the operation would be the best preparatory technique. These were as follows: (1) theories and techniques involved, (2) sensations that might be experienced, and (3) postoperative benefits that the patient might expect.

I deliberately made the patients extremely dependent on me and me alone, because I would be in intimate contact with them during the operation. To accomplish this I devised a method by means of which the patient's attention was focused as much as possible on me and on the operation. I attempted to eliminate all other matters, past or present, from the overt psychologic scene. The operation "became the patient's entire life" for a period of days.

This was often not too difficult a task. Many patients looked forward to the operation as their last attempt at salvation, because they had been through many types of therapy over a period of many years without success. Also, in spite of their anticipations of help through surgery, most were terrified by the thoughts of an intracranial operation and therefore latched eagerly onto an authoritative physician who promised help and protection during the operation and who was willing to explain the mysteries of lobotomy.

The preparation consisted of a three- to twenty-one-day period of repetitive explanations. For the vast majority, the optimum duration of the preparatory period was approximately seven days. I found that if the period was too short the patient's dependence on me was poor. On the other hand, if the preparation was too long, the stark reality of the operation became a daily threat that exhausted the patient and nullified the benefits of the doctor-patient relationship. In the latter situation, the individual approached the day of surgery in a very anxious state with his psychic defense mechanisms strained by an overly long period of expectation.

In this preparatory technique the patient was given information that would prepare him for each phase of the operation. The anticipation of a previously unknown painful sensation precipitates tremendous anxiety in any subject, particularly one who is to undergo surgery. This could be avoided, or at least greatly diminished, by proper preoperative explanations given patiently and repeatedly.

To this end, all such words as *cut, knife, drill, saw,* and *blood* were avoided religiously during the period of preparation and during the operation. All descriptions of unpleasant sensations were deemphasized. The theory behind the operation was explained in broad, generalized, but correct terms.

TABLE 12.1 Initial Evaluation of Patient

Case No.	Components of Anxiety				Fear of Loss of Reality Contact	Intellectual Organization	Drive	Ability to Verbalize	Affect Syndrome		
	Motor	Affect	Verbal	Reality Contact					Anxiety	Rage	Depression
1	2–3	2–3	2–3	1	3	1–2	2	2–3	3	2	2
2	2	3	2	2	2	1–2	1–2	1–2	3	3	3
3	2	3	2	2–3	2	2	3	2	3	3	3
4	2	2	2	3	1	2	3	2	2	2	2
5	2	3	1	1	2–3	1	2–3	1	3	3	2
6	2	4	2–3	2	3	1	2–3	2	4	3	3
7	2–3	4	2	3	3–4	1–2	1–2	1–2	4	2	3
8	2–3	3	3	2–3	3–4	2	2	2	3	2	2
9	2	3–4	2	1	2–3		2	1	4	2	2
10	3	3	2	2	3–4	1–2	2–3	3	3	3	3
11	2–3	3–4	2–3	2–3	4	1	1	2–3	4	2–3	2–3
12	3	3	2	1	2	1	2	1	4	2	2
13	4	3	3–4	3–4	4	3	3	1	4	4	2
14	2	3	2–3	2	4	1	2	2–3	3	2	2
15	2	3	3	2	2	2–3	2	3	3	3	2
16	3	3	3	2	3	2–3	2–3	2	3	3	2
17	2–3	4	2	2–3	4	1	1–2	1	4	2	4
18	3	4	3	2	4	1	2	1–2	4	3	4
19	2	2	3	2–3	1	1	2	1	3	2–3	1–2
20	3	3–4	3	2–3	4	1	2	3	3–4	2	3
21	3	2	3	3	2	3	3	3	3	2	3–4
22	3	2–3	3–4	1	3		1	1	3–4	3–4	2
23	2	2–3	2–3	2–3	2	3	3	2–3	2–3	3	3
24	2	2	2–3	2–3	3	2	2–3	2–3	2–3	3	2

Row											
25	2–3	3–4	2	1	3	1	3	1	2	3–4	3
26	3	3–4	3	1	4	2	2	1	3	3–4	3–4
27	2	2	2	3	1	1–2	2	3	2	2	2
28	1	2	2	1–2	3	1	2	1–2	2	2	3
29	3–4	4	3–4	2–3	4	2–3	3–4	2–3	3–4	4	4
30	3	3	2	3	4	1	2	3	2	3	2–3
31	3	4	3–4	1	4	2–3	3–4	3	3	4	4
32	2	4	2	1	4	1	2	1–2	1–2	2	3
33	2	2	1–2	3	1	1	1–2	2	1	3–4	2–3
34	3–4	3–4	1–2	2	4	1–2	1–2	2–3	1	3–4	3
35	2	2	3–4	2	1	1–2	2	3	3–4	2	1
36	2	3	4	2	2	2	2	4	3–4	3	1
37	3	3	2	1–2	3–4	2	1	3	1	3	3
38	2	3	1–2	1–2	4	1	1	2–3	2–3	2	2
39	2	3	2	2	4	1	2	1–2	1–2	3–4	3–4
40	3	4	2	1–2	4	2	1	1	1	2–3	3
41	2	3	3	3	1	1	2	2	1–2	3–4	3
42	3	3	2	2	3	2–3	3	3	3	3	3

The following section is an encapsulation taken from many direct recordings of my instructions to the forty-three schizophrenic patients who were prepared specifically for a craniotomy under local anesthesia.

INITIAL PREPARATORY SESSION

The patients were approached in a warm, friendly, reassuring, but authoritative fashion. Simple, nontechnical terminology implying an understanding of the great emotional pain plaguing the patient was used.

I am Dr. Lesse. I am the doctor who accompanies everyone through the treatment for which you entered this hospital. You and I will be very close with each other. I want you to feel free to speak up and ask questions at any time. I know just how worried you are about this treatment. I know also that you have heard many confusing ideas about the therapy, but I assure you that as you know more about it you will not find it so frightening.

First of all you will be helped. Now, I know you have asked yourself, "Just how is this treatment going to help me?" I know you have been through many types of treatment and all were held up to you as cure-alls. Well, the idea behind this treatment is very simple. It helps by decreasing the amount of tension, fear, and anxiety that you feel. I am referring to that tension that sometimes "runs away with you" so that you can't even think straight. Intelligence alone doesn't mean a thing when a person is overwhelmed by fear. [Usually the patients understood these simple terms and were interested in learning more. Anyone who proclaimed sympathy for their painful emotional state could obtain their attention immediately.]

I appreciate that when an individual is very tense, this tension seems to override everything. We will decrease this tension in order that your good common sense can once again take over. I don't mean that we will remove normal feelings. For example, if, after the treatment, you cross a street and a car comes directly toward you, of course you will be frightened, but that's normal fear. (Invariably, the patient nodded or verbalized his agreement.)

During this initial phase of treatment the patients were encouraged to relate their main fears relating to psychosurgery. The more common ones were:

1. Fear of disfigurement (fear that the scars would be noticeable). This was most prevalent among balding men.

2. Fear of pain.

3. Fear of loss of reality contact (this was most prevalent among those who had had difficulties with reality control).

4. Fear of losing control, of running amuck, of "becoming a monster."

5. Paranoid patients often feared that they would be "controlled" after surgery and that the surgeon would be influenced by electronic or telepathic means to destroy their brains.

7. Fear of death (this was surprisingly infrequent).

8. Fear that intelligence would suffer (this occurred only in three patients).

9. Fear that the personality would be changed (some expressed fears that their personalities would not be changed).

The fear of losing control was the most terrifying of all.

The various fears were managed in general in the following manner:

Your hair will grow over the treatment area. The treatment region will be entirely behind the hairline. We do not remove anything. If you have the idea that something will be removed, you can forget it. All we do is to separate certain fibers. The separation of the fibers decreases your tension. Your intelligence and memory are not affected. In fact, when your tension is reduced your thinking and memory may be better than they have been for some time.

To those who had difficulty with reality control or fears of running amuck:

Your feelings of haziness or unreality result from your great tension and anxiety. This will disappear as the anxiety is reduced by the treatment. Have no fear about doing anything violent. I will be with you during the entire procedure, and we will work it through together. I will be no more than a few inches from you during the entire process [this was true]. You know, many patients feel better in the operating room even before they return to the ward [this was also true].

I want you to appreciate this. With the techniques that we use, there will be no nausea and vomiting that you usually associate with an operation. You will be out of bed in twenty-four to forty-eight hours. If you expect to have much pain during the procedure you are very mistaken. But we will talk more about this the next time we meet.

I found that this was as much as the patient could tolerate during the first meeting. To go further during this initial conference often produced restlessness and increased anxiety. The purpose of the first meeting was to whet the patient's enthusiasm, to make him feel that there was some *one* person interested in his personal problem, one who would prepare him and see him through the operation and who would give him some explanation of how this mysterious "last-chance" treatment could help him. I encouraged the patients to call on me at any time to ask questions.

SUBSEQUENT PREPARATORY INTERVIEWS

On the second and following days a variation and elaboration of the first day's session was repeated. The patient's past fears and problems were passed over as if they were of little moment. Fantasies and dreams were minimized unless there was some clear association with the operation, and then they were interpreted within the framework of the operative preparation, always optimistically.

A full, detailed description of the operation and the sensations that would be experienced was presented in nontechnical terms. All the sensations were accurately described, but they were treated casually.

The step-by-step events that occurred during the morning of the operation were clearly outlined including the action and purpose of the various medications to be used. Detailed descriptions were given of the anesthesia and operating rooms, of the physicians and nurses with whom they would have contact. This description tended to relieve the constant fear that accompanies surgical patients, in general, and schizophrenic patients, in particular, when they are moved through rooms filled with aswesome equipment and impersonal, masked staff members.

The events of the head preparation, the infusion, the application of multiple pieces of recording equipment, the positioning of the patient on the operating table, and the limb restraints were carefully explained. I described all these events as being for the benefit of the patient.

The day before the treatment, your hair will be cut short, but it will grow back quickly. That night I want you to sleep soundly, and I will give you something to guarantee this. On the morning of the treatment you will receive an injection that will make your mouth dry [atropine sulfate]. I will do this purposely in order that you will not be bothered by an excess of saliva.

For those patients who I felt would benefit from preoperative sedation I explained:

You will be given an injection [sodium amytal] that will make you slightly drowsy and quite relaxed. However, you will not fall into a deep sleep and as I talk to you you will be able to reply and think clearly. This is very important because your cooperation is necessary.

Remember, it is important that you tell me what you are thinking and how you feel at all times. Do not keep your thoughts to yourself. This is the time, if there ever was a time, to express yourself. Do not select those thoughts that you express; let them slip off your tongue. We are depending on you to help us.

You will be taken to a room, light gray in color, where there will be a number of doctors and nurses, all of whom you will meet. [The names of the staff were mentioned to familiarize the patient with the people who would be about him on the day of operation. A brief description of the various personnel was also included.]

Your hair will be made shorter. [In reality, the scalp was shaved.] Patients often asked, "You mean it will be cut off completely?" This was countered with the simple reassurance that it would grow back quickly.

Certain medications will be put on your head to make the skin sterile. A needle will be put in your left arm. You will see this needle attached to a bottle in which there will be sugar and water. This feeds you and keeps you moist during the treatment. By this technique I can also give you all the medications that may be necessary.

Next a blood pressure cuff will be placed on your right arm. A narrow rubber tube [pneumometer] will be placed around your chest. This records your breathing. On either palm I will palce a metal disk [psychogalvanometric disk]. All these gadgets help us to obtain valuable information. Nothing can go wrong! You will be in a comfortable position.

To those patients who were afraid that they would accidentally move about on the table, the following statement was given with great reassurance:

Don't worry about that! You let me take care of this matter. You will not move your head. You will have a loose cuff on either wrist. This is not to hold you down. Please understand this. Its purpose is to prevent you from accidentally scratching your nose or something of that nature. Also a wide band will be placed over your thighs. This will remind you not to squirm too much, but you will be able to move your feet and legs. If you are not comfortable at any time let me know. I can correct it. Remember, I will be next to you all the time.

Now you will be taken into the treatment room. It is cheerful, comfortably air-conditioned, light gray in color. You and I will have an arrangement whereby we can hear each other clearly, but others in the room will be heard only as muffled voices. I will be with you every moment. If you are worried or uncomfortable let me know. I can take care of anything that comes up.

The sensations that would be experienced during the injection of the local anesthetic into the scalp were described as follows:

The first thing you will feel will be a little pinprick on the top of your head. You have had blood counts here, haven't you? It will feel just like that. Have you ever had a tooth pulled with Novocain? We use medication that has the same sensation. Your head will then feel tense. That is the medication going in. Your head will feel tense from your eyebrows to your ears. Some of the tension then wears off and then you will feel nothing.

The various operative steps—such as the incision, application of hemostatic clips, the reflecting of the scalp, incision of the periosteum, drilling, sawing, and reflecting of the bone flap were described in vague, generalized terms. The various sensations that the patient would experience during these steps were described in an accurate but underplayed manner. For example, the sensations caused by the incision and reflecting of the scalp were described as the "pressure of the surgeon's fingers" and not as being caused by a knife.

You will feel the pressure of the doctor's fingers and hands on your head. He is searching for landmarks. It will feel like the pressure of a thumb or little finger or of a whole hand. This pressure goes on for a considerable period of time. Some patients say that it aches; some say that it doesn't annoy them at all. If you expect anything painful you are mistaken. If you are uncomfortable in any way let me know immediately and I will take care of it.

It will be noted that all references to sharp instruments are omitted. In no instance did a single patient refer to the use of a knife.

It was not easy to formulate a description that would convey an impression of the sensations that were experienced during the drilling and sawing of the calvarium without frightening the patient. One need only recall the discomfort that accompanies the drilling of a tooth to appreciate the physical and psychological stress produced by the drilling and sawing of the calvarium. I found the following technique very successful:

After the period of pressure is over we will use a machine that vibrates. [Hereafter the term "vibrating machine" was mentioned frequently. Any mention by the patient to sawing and drilling was pushed aside. The patient's desire not to face the realities of the craniotomy made it relatively easy to refer to the cutting of bone as "vibration."] This vibration goes on for about ten minutes. However, it is not constant. The actual vibration lasts about two to three minutes.

Manipulation of the dura often can be uncomfortable. Therefore, the patients were told that they might "experience a few aches" after the brief period of vibration was terminated. Because electrocortical stimulation and the lobotomy itself were not associated with much discomfort little more was said in preparation for the lobotomy per se.

After the calvarium was reflected our research team was ready to stimulate various areas of the temporal and frontal cortex. This required an alert and cooperative patient. He would have already been through the stress of a one-and-one-half to two-and-one-half-hour craniotomy at that particular moment. The patient was a member of the recording team and therefore a preoperative briefing about this part of the operation was necessary.

After the vibration is completed the procedure is almost over. However, we will have come to that point where your cooperation will be most important if we are to help you. I will ask you to count "one, two, three," and so on. I want you to tell me immediately if you experience anything, hear anything, see anything, think anything, feel anything, smell anything. If you do, stop counting immediately and tell me what experiences you have had. [To explain further, we had the patient count prior to the onset of each electrocortical stimulus. Any interruption in counting that might denote a change in consciousness or interruption by some mental aberration could then be recorded.]

That is all there is to it. You will remain in the treatment room for a period of time, and then you will be taken back to your room. You will be somewhat drowsy, but as I have mentioned you will most likely be out of bed on the following morning. On occasions, some patients have a dull headache. However, it is mild and will be relieved with aspirin. In a few days, at the very most, the headache will disappear entirely.

This entire explanation was repeated daily. In addition to that which has been described above, numerous questions were asked and answered. The success of the technique depended on the fact that these patients had been through a long period of emotional pain. Their desire to be helped plus the process of conditioning described above led to an extreme degree of dependence on me. It was so extreme that it was rare for a patient to enquire who would perform the operation. I, as the physician who had prepared the patient, received all the blame for any discomforts during the operation.

IMMEDIATE PREOPERATIVE PREPARATION

The evening prior to the operation all the patients scheduled for surgery received adequate oral sedation to ensure a restful night.

On the morning of the operation, preoperative medications were given. The big decision now was whether to sedate and, if so, how much and what kind of sedation was necessary. My decisions were influenced by the individual patient's reactions to intravenous sodium amytal and intravenous amphetamine, which each one had received as part of his earlier work-up. Those patients who had shown a decrease in anxiety and better psychic integration when sedated received sodium amytal (amobarbital sodium, Lilly) 0.25 to 0.5 gram intramuscularly one hour before going to the operating room.

On the other hand, there were patients who had definite difficulties with reality contact attended by increased anxiety when barbiturates were given. These required reinforcement of their states of consciousness by amphetamines. They were given very small doses of sodium amytal intramuscularly (up to 0.25 gram) purely to decrease the change of seizures that might result from local anesthesia with 1 percent procaine. At times these patients also received 0.010 gram of amphetamine intramuscularly to reinforce their states of consciousness.

All patients received atropine sulfate (0.0004–0.0006 gram) intramuscularly one hour before going to the operating room (homatropine bromide worked very adversely). Demerol (meperidine hydrochloride, Winthrop) (0.075–0.1 gram) was given intramuscularly on call. The Demerol gave a mild analgesic coverage. In patients with low pain thresholds it was preferable to withhold the intramuscular injection of Demerol and to give fractional doses of Demerol or morphine intravenously during surgery.

Control of the Patient During Operation

There was a high degree of coordination with a minimum of talking on the part of the large operating team and research staff. If such words as *cut*, *drill*, *sawing*, and *blood* had to be used, they were spoken in a hushed voice so that the patient would not hear them. Excessive noises tended to focus the patient's attention on the operation and on its attendant discomforts.

Of the forty-three patients specifically prepared to have psychosurgery performed under local anesthesia, only nine required a general anesthetic before the lobotomy was completed.

Certain techniques were found to be useful during the operative procedure. I had a thorough knowledge of how each patient reacted under stress. A quick evaluation of the individual patient's pain threshold was possible at the time the "cut down" for the placing of the intravenous needle was performed. This evaluation was very important as patients with a low pain threshold often required frequent small injections of Demerol or morphine. I knew that those patients who had difficulty with reality contact, when consciousness was impaired, had to be kept alert. Similarly, I was ready to distract or sedate those who mounted great anxiety when an awareness of the operation became too all-consuming and terrifying.

The following psychologic techniques were most frequently employed:

1. Frequent definite reassurance.

2. Encouragement to free associate (some obsessive-compulsive patients spoke incessantly).

3. Restatement of the need for the patient's cooperation for best results.

4. Forewarning the patient of sensations he was about to experience.

5. Encouraging patient's secondary defense mechanisms: obsessive thinking, compulsive acting, and delusions and hallucinations. (I had obtained a thorough knowledge of these mechanisms prior to the operation. I did not encourage them, if the manifest content was frightening.) Hypochondriacal mechanisms were never encouraged.

6. Distracting techniques: abstract discussions, discussion of some point in the patient's history, discussion of patient's future plans, free discussion, even of current events, and simple mathematical or other intellectual problems.

7. Pain: Some patients as they experienced increased anxiety or pain would squeeze my hand in an attempt to hurt me. This would be very distracting for them and was encouraged if necessary. In some instances it represented the patient's anger toward me. In other instances it was a mechanism by which the patient attempted to maintain reality contact; patients often asked me to cause them pain by squeezing their hand. This too, at times, was employed in order to distract the patient from the reality of the operation.

8. Simple, forceful commands.

9. Use of the patient's poor conception of the passage of time. (During the operation the patient, if necessary, was told that ten minutes represented merely one minute.)

10. Reassurances as to the success of the operation.

11. Sensory stimuli to maintain reality contact.

The auditory and tactile stimuli enumerated above enabled the patient to maintain his "psychic bearings."

Figures 1.1 and 1.2 demonstrate the physical setting in which the surgery was performed. These photographs illustrate the close contact that was maintained between the patient and me.

SUMMARY

The procedures of preparation and management that I have described were very effective in thirty-four of forty-three severely ill schizophrenic patients. As I mentioned earlier in this chapter, variations of these techniques can be utilized in a highly successful fashion both in clinical and in laboratory research investigations. These techniques require a great deal of time and patience on the part of the research investigator; however, they enable detailed studies of severely ill, extremely anxious psychiatric patients over a limited period of time.

13

THE AMBULATORY MANAGEMENT OF PATIENTS WITH SEVERE ANXIETY REACTIONS

In terms of the central theme of this chapter, namely, the ambulatory treatment of patients with severe anxiety reactions, one must have immediate, intermediate, and long-range goals. Procedures may be more or less effective with regard to the attainment of one or another of these aims. In current practice those who utilize the various psychiatric treatment techniques have usually focused on one or another of these temporally oriented aims. Therapists utilizing mechanical techniques or drugs alone have emphasized immediate and, to a lesser degree, intermediate results. Some have paid little attention to the long-range outlook or have implied that if one attains an immediate result a long-range beneficial outcome is guaranteed or that the patient can be helped in the future by a repetition of the same procedure. (I am aware that, with certain types of patients, psychiatrists utilizing maintenance electroshock or maintenance drug therapies are indeed focused on long-range results.)

In an opposite vein, there are psychotherapists who in their treatment of severely anxious patients focus primarily on intermediate or even long-range results, and who by the very nature of their techniques are far less interested in any significant immediate change in the patient. Therapists utilizing intensive reconstructive analytic techniques, particularly the group that utilizes the so-called classic psychoanalytic procedures, imply that the relative paucity of immediate symptomatic relief is well worth the price one must pay during the reeducation procedure. Indeed, in the long-range psychoanalytic therapies a rapid amelioration of anxiety and secondary symptoms is considered by some to inhibit the long-range goal.

More recently the emphasis by those interested in conditioned reflex-ology have stressed immediate goals, including the rapid amelioration of overt anxiety, with the unwritten implication that once these goals were attained the patient would be able to manage the future with a high level of adaptative capacity.

In the management of the vast majority of patients manifesting marked anxiety, the therapeutic aims must be adaptationally oriented, whether one is interested in the immediate, intermediate, or long-range phases of therapy or a combination of all. In the past, the term *adaptational* has been used purely in terms of psychosocial factors. Ideally, the concept of adaptation should refer to a dynamic interrelationship among physio-dynamic, psychodynamic, and sociodynamic factors, for this concept assumes an indivisible mutual interdependency between all human func-tions. These various terms may be defined as follows:

1. *Physiodynamics* refers to the state or changing state of the individual's anatomic structures, physiologic and biochemical functions, and their mutual interdependence in relationship to one another and in relationship to psychodynamic and sociodynamic factors.

2. *Psychodynamics* refers to the state or changing state of the individual with regard to all psychic functions (conscious and unconscious) and their mutual interdependence in relation to physiodynamic and sociodynamic factors.

3. *Sociodynamics* refers to the state or changing state of the individual's total external environment and its mutual interdependence in relation to physiodynamic and psychodynamic factors.

The central theme to be stressed here is that, whenever there is an altera-tion in one area of human function, there is inevitably an alteration in other aspects of the same function and in all other functions, both internal and external, until a state of relative equilibrium is reached. These changes operate and affect every aspect of the individual's life and in turn that of society in an indivisible feedback fashion. In this fashion a dynamic, ever-changing equilibrium is maintained. The equilibrium, being dynamic, is momentary, and over time a picture of constant flux emerges.

In terms of adaptation, all therapies employed in the ambulatory treat-ment of severely anxious patients should strive for an optimum rather than maximum result. The struggle for the maximum during the past decades has been self-defeating, because fragmentary results often were accepted without careful evaluation and were offered as examples of a type of maxi-mum. The search for the maximum always has been associated with a need for self-deception, because those who strive for the maximum usually press a procedure beyond realistic limits, and what they fail to attain in reality they often make up in fantasy.

The search for the optimum in the treatment of ambulatory patients should have efficiency as one of its guiding principles. This goal has various qualities, some of which are as follows: (1) a therapy ideally should be efficient as to the prevention of reoccurrences of illness; (2) it should be efficient as to the time required to obtain a certain goal; (3) it should be efficient as to the use of available psychotherapeutic manpower; (4) it should be economically efficient (meaning the required outlay in time and money); (5) it should be culturally efficient. In a polyphasic society, such as the United States, all psychotherapeutic techniques cannot be considered adaptable with equal efficiency to all socioeconomic spectrums of our culture.

Symptom Amelioration Versus Reeducation

These two roles of therapy have been considered by many as an either/or process rather than as a broad spectrum goal in which both are important.

In general, until recent years the removal of symptoms was considered as the stepchild of organized psychotherapy. During the past decade, those schools dealing with condition reflexology of various types, led by men who are primarily research psychologists, have reemphasized the importance of symptom amelioration, but at the same time have been relatively blind to the question of reeducation considered from a broad socioadaptive standpoint.

Conversely, therapists adhering purely to the various psychoanalytic concepts seem to forget, in many instances, that it is primarily the removal of presenting symptoms and signs for which the patient enters therapy, and, if a therapy accomplishes nothing else, it should at least blunt or completely remove these presenting phenomena.

The immediate, or short-range, goal of all therapies should have incorporated into their basic structures the aim of decreasing the level of anxiety as quickly as possible so that the presenting secondary symptoms and signs may be ameliorated. It is my impression that, as far as most therapies are concerned, the amelioration of presenting symptoms and signs is not directly dependent on the frequency and duration of treatment. There is a small group of patients who, in addition to an amelioration of the presenting symptoms and signs, obtain a thorough physiopsychosociodynamic reeducation so that they are able to face the stresses of everyday life on a more mature plane, thereby preventing reoccurrences of their presenting problems.

Considered in this light, one arrives at the conclusion that *the process by which the level of increased anxiety is decreased in the initial phases of therapy is relatively unimportant. There is no evidence, at this time, that the final benefits of therapy, even therapy that has reeducation as its primary aim, is enhanced by a prolonged introductory period of anxiety decompression requiring many months as compared to a process in which anxiety may be effectively decreased in a matter of days or weeks. Indeed, the contrary may be more correct: namely, that the more rapid the level of anxiety is decompressed, accompanied as it is by the removal of secondary symptoms and signs, the more efficacious the long-time reeducation program may be.*

It should be noted that *the duration and frequency of treatment does not indicate necessarily the intensity of treatment, particularly with regard to psychotherapy.*

SELECTION OF THERAPIES FOR SYMPTOM AMELIORATION

Ideally, the technique that one utilizes for the rapid amelioration of marked anxiety and the removal of secondary symptoms should have the capacity for being expanded in scope so that it becomes a reeducation process by means of which long-range goals may be attained.

The selection of a particular technique, of course, depends on many factors. It depends on all the factors considered in Chapter 10, "The Placebo Phenomenon," in addition to a consideration of specific therapeutic capacities accruing to a particular technique. Therefore, in addition to treatment specificity, placebo factors that pertain to the therapist, to the patient, to the milieu, to the initial values, and to the question of spontaneous rhythms should be weighed in the selection of a particular treatment for the removal of presenting symptoms.

Particular attention should be paid to the initial quantitative level of anxiety and as to whether this anxiety is increasing or decreasing at the onset of therapy. All treatments "look good" when they are instituted in patients who are improving. From a research standpoint, only patients who are becoming worse should be selected for the testing of any given treatment.

With marked initial levels of overt anxiety, the use of tranquilizing drugs, in combination with various types of psychotherapy, particularly supportive psychotherapy, has proven to be most effective. On occasions, if anxiety is extreme, the tranquilizing drugs or sedatives initially may have to be administered parenterally. However, in most patients, no matter how severe the presenting level of anxiety, orally administered tranquilizers, together with supportive psychotherapy, is sufficient to significantly ameliorate presenting symptoms and signs, usually in a matter of one or two weeks, often in a matter of days.

Some psychotherapists interested in conditioned reflexology, will argue that the use of their techniques eliminates the need for various tranquilizing drugs. This is a mistake, particularly if one treats patients whose presenting symptoms are in a psychotic matrix. In patients in whom the presenting level of anxiety is only moderate or slight, the various tranquilizing drugs are more often a hindrance than a benefit. This is particularly true when the presenting symptoms and signs take the form of social or sexual maladaptation.

It should be pointed out very clearly that *the greater the degree of presenting anxiety, the more efficient any given therapy is, whether it be organic or psychotherapeutic in nature.* Stated in another fashion, the higher the initial level of anxiety, the more efficient any particular treatment will be with regard to the removal of presenting symptoms and signs. The use of the tranquilizing drugs in only slightly anxious patients is a therapeutic error that is repeated all too often by those who do not fully understand the function of the tranquilizing drugs.

Some psychotherapists quickly point out that there are dangers in the rapid decompression of anxiety with its concomitant removal of presenting symptoms and signs. They claim that in the absence of any effective residual psychic pain the patient will have little or no motivation to remain in therapy and, as a consequence, may proceed in treatment without any enthusiasm or even run away from it. This is true in many instances. On the other hand, if painful symptoms persist over a prolonged period of time despite active treatment, patients tend to seek additional or different kinds of help.

Realistically speaking, one should search for the optimum level of patient change that will remove or substantially blunt the patient's presenting anxiety and secondary symptoms and signs without effectively destroying his capacity to participate as an effective member of the therapist-patient team. This will be discussed further in the chapters dealing with psychotherapy in combination with various psychotropic drugs.

One point is definite, the initial aim of treatment, whether it be psychotherapy alone, organic therapy alone, or a combination of both, should be the lessening of the initial level of anxiety to the point where the patient can cooperate effectively in a psychotherapeutic relationship. It becomes obvious that in this theoretic framework, drug therapy is not considered an end in itself, but rather a vehicle to rapidly aid a very anxious patient by decompressing the initial level of anxiety—with concomitant removal or blunting of the presenting symptoms and signs—so that he can effectively cooperate in a psychotherapeutic milieu that has reeducation as its central purpose.

Drugs, therefore, should be an appendage to psychotherapy and not a substitute. Where conditioning therapies are utilized for the initial removal of the presenting symptoms and signs, the therapists must be prepared to alter the nature of their therapies if they are to include a program of psychic reeducation. At present most of those employing conditioning techniques have shown little or no interest in this type of long-range goal.

In any case, *it should be noted that the removal of the presenting symptoms and signs purely indicates that the level of anxiety has been decreased and nothing more. This is the same whether drugs, electroshock therapy, or any type of psychotherapy has been used.*

Following the removal of the presenting symptoms and signs, the therapist still is faced by a patient who has decompensated in response to various psychosocial factors that are usually based on a combination of genetic, congenital, and developmental maladaptations. It is in the application of techniques whose primary long-range goals are to prevent reoccurrences of emotional difficulties that the admonition concerning careful socioeconomic and sociophilosophic applicability between technique and patient applies. Most therapies that are utilized primarily for the removal or blunting of the initial level of anxiety and presenting symptoms and signs are adaptable to patients coming from all socioeconomic and sociophilosophic environments.

The reeducation process on which maturation depends is primarily a process of psychosocial deconditioning and reconditioning. In all educationally oriented therapies, insight must play a role. Depending on the socioeconomic background of the patient, various insights will be brought to the fore; some will be emphasized, whereas others will be deemphasized. Also depending on the socioeconomic and sociophilosophic background, the sources of stress will vary, for the prime sources of stress are not the same in all environments, a fact that is too often overlooked in our training of students from different cultures.

In previous papers (Lesse, 1964, 1969) I have expressed the view that the psychoanalytic and psychoanalytically oriented types of psychotherapy appear to be best suited for patients who come from backgrounds in which there has been an individualistically directed orientation. To the contrary, patients who come from more group-oriented backgrounds should be treated by techniques in which group adaptation is stressed. Stating this in a different fashion, emotional decompensation in group-oriented and group-dependent individuals is primarily owing to group maladaptation, which may be in the form of an excessive expression of individualism. In most instances, psychic decompensation among individualists is owing to the fact that their capacities to function as individuals are not in keeping with the demands that are placed on them.

In all therapies, it is necessary to have the patient understand the limitations of their adaptive capacities in relationship to the presenting sources of stress. It is important for all patients to function within their ego capacities at any given moment. Similarly, an awareness of the earliest signs of abnormal anxiety, scondary to various types of stress, should be emphasized until it becomes a cardinal point of appreciation in all patients.

CONCLUSION

It has not been my intention in this chapter to avoid or deprecate the importance of the intrapsychic aspects of emotional illness or to play down the necessity to understand the psychodynamic mechanisms that play a role in a given patient. This is beyond the scope of this particular chapter, and there are a multitude of papers and books written by members of various schools of psychotherapeutic thought that emphasize the many theories of psychodynamic interpretation. Also, I do not mean to imply that the therapist's interpretations to the patients are of small moment. Rather, it has been my purpose here to emphasize the fact that socioeconomic and sociopolitical factors must be considered in the selection of specific psychotherapeutic techniques that have as their aim the broad psychic reeducation of patients. The very nature of a given psychotherapeutic technique will aid or hinder a patient in his adaptation to a given economic or political environment.

It would not be too rash to state that most men must adjust to their times and environment to find a modicum of security and contentment. It is one of the obligations of the psychotherapist to aid the patient in this type of adaptation. Most persons do not have the emotional capacity to function as individuals in a competitive society, as recent historic trends in the United States illustrate. The psychotherapist must be cautious lest he encourage and unintentionally direct the patient to attempt a type or adaptation of which he is incapable. This type of error is very common in the United States, owing in part to the fact that many psychotherapists are rock-bottom, self-employed individualists who have relatively little personal contact and understanding of persons from other socioeconomic environments. It is small wonder that most psychotherapists are insufficiently aware of the polyglot economic and philosophic environments from which their patients come, and to which most must return.

In an opposite vein, it would be a gross error to assume that all persons should be adjusted by their psychotherapists to their culture. Indeed, there are some who will never find contentment unless they attempt to extend the physical, economic, political, or philosophic boundaries that limit their society. However, such men are individualists and their number is small and must not be confused with a much larger and more dependent group.

It is within the psychotherapist's province, in most instances, to determine which patients should adjust and which patients need not adjust to their environment in their search for contentment and security. If this sounds presumptuous, then most physicians are presumptuous when they determine the role a patient with limited physical capacities (that is, patients with cardiovascular, cerebrovascular, or pulmonary insufficiency) should follow if he is to survive or live free of distress. It would appear that the psychotherapist's duties should be just a broad as those of the physician who deals with somatic ailments.

In the following two chapters, the use of psychotherapeutic techniques in combination with various psychotropic drugs will be described. These techniques are uniquely suited for use in the treatment of patients with severe anxiety reactions, particularly those patients seen on an outpatient basis. These techniques may also be adapted for use in a hospital setting. They have the advantage of producing a rapid amelioration of the initial presenting symptoms and signs. They also can be expanded as the patients improve in order that effective psychosocial reeducation can be accomplished.

14

PSYCHOTHERAPY IN COMBINATION
WITH TRANQUILIZERS

The treatment of patients in whom marked, overt anxiety is a prominent feature of their clinical syndromes is very likely the most common problem confronting psychiatrists and clinical psychologists. Depending on the therapist's personality and earlier training, a broad spectrum of treatment modalities may be brought into play. Some psychiatrists who are purely organicists in their orientation will automatically administer tranquilizing drugs or electroshock therapy, and these treatment procedures will be the sum and substance of their planned therapy.

Other psychiatrists and psychologists will only employ purely psychotherapeutic techniques in the management of severely anxious patients whether the prime nosologic problem is psychoneurosis, schizophrenia, or sociopathy.

These polarized therapeutic conceptualizations of the treatment of patients manifesting severe anxiety are anachronistic at our current level of psychiatric development.

In the last chapter I emphasized that the optimum procedures in the treatment of severely anxious patients were those flexible enough to fulfill immediate, intermediate, and long-range therapeutic goals. In my experience, psychoanalytically oriented psychotherapy employed in combination with properly chosen and administered tranquilizing drugs is the optimum therapeutic technique for the effective management of the vast majority of patients in whom severe or even massive anxiety is a prominent clinical feature.

This chapter is devoted to a step-by-step description of the technical intricacies involved in the use of tranquilizers in combination with psychoanalytically oriented psychotherapy. It is a digest of my sixteen years of experimentation and experience with this treatment procedure in the management of several hundreds of severely anxious patients who had a broad spectrum of psychiatric illnesses.

The combined tranquilizer-psychotherapy procedure is a complicated method from a theoretic basis, because it involves the compounding of biodynamic, psychodynamic, and sociodynamic elements into a single unified treatment approach. To help the reader appreciate some of the difficulties involved in the evolution of this combined technique I would like to review some of the problems and confusions that have tended to polarize many, if not most, psychotherapists and psychopharmacologists.

Despite the fact that millions of very anxious patients have received tranquilizing drugs since their introduction in 1952, relatively few papers have appeared in the literature that give a detailed account of the combined uses of psychotherapy and drug therapy. This does not mean that psychotherapy is combined infrequently with psychopharmacologic agents in the treatment of severely anxious patients. Indeed, it is fair to say that some form of psychotherapy is administered to all anxious patients receiving drugs. However, in many instances the organically oriented psychiatrist is unaware or has little interest in the fact that he is employing psychotherapeutic techniques. It may well be that many of the positive reports testifying to the beneficial effects of drugs may actually result from an unintended psychotherapeutic intervention, with the psychotherapy being in the form of suggestion, persuasion, or direction.

When psychotherapy is not intentionally employed as part of a broad drug therapy program it must be considered as an unintended placebo. One might say then that there are only two types of psychopharmacologic therapy, and both are indeed combinations of psychotherapy and drug therapy. They may be classified as (1) unintended psychotherapy in combination with drug therapy and (2) intended psychotherapy in combination with drug therapy.

Because, according to this concept, all drug therapy is in reality combined drug therapy and psychotherapy, it is my firm contention that it should always be given as intended, planned, combined therapy. Even where intended combined therapy is employed there will be unintended placebo effects, but these should be fewer than if the combined procedure is unintended.

At present, few psychiatrists use combined therapy in a planned, intended fashion. Dynamically oriented psychotherapy has not been purposefully combined with psychopharmacologic therapy owing mainly to the lack of broad training that is necessary if one is to employ this technique. Psychiatrists, in order to utilize this combined procedure effectively, must have extensive experience with the organic therapies and with dynamically oriented psychotherapy, particularly brief analytically oriented psychotherapy. Unfortunately, most psychiatrists adhere either to the organic treatments or to the psychotherapies and use combined therapy only unintentionally.

There are different conceptual approaches to the use of tranquilizing drugs. Many psychiatrists use psychotropic drugs as an end in themselves with the sole purpose being to eliminate target presenting symptoms. Though some psychiatrists may claim that they use these ends purely as measuring devices, this, in fact, represents their sole aim, the implication being that if symptoms are ameliorated the patient will be able to adapt to his environment. This philosophy, held currently by many neuropsychopharmacologists, is a very narrow, archaic concept in view of our knowledge of the dynamics of emotional illness and our understanding of the process of psychosocial adaptation.

As I discussed in Chapter 13, the removal of target symptoms does not necessarily indicate that the patient will be able to adapt successfully to his environment. It has been shown that symptomatic relief results primarily from a patient's expectation of help, that it commonly occurs rapidly and is independent of the particular type of therapy employed. The same results can be duplicated in some patients by the administration of placebos. On the other hand, improvements in personal functioning occur more gradually and seem to be related to the nature of the therapeutic experience to which the patient has been exposed, suggesting that they may result from a learning process.

Psychotropic drugs should not be considered at any time as an end in themselves, but rather should be used as a vehicle to enable the patient to function in a cooperative fashion in a psychotherapeutic relationship. In this broader and more inclusive conceptual scheme, the question is not whether psychotherapy should be used in combination with tranquilizing drugs. On the contrary, the pertinent question is "What type of psychotherapy should be employed in conjunction with the psychopharmacologic drugs?"

My initial studies on the use of psychotherapy in combination with tranquilizers in the treatment of severely anxious patients began in the early months of 1954, shortly after chlorpromazine was available for research work in the United States. My papers dealing with the technique of psychotherapy in combination with tranquilizing drugs (Lesse, 1956, 1957) were the first detailed studies of this subject to appear in the psychiatric literature.

The initial criticisms with regard to the use of the tranquilizers to ameliorate marked anxiety came from diehard psychoanalysts of the classical school who had little or no experience with the various psychotropic agents, but who saw these medications as threats to the purity of their particular psychotherapeutic tool, feeling that any medication would interfere with the results that might have been gained from psychoanalysis. These statements reminded me of the ecclesiastic protests against the use of anesthetics more than a century ago. As time went on, even diehard, conservative psychotherapists grudgingly found it necessary to use tranquilizing drugs in patients who continued to deteriorate while in therapy. Unfortunately, their use of the medication was in the spirit of helplessness, and the drugs were often used inappropriately.

Our understanding of the mechanisms by which tranquilizers operate to ameliorate anxiety are still purely theoretic, even though many biochemic and psychodynamic theories have been proposed. Similarly, the mechanisms by which the various psychotherapies help still remain mysteries despite a wealth of purely psychologic theories and a number of psychosomatic and somatopsychic concepts. Therefore, both processes still operate through empiric means.

Expressed in a broad fashion, it is likely that the various tranquilizers operate by compensating for biochemic insufficiencies or excesses. These insufficiencies or excesses possibly cause disturbances in neurohumoral mechanisms probably mediated through the hypothalamic-reticular network with psychophysiologic manifestations such as anxiety, being the clinical expression of the disturbances. The secondary symptoms and signs are, in turn, possibly reflections of hierarchically higher neurogenic regulatory mechanisms.

COMBINED THERAPY IN PATIENTS WITH MARKED ANXIETY

The combined process can be introduced at any of three phases of the therapeutic procedure, namely, at the inception of therapy, during the course of treatment, or as maintenance therapy.

THE INCEPTION OF TREATMENT

Combined therapy logically should be instituted at the beginning of the therapeutic procedure in patients who are too overtly anxious to be amenable to psychotherapy alone on an ambulatory basis. It is especially effective if the motor component of anxiety is extremely marked. At this phase of treatment the therapist is primarily interested in short-term goals related to the amelioration or blunting of the initial level of anxiety and the secondary symptoms and signs that are the secondary defenses against this anxiety.

Prior to the advent of the tranquilizers, when psychotherapeutic techniques were employed alone, weeks or months were often spent in ameliorating the level of anxiety to the point at which the patient had sufficient ego strength to cooperate effectively in a dynamically oriented psychotherapeutic relationship. In a great many instances the early administration of tranquilizing drugs greatly shortens the period of anxiety decompression and thereby enables the patient to cooperate effectively and meaningfully more quickly. Since the advent of the combined technique, many patients who formerly would have required hospitalization can be managed on an ambulatory basis. The proper use of the combined technique prevents the necessity for hospitalizing many severely anxious schizophrenic patients and some patients with agitated depressions who otherwise would have been exposed to the psychic trauma and economic drain that is often associated with institutionalization.

Combined therapy is particularly effective among those severely anxious patients who are commonly diagnosed as having schizophrenia, pseudoneurotic type. I would go further and state that, from my point of view, the combined therapy technique is the treatment of choice for most pseudoneurotic schizophrenics who overtly manifest a marked degree of anxiety. I have also found that many severely decompensated schizophrenic patients, whose illnesses were previously considered incompatible with ambulatory psychotherapy, often become suitable candidates for analytically oriented therapy when it is combined with tranquilizing drugs, particularly those of the phenothiazine group.

Combined therapy is a necessity in the management of many very anxious patients who have organic mental reactions. Prior to the advent of the tranquilizing drugs, outpatient electroshock therapy or hospitalization was mandatory for a very large group of these individuals. At the present time, a high percentage of those anxious patients with organic mental illnesses, particularly those that fluctuate in appearance and in intensity, can be managed very effectively by a combination of tranquilizing drugs and supportive psychotherapy.

Though combined therapy has its most dramatic effects in the outpatient treatment of anxious psychotic patients, it is also indicated at the very inception of treatment with some extremely anxious psychoneurotic patients. Weeks and even months of painful anxiety that severely limits the benefits of all psychotherapeutic efforts may be greatly shortened if combined therapy is diligently employed.

The combined therapy approach is also indicated at the inception of treatment with very anxious, acting-out adolescents and some hyperactive children where the acting out and hyperactivity is a secondary defense mechanism against a marked increase in the degree of anxiety.

THE COURSE OF TREATMENT

The tranquilizing drugs also may serve a purpose when introduced during the course of analytically oriented psychotherapy or even during the course of intensive, reconstructive, psychoanalytic psychotherapy. They should be considered when the level of anxiety escalates sharply or persistently secondary to an increase in environmental stress or psychotherapeutic events. The introduction of the tranquilizers may often literally save psychotherapy, when judiciously introduced. This is particularly so in the ambulatory management of anxious schizophrenic patients.

The insights unveiled during the course of dynamically oriented psychotherapy may precipitate a marked or even massive elevation in the intensity of anxiety in some neurotic patients, and most particularly in a large group of schizophrenic patients, no matter how diligent and careful the therapist may be. This marked increase in anxiety may be attended by the appearance of a strong negative transference and a decrease in effective free association. The tranquilizing drugs, when properly utilized, by rapidly reducing the level of anxiety not only may ameliorate the secondary signs and symptoms associated with the increased level of anxiety, but also may ameliorate the destructive effects of a strong negative transference and permit more significant free association.

MAINTENANCE THERAPY

Many patients require intermittent psychiatric treatment throughout their lives. This is particularly true with schizophrenic patients. To a lesser degree it pertains also to a segment of the population of neurotic patients who have been chronically ill. In the next chapter, an analogous problem will be discussed in connection with patients with recurrent depressions.

An experienced therapist learns to recognize and appreciate which patients require scheduled visits and which patients may be permitted to use their judgment as to when they should seek help. As I have noted before it is imperative that patients be taught to recognize the earliest evidences of mounting anxiety and the threshold beyond which they should return for further treatment. The importance of the automatic recognition of the earliest signs and symptoms of mounting anxiety was discussed in the previous chapter.

The nature of maintenance therapy will differ depending on the patient, the therapist, and the environment. Some patients are unable to function successfully vocationally, socially, or sexually without maintenance drug therapy even in the face of routine, everyday responsibilities. Usually the required dose of a tranquilizer for maintenance purposes is far less than the amount needed to ameliorate the original anxiety. Indeed, a less potent tranquilizer than that originally required, one that may also have less severe side effects, may be sufficient during the maintenance period.

There are literally tens of thousands of patients who are on a continuous program of tranquilizing drugs. Very often, when they evidence psychic decompensation, the problem may be met by a simple increase in the dose of the prescribed drug. On occasions it may be necessary to change the drug with a different biochemic agent being substituted. The psychotherapeutic techniques utilized in combination with the drugs will differ depending on the intensity and rate of increase in the level of anxiety and the patient's immediate response to the tranquilizers. If the level of anxiety is readily controllable, an analytically oriented psychotherapetic approach in which reeducation is continued, is feasible. If the level of anxiety is very pronounced, a return to a supportive psychotherapeutic approach will be necessary.

Certainly not all patients require maintenance drug therapy but instead can be managed with various types of psychotherapeutic techniques alone, the visits being scheduled periodically or as required by evidences of psychic decompensation. Usually, maintenance psychotherapy merely reinforces previously learned processes. Less frequently, the widely spaced maintenance visits may further the learning process by bringing to light insights that advance psychic maturation.

If the presenting level of anxiety is severe or if the rate of increase is pronounced, the therapeutic process will become more supportive until the overt manifestations of anxiety are significantly reduced. Very commonly it is advisable to supplement the psychotherapeutic regime by the addition of a tranquilizer depending once again on the degree of manifest anxiety and the rate of acceleration in the degree of anxiety. If the level of anxiety is not marked, small amounts of the original drug or even a less potent tranquilizer usually are sufficient to block or ameliorate the presenting symptoms and signs. In any case, when employing any drug, one must use the appropriate preparation in sufficient amounts.

SELECTING THE PROPER TRANQUILIZER

It is beyond the scope and purpose of this book to enter into a discussion of the minutae of the biochemical structures or actions of the various tranquilizers or to discuss in detail the therapeutic pros and cons of various preparations. A detailed description of the structure, actions, and application of a multitude of tranquilizing preparations has flooded the literature ad nauseum.

My rules for the selection of a particular type of preparation are very simple. Wherever there is a clear-cut evidence of marked to extreme overt anxiety, measured according to the parameters discussed at length in previous chapters, usually accompanied by one or more secondary symptoms or signs, I select one of the phenothiazine preparations—Thorazine (chlorpromazine), Stelazine (trifluoperazine), Trilafon (perphenazine), Compazine (prochlorperazine), and the like. In patients in whom anxiety is obviously very pronounced I find that chlorpromazine, the first of the phenothiazines to be introduced, is still the most reliable and effective preparation. The initial soporific side effect commonly associated with chlorpromazine may be beneficial. As the dosage of the phenothiazines is increased, particularly in the case of chlorpromazine, one may find it necessary to add one of the amphetamine preparations to combat fatigue. Similarly one of the anti-Parkinsonian drugs may be required to prevent or ameliorate extrapyramidal-like manifestations.

Where the level of anxiety is moderate, and the patient has not responded to psychotherapeutic procedures alone, drugs such as Librium (chlordiazepoxide) or Valium (diazepam) may be utilized. On occasion one may use one of the substitutive diols (Mellaril), when the level of anxiety is moderate to severe.

Meprobamate is ineffective in most instances, or effective primarily by means of a placebo reaction, and should be avoided as a general rule. In my experience almost any patient can be managed just as effectively by psychotherapeutic means alone as by psychotherapy in combination with meprobamate.

Recently, a number of neuropsychopharmacologists have expressed the opinion that there is a difference between neurotic and psychotic anxiety, with the so-called minor tranquilizers being prescribed to patients with neurotic anxiety and the so-called major tranquilizers being prescribed to anxious schizophrenic patients. Included under the major tranquilizers are the rauwolfia alkaloids and the phenothiazine derivatives and analogs; the minor tranquilizers include the substitutive diols, chlordiazepoxide, diazepam, and the like. It has been claimed that the major tranquilizers do more than simply tranquilize excited patients, that they have a broader effect that could be characterized as antischizophrenic or antipsychotic.

This concept is open to serious questioning. In my studies, as I have indicated in previous chapters, I found the process of symptom amelioration in both neurotic and psychotic patients to be very similar. *If neurotic patients are extremely anxious, the so-called minor tranquilizers are of relatively little benefit and the major tranquilizers usually must be employed.* Conversely, there are ambulatory schizophrenic patients, seen in private or clinic practice, who will respond to chlordiazepoxide or diazepam if the degree of manifest anxiety is not severe.

ANALYTICALLY ORIENTED PSYCHOTHERAPY IN COMBINATION WITH
TRANQUILIZERS

INITIAL PHASE

This combined technique is optimumly suited to patients whose illnesses are characterized by marked or extreme overt anxiety together with various secondary symptoms and signs. Indeed, it is the preferred technique for such patients. The prime purpose during the initial phase of treatment is to ameliorate the severe pathologic level of anxiety, this decrease being accompanied by a blunting or removal of the secondary clinical manifestations.

When this is accomplished, the therapist should not be deluded that he has caused a grand metamorphosis that will stand the ravages of time and stress. All that has been accomplished is the lessening of the patient's psychic pain as evidenced by marked anxiety and those symptoms that are secondary defense mechanisms against this anxiety. This may be likened to the lowering of a fever, rapid pulse, or increased respirations secondary to an upper respiratory infection. It may be also compared to the alleviation of diarrhea, epigastric pain, or dyspepsia associated with gastrointestinal deficits. These changes may or may not mean that the primary cause of the ailment has been affected. The initial improvement in the presenting symptoms certainly does not mean that the patient recognizes the source of his problems, nor does it guarantee that he will be able to control or avoid the internal or external environmental sources of his difficulties.

The initial process of the combined therapeutic procedure usually lasts from one to three weeks. It is rare for this phase to be of longer duration. The psychotherapeutic aspect is strongly supportive and is conducted in a face-to-face setting. Under no circumstance should the patient be placed on a couch at this point, for it is imperative that the therapist be sharply aware of all clinical changes, whether the information is transmitted to him by visual, auditory, or tactile means.

The therapist should be aware, particularly at the very outset of therapy, that all the factors discussed in Chapter 10, "The Placebo Phenomenon," are likely to influence the course of treatment. It is important for the therapist's immediate expectations and goals to be in harmony with those of the patient.

The recording of the anamnesis is an intimate part of the technique of anxiety reduction. The therapist should take great pains to reassure the patient as to a positive outcome. During the initial interview the therapist must obtain a detailed qualitative and quantitative analysis of the anxiety that is present, together with a sharp awareness of the sequence of appearance of the secondary defense mechanisms. He must also evaluate as clearly as possible the sources of stress, both chronic and acute. In addition to an awareness of the initial value or level of anxiety, it is urgent for the therapist to know prior to the institution of therapy whether the level of anxiety is increasing, has already plateaued, or is decreasing. The therapist may require a number of visits before he can accurately ascertain the direction and rate of change in the quantitative degree of anxiety. The therapist should be aware also as to whether the anxiety and secondary symptom formation is in a psychotic or neurotic framework. (Though this determination cannot be made in some instances during the initial interview, a tentative evaluation is a great aid.)

Prior to the termination of the first interview the patient should be reassured by the therapist that the degree and nature of his psychic pain is appreciated and that he can and will be aided in the relief of his problems with particular reference to the presenting symptoms and signs. These reassurances are not wild promises in most instances, because the vast majority of patients can be helped to attain symptomatic relief by the tuse of the combined therapeutic approach usually within a period of several weeks, and often sooner.

The patients should be seen three times during the first week of combined therapy (occasionally two visits during the first week may be sufficient). This peimits the therapist to adjust the dosage of medication, obtain further history, and continue the supportive psychotherapy begun during the initial interview.

In very anxious patients the tranquilizers are prescribed at the time of the initial interview. The psychiatrist should have a thorough knowledge of the drug that he is employing both from a therapeutic standpoint and with regard to possible side effects. He must be confident in his handling of the medication. It is imperative also that he be experienced in the technique of brief analytically oriented psychotherapy. He should understand the capacities, as well as the limitations, of both the organic and psychotherapeutic aspects of the procedure. The therapist should also understand the benefits and limitations of hospitalization, for with many of these patients, should their ailments worsen instead of improving, emergency hospitalization may be necessary. Finally, the therapist should be cognizant of the benefits of ambulatory electroshock therapy, for some of the psychotic patients who continue to regress or show no significant improvement may be excellent candidates for electroshock therapy as far as the amelioration of the initial levels of anxiety and secondary symptoms and signs are concerned.

Under no circumstances should a potent tranquilizer be used as an intended placebo; this maneuver is used too frequently by those who have vested interests in a fixed psychotherapeutic approach. Before prescribing the drug, its nature and purpose, especially its potential positive benefits, should be described to the patient in general terms.

The mechanism by means of which the combined technique operates can best be described to the patient in terms of anxiety reduction with symptomatic relief being secondary to this amelioration. Many patients come expecting medication. Indeed, many may request one particular "magic pill." The degree to which the public has been exposed to various medical techniques by advertising media has been described in Chapter 10. Environment may exert a negative effect on the patient. Some patients come with great antipathy to drug therapy or psychotherapy or to a particular type of drug therapy or a particular type of psychotherapy. This is especially true if they have had any prior treatment. Such a situation may complicate the initial therapeutic situation to varying degrees.

The most common potential side effects that may occur secondary to a particular drug should be presented simply and honestly. The descriptions must take into account the patient's preconceived conceptualizations, correct or incorrect. Every therapist should be prepared for possible difficulties arising in anxious patients who have hypochondriacal manifestations as part of their secondary defense mechanisms should side effects occur. Finally, one should be aware of difficulties that may arise among severely anxious schizophrenic patients, particularly among those in whom there are evidences that a decrease in the level of consciousness may be followed by difficulties in reality contact. Some very anxious patients who have organic mental deficits also are prone to pose problems should the tranquilizers have a potent soporific side effect. Finally, patients with a very pronounced obsessive-compulsive matrix may pose a problem in the very initial phase of therapy as a manifestation of their fear of losing control secondary to the use of any drug.

At the time of the initial interview, if it is feasible, there should be an attempt to manipulate the patient's environment. As a general rule the patient should be admonished to temporarily decrease his vocational and social responsibilities and activities. In some instances, the patient should be confined to his home.

Patients are all relatively helpless at the outset of therapy. Most have infantile magic expectancies for help. Many will cooperate and follow the therapist's suggestions blindly in the hope of finding relief from their psychic pain. Others, particularly very anxious schizophrenic patients, may be so frightened as to hold all therapists suspect, even though they promise help; indeed, some schizophrenics will fight the new therapist tooth and nail, and a few will run away from treatment. These and other types of negative expectations are commonly enhanced if the therapist and the patient come from different socioeconomic and sociophilosophic backgrounds.

One of the primary aims during the initial phase of treatment is to foster a very strong, positive transference reaction. The accomplishment of this aim is rendered relatively easy if the therapist's and patient's initial goals are in harmony and the prime basis for concomitancy at this point is an expectation of rapid amelioration of the presenting symptoms and signs. If the initial aims are divergent therapy will be star-crossed from the very beginning. Unfortunately, a negative transference reaction is likely to occur if the therapist states, in effect, that "the main purpose of treatment is reeducation and this will take a long, long time." The severely anxious patient's prime desire at this point is symptomatic relief, and he should be approached overtly with the general idea that "I will relieve you of your pain."

This simple goal transcends all socioeconomic and sociophilosophic differences that may exist between the patient and the doctor. It does not interfere or negate long-range goals aimed at psychosocial maturation as some psychoanalytic psychotherapists appear to believe.

Complications can be expected to arise in patients in whom there is a chronic, malignant masochistic trend. The very reassurance offered by the therapist may temporarily increase the level of anxiety in these patients, but through the combined treatment process even deep masochistic elements can be blunted, in most instances, as the level of anxiety is reduced below a certain threshold.

The rapid decrease in the quantitative degree of anxiety in itself encourages a strong, positive transference reaction. Transference relationships in very anxious patients, particularly in schizophrenic patients, initially may be quite tenuous. A strong positive transference is not established until the patient no longer feels he is in constant jeopardy.

The rate at which the level or intensity of anxiety is reduced has an important bearing on the patient-psychiatrist relationships. In general, *the more rapid the rate of anxiety amelioration, the more marked the initial positive transference reaction.* This is particularly true of any patient who manifests a very high initial level of anxiety. One might correctly postulate that the rapid reduction of psychic pain satisfies the patient's magical expectations. The only danger that may occur secondary to this magic clinical change is a feeling of omnipotence and overconfidence with a premature lowering of vigilance that may arise in some therapists.

By the use of this combined tranquilizer-psychotherapeutic approach a working relationship between doctor and patient that would have taken months to establish with psychotherapy alone may be accomplished in a matter of weeks. Many patients react to the rapid relief of painful anxiety with unquestioning gratitude and a desire, indeed an eagerness, to relate to the psychiatrist. This quickly establishes and enhances the strong positive transference. It occurs at times as part of the magical expectancy with the therapist being viewed as an all-powerful father who is infallible in the patient's judgment.

Under these conditions it is rare to see a strong negative reaction or transference develop in the patient. Even when the patients recount anxiety or anger-laden traumatic childhood experiences associated with their parents there is no significant shift of the abreacted hostility to the therapist in contrast to the situation that commonly arises in the absence of combined therapy. In other words, the negative transference trend is blunted. (This very primitive, child-like dependency in a number of instances can be a drawback to therapy if it is permitted to remain undiluted. As will be noted later, the therapist must actively and repeatedly make the patient aware of his dependency feelings. If this is not done, therapy at times can stagnate and the patient's ego capacities will atrophy.)

I cannot stress too forcefully that the initial phase of the combined technique produces rapid clinical changes that are ever changing and that have a momentum far greater than that seen when psychotherapy is used alone. This puts greater demands on the therapist. Indeed, some therapists are poorly equipped psychologically to effectively handle this type of procedure.

During every visit, by direct questioning and careful observation, the degree of the patient's anxiety, the nature and status of the secondary symptoms, the vocational, social, and sexual behavior, and the dream material are reviewed in detail. Close contact is made, where possible, with the patient's family and friends. I appreciate the fact that relatives and friends may be poor informants, but the nature of the information to be gathered is simple and can be readily correlated with the data obtained from questioning and observing the patient.

In view of the rapid change in the patient's clinical status, the therapist may be prone to overestimate the patient's capacities for vocational and social adaptation. However, I repeat, once again, that at this point the improvement is primarily symptomatic in nature, with the patient having little or no understanding of the nature or origins of his problems. It is safer to be conservative in the estimation of a patient's ego capacities. At this point in treatment overoptimism could result in anxiety to the point of panic, if the patient is exposed prematurely to excessive vocational or social stress.

The rate of change that occurs as a result of the combined technique can be controlled. This pacemaker can take several forms. First, the dosage of the tranquilizer can be varied. A rapid build-up is often necessary during the first week with changes being made daily or every few days until the intensity of anxiety is very definitly ameliorated. After the level of anxiety is decreased, the total daily dosage of medication may be lessened. The total daily dosage has to be titrated against the degree of overt anxiety.

From a psychotherapeutic standpoint, the level of anxiety can be affected by the relative control or encouragement of the process of patient catharsis. In some patients a free outpouring of affect-laden material may be an effective tool leading to anxiety decompression. However, at times it can cause a negative feedback reaction and actually increase the level of anxiety leading to a new pananxiety state. In such instances the therapist may aid anxiety amelioration by limiting the nature and rate of catharsis. Systematic autorelaxation exercises, vigorous physical outlets, and occupational diversions are good temporary channels that may serve as braking mechanisms. It should be understood that this process is very fluid and depends entirely on the rate and direction of the patient's clinical change. The rate of clinical change can also be affected by controlling the patient's activities relevant to work, socialization, and sexual relationships.

It can be affected to a lesser degree by interpretations. At this phase of treatment interpretations should be made sparingly. The therapist must be careful not to precipitate insights that the patient is emotionally incapable of handling. Interpretations, when they are given, should deal with the here and now. When they involve situations from the patient's past they should be pertinently related to the patient's current behavior or life situation. Poorly timed and poorly conceived interpretations may precipitate a massive panic reaction.

The reporting of dreams is encouraged even in the initial phase of therapy. As I described in detail in Chapter 7, "Dreams," as the level of anxiety is rapidly decreased, there is a greater awareness of dream material. The therapist should be cautious and not overwhelmed by this seeming deluge of dream recall. Once again, at this point he should refrain from making profound interpretations that the patient may not be able to tolerate. *At this phase of treatment dreams should be viewed primarily as a source of psychodynamic information and secondarily as a means of anxiety decompression.* Interpretations, when deemed pertinent, should be related to the current scene and should be gauged according to the patient's capacities to tolerate an awareness of the latent content.

As I have emphasized in Chapter 7 and as was emphasized years ago by Gutheil (1951), the most important aspect of the manifest content of dreams is its emotional charge as evidenced by the amount of movement, affect, pressure of speech, color, and so forth. In general, if one interprets the intensity of the emotional impact, it is not likely that the interpretation will increase the general level of clinical anxiety. In addition to the safety factor, the interpretation of the emotional charge as evidenced in the manifest content of the dream has great impact on the patient in the initial phase of combined therapy and may effectively aid the process of anxiety amelioration. It also serves as one of the bridges to the psychoanalytically oriented phase of treatment.

Nightmares serve directly and rage-filled dreams indirectly as indicators of the intensity of anxiety. I repeat once again that all nightmares and rage-filled dreams are not of equal weight. A quantitative and qualitative change in the nature of the nightmares or rage-filled dreams may be the earliest evidence of clinical improvement. I would like to reiterate also that in the initial phase of combined therapy the appearance of nightmares or, less frequently, rage-laden dreams in some patients in whom they had previously not been reported paradoxically may represent a state of improvement as described before in the section of Chapter 7 on "Anxiety Beyond Nightmares."

Dangers Associated with the Initial Phase

Many complications can occur during the initial phase of treatment. Most can be anticipated and avoided. Others can readily be corrected.

Excessive Tranquilizing. At times the dosage of the tranquilizers may be increased too rapidly, or as the overt level of anxiety is decreased the drug level may be kept at levels more appropriate for the period when the overt level of anxiety was much greater. It is imperative that the dose of medication be optimally titrated according to the intensity of manifest anxiety. This titration should proceed gradually, never precipitously.

In part, one can be guided by observing the degree to which secondary symptoms and signs have been ameliorated. If secondary symptoms and signs are still present one must be very cautious before contemplating drug reduction. An understanding of the threshold of anxiety associated with various symptoms and signs, as described in previous chapters, is imperative at this point.

One must be particularly cautious in the reduction of drug dosage in schizophrenic patients, for at times an excessively rapid decrease in medication may precipitate a panic episode. On the other hand, overtranquilizing may cause a paradoxic, massive pan-anxiety state in schizophrenic patients if the soporific side effects of the drug lead to difficulties in reality control. On occasions this may be relieved by the addition of small amounts of amphetamine.

Excessive tranquilizing also may produce a degree of placidity and passivity that will block further effective treatment. The overly rapid amelioration of anxiety may lead some patients to minimize the severity of their illnesses. Indeed, in some, one can observe the unfolding of a complete scheme of denial of illness. Some will run from treatment. Others may remain purely to receive the medications. It was interesting that these patients were afraid, in many instances, to have other physicians take over the administration of drugs. This is an example of what I have called *drug transference* in which the therapist becomes merely the purveyor of a "magic elixir."

Insufficient Dosage of Tranquilizer. The danger of an insufficient dosage is self-evident. If the therapist utilizes the information that can be garnered from the chapters dealing with decompression of anxiety, he should have little difficulty in administering the amount of drug necessary for the amelioration of a certain quantum of anxiety. I repeat that the therapist must know his drug, its benefits and its limitations.

Side Effects of Medication. All drugs that have any potency may have adverse side effects. Most that occur as a result of the administration of tranquilizers are fortunately mild and transient. The patients should be forewarned to minimize the anxiety that is associated with the appearance of side effects.

The management of side effects depends on their nature and severity and the patient's attendant emotional reactions. As mentioned above, most sequelae are mild, transient, and disappear spontaneously. In other instances, the addition of counteracting drugs may rapidly ameliorate the adverse side effects. The prompt use of counteracting drugs depends on the therapist's knowledge of the tranquilizer.

As side effects appear the therapist should interpret them clearly to the patient so that they are not falsely conceived by the patient as being an integral part of his illness. This is particularly important in patients who have hypochondriacal defense mechanisms. It is also important in patients who have an obsessive-compulsive personality matrix, for they may conceive that side effects are a further indication of their lack of control. Paranoid schizophrenics may interpret side effects as evidence of the therapist's malevolence toward them.

As the result of any one of these situations, the side effects may cause a paradoxic feedback mechanism that will actually increase the level of anxiety despite the fact the tranquilizer may have produced, initially, an excellent response in the patient. On occasions, this feedback mechanism may be of such degree as to necessitate the termination of combined therapy. Fortunately, this is rare. At times, the nature and severity of the side effects may permit a change in tranquilizers. This can be done effectively in many patients, but in some instances the entire therapeutic scheme collapses.

Excessive Positive Transference. In some instances the patients develop a degree of dependency that renders them affectively almost inert. In general this is not a problem during the initial phase of treatment; it usually becomes a major concern during the second or psychoanalytically oriented phase of treatment. Quite often this difficulty may be associated with over-medication and can be corrected by a reduction in the daily dose of tranquilizer.

Excessive positive transference often can be prevented by the manner in which the initial phase of psychotherapy is conducted. An excessively strong positive transference reaction does not occur overnight, and in those patients in whom it appears to be progressing too rapidly, active interpretation of the overdependency can be introduced gently and gradually. Such dependency represents a therapeutic hazard in those patients in whom the infantile magical expectancies are so pronounced at the very outset of combined therapy that they dominate the therapeutic relationship. There is a very small percentage of patients in whom therapy must be terminated owing to this development. As far as symptom relief is concerned, patients such as these often can be managed by the use of drugs and the simplest type of directive therapy. Before any further attempt at a more definitive type of psychotherapy it may be necessary to refer such patients to another therapist.

Drug Transference. As mentioned earlier, drug transference pertains to situations in which patients will remain in therapy with a given psychiatrist because they associate him with the administration of a successful drug and are afraid that the same drug will not be so effective if administered by a different physician. In these instances, the therapist becomes merely the purveyor of a pill. At times drug transference may be confused by the therapist as representing a true, strong, positive transference. When such misinterpretations are marked, owing to the therapist's own emotional needs, effective treatment is bound to collapse. With the use of drugs, as with all types of treatment, accurate observations, undiluted by exaggeration due to immodesty and neurotic wishful thinking, are necessary for optimum benefits.

Premature or Excessive Environmental Commitments. The rapid amelioration of the initial level of anxiety and secondary symptoms and signs is interpreted by most patients as a sign of a "return to health." When this occurs, almost all patients, if left to their own design, immediately will attempt to resume full vocational and social activities. Indeed, many will strive to "make up for lost time." They will try to compensate for that period of time in which their psychic difficulties limited effective activity.

I cannot emphasize too urgently that, following the initial symptomatic improvement secondary to drug therapy, premature resumption of routine responsibilities may lead to a massive psychic collapse. It is one of the main tasks of the psychotherapist, at this phase of treatment, to guide the patient's vocational and social performance with a firm hand until the patient demonstrates firm evidence of increased ego capacities. The failure on the part of psychiatrists to follow these suggestions is one of the commonest causes of failure in drug treatment.

Family Interference. The rapid amelioration of the presenting symptoms and signs is considered to be synonymous with the cure in the minds of most relatives and friends of patients, and they often become a negative influence with regard to the patient's remaining in therapy. Even those relatives who become temporarily chastened in their roles as amateur psychiatrists when the patients are extremely ill quickly resume "practice" after there is evidence of symptomatic improvement.

To a degree this can be forestalled by predicting for the patient and family at the first visit that symptoms and signs will probably disappear very quickly but that any cessation of treatment at that point would be fraught with danger. This admonition may now be repeated, if unintentionally malevolent advice from the family threatens to interfere with further treatment. Both the family and the patient should be warned in no uncertain terms of the consequences of premature termination of treatment.

To a small number of patients together with their "household advisors," all warnings will be of no avail, and the patient will precipitously terminate therapy. In many instances a rapid exacerbation of all symptoms and signs will occur with the family and the patient returning for further help. From bitter experience I would advise all psychiatrists who anticipate utilizing the combined therapeutic procedure not to permit a reoccurrence of this situation. If the patient runs away from treatment on a second occasion it is far better to refer him to another therapist or to recognize that, at least in your hands, combined therapy cannot be effectively promoted with this specific patient.

PSYCHOANALYTICALLY ORIENTED PHASE

There is no sharp demarcation between the initial and secondary, or psychoanalytically oriented, phase of treatment. Rather, the change takes place gradually, with the psychotherapeutic process becoming less and jess supportive. The change usually begins from one to three weeks after the onset of treatment, after there has been definite evidence of a marked decrease in the quantitative degree of anxiety and a significant amelioration of secondary symptoms and signs. In some instances the secondary symptoms and signs may be completely gone. In other patients one or even two of the symptoms may be present but only intermittently and denuded of their pretherapeutic level of affect.

Aberrations such as delusions, illusions, and hallucinations should be ameliorated completely before the analytically oriented phase of the treatment begins. Psychosomatic symptoms and signs may be ameliorated completely at this point if they are acute in nature. In situations in which they are chronic with evidences of secondary tissue change, the psycho-analytically oriented phase of therapy may begin after there is a relative quiescence in the symptoms or signs and evidence of a marked decrease in the anxiety associated with the particular psychosomatic disorder.

Therapy continues in a face-to-face confrontation throughout the early phase of psychoanalytically oriented treatment. At a later period, the couch, whether for the benefit of the patient or the therapist, may be used at the therapist's discretion.

The prime aims of the psychoanalytically oriented phase of treatment are (1) reinforcement of anxiety decompression begun in the initial phase of treatment and (2) reeducation with the aim of increasing the patient's psychosocial maturation.

As treatment progresses the first goal becomes less and less important as the second goal becomes increasingly realized. I would like to reaffirm that at the onset of this second phase of treatment the patient has little or no insight as to the sources or psychodyanmics of his difficulties. Improvement, thus far, has resulted from the tranquilizer, the supportive psycho-therapy, and various placebo effects.

This is a dangerous point for a therapist to become overwhelmingly enthusiastic and undercautious, particularly if he becomes enamored with his own magical powers. Poor judgment, in this regard, may lead to a precipitous collapse of all that has been attained. At this point, the patient still has relatively fragile ego capacities.

The psychotherapeutic support that characterized the initial phase of therapy can be gradually relaxed when there is adequate indication of increasing ego strength. This is measured to a great extent by the degree of overt anxiety and the patient's vocational, social, and sexual adaptation. Therapy remains ego supportive in nature but to a gradually lessening extent. Free association is encouraged but in a guided fashion.

The clinging positive transference relationship is given active attention. As noted before, if it continues in an undiluted form, therapy will become paralyzed. The positive transference is actively interpreted and dissipated, for its existence is a constant threat to the effective continuation of the psychoanalytically oriented phase of treatment. Its presence is a residue of magical expectations and is antithetical to any psychotherapy that has emotional maturation as a goal.

As mentioned before, in the presence of a very strong positive trans-ference reaction there is often a marked inhibition of any negative or hostile responses. I do not mean that repressed hostility is completely inhibited. To the contrary, marked anxiety has a hostility-inhibiting effect in many patients, and during the initial phase of therapy, as the level of anxiety is rapidly reduced, anger directed toward persons other than the therapist may come forth.

The decompression of anxiety during the initial phase of treatment is often followed by a free flow of repressed hostility, but this hostility is rarely directed toward the therapist in the form of a strong negative transference reaction. This situation poses a therapeutic problem in a number of instances if it persists in the psychoanalytically oriented phase of treatment. Manifestations of negative transference, when kept within reasonable bounds, afford an excellent means for the controlled discharge of hostility and at the same time serve as a valuable medium by means of which the patient obtains significant insights.

As the excessively positive transference is reduced in intensity the therapist usually can expect the appearance of a negative transference reaction. However, it will usually not be so intense as it might have been if a tranquilizer had not been used in the initial phase of treatment. This poses an active task for the psychotherapist to guide the release of hostility in such a manner as to benefit the patient, while at the same time avoiding an indiscriminate and inappropriate outburst of rage against family and friends. I have noted only a few instances, in my studies, in which the released hostility could not be managed by diligent guidance even with schizophrenic patients.

COMMUNICATION ZONE

The term *communication zone* refers to a quantitative degree of anxiety in which the patient appears to communicate most freely. In some patients the range appears rather broad, whereas in other patients, it is relatively narrow. Psychotherapists, beginning with the classical psychoanalysts, correctly warned that, if the patient's level of anxiety is depressed to too great a degree, the patient will not communicate efficiently. Relatively few psychotherapists have drawn attention to the fact that when patients are extremely anxious there is also relatively little effective communication.

Though the pattern is highly individualized, in many instances I find that there is a certain threshold of anxiety below which the patient will communicate with greater freedom. The rate of change in the quantitative degree of anxiety also appears to effect communication. The level of communication is greatly enhanced as an excessive level of anxiety is decreased and is less evident as anxiety establishes a plateau effect. Similarly, as the quantitative degree of anxiety is increased in patients who present a flat affect a zone of anxiety will appear characterized by relatively free communication that may disappear if an excessively high level of anxiety is attained. I repeat, once again, that this is a highly individualized process that requires greater study.

INTERPRETATIONS

With regard to interpretations made by the psychotherapist during the combined therapy technique, the same general rules pertain as in any other brief psychoanalytically oriented procedure. It should be remembered, once again, that the process of change is much more rapid here than in the usual psychotherapeutic process. The therapist must be very cautious lest he permit the development of a free-floating pananxiety state secondary to interpretations that the patient is unable to accept at a particular state of emotional maturation. As in dream interpretation, the interpretation of other material should focus on the here and now with past events and associations being related as much as possible to current processes. At all times, evidence of increasing anxiety, as described in previous chapters, should be probed.

Vocational and social adaptation with pride and pleasure in relationship to past and present relationships are stressed with prime emphasis being on current processes. The necessity to function within one's current psychic capacities is prominently emphasized throughout this analytically oriented phase of treatment. The patient is conditioned, so to speak, to an awareness of the earliest evidences of increased anxiety secondary to any type of environmental stress. As the patient attains a more mature level of awareness he learns to anticipate situations more positively. Usually at this point the amount of anxiety precipitated by a particular situation is relatively slight. The final attainment of maturity with regard to a particular situation is attained when the patient is automatically able to manage a situation without significant anxiety.

If the tranquilizing drugs are introduced during the psychoanalytically oriented phase of treatment for the first time, or if they are reintroduced after having been discontinued, the degree of the positive transference that occurs is not so profound as noted when drugs are introduced in the initial stage of the combined therapy program. Similarly, in such instances it is rare for a strong drug transference to occur. The patients in this situation usually maintain a realistic attitude toward the medications, and they merely credit the therapist with good judgment for having employed the tranquilizers.

The use of the tranquilizing drugs in combination with psychotherapy effectively permits a broad range of very anxious individuals to be treated on an ambulatory basis. These patients formerly would not have been amenable to therapy in a psychiatrist's office or in an outpatient department. Even in those instances in which effective therapy could be accomplished after long, painful, and expensive months of intensive psychoanalytic psychotherapy, the entire process of treatment is made much more efficient while sacrificing none of the long-range benefits. Indeed, if we honestly recognize the frequency with which patients exacerbate despite the therapies employed, the use of combined therapies adds a dimension in the psychiatric armamentarium that is far superior to drugs or psychotherapy alone.

15

PSYCHOTHERAPY IN COMBINATION
WITH ANTIDEPRESSANTS IN THE TREATMENT
OF AGITATED, DEPRESSED PATIENTS

Marked overt anxiety is commonly a hallmark in certain types of depressive syndromes. It is a prominent characteristic of agitated depressions, probably the most common psychiatric ailment observed in individuals over the age of forty. This psychologic illness formerly carried the label of *involutional depression* and, during the early part of the twentieth century, was estimated to occur twenty times more frequently in women than in men. At present, however, in my experience with this syndrome the female-male ratio has dropped to 5:1. This is a reflection of the changing psychosocial scene.

The relationship of anxiety and depression has been the subject of much research and of many serious discussions that have involved psychotherapists, biochemists, and even neurophysiologists. No definitive answers have been forthcoming. Clinically, anxiety and depression are seen in various combinations. In some instances an increase in the intensity of anxiety and depression parallel each other in a crescendo fashion as the patient decompensates in response to real or apparent stress. On other occasions one may observe a seemingly paradoxic relationship in which the intensity of overt anxiety appears to decrease as the patient becomes more depressed. In an opposite vein, one may also observe an apparent decrease in the severity of depression as the patient manifests a marked increase in the degree of anxiety.

In this chapter I aim to present the results of my research with a large group of very anxious, severely depressed patients who were treated by me during the past eleven years on an ambulatory basis with antidepressant drugs in combination with psychoanalytically oriented psychotherapy. When anxious, agitated, depressed patients are treated by the combined psychotherapy-drug technique, tranquilizers as well as antidepressant drugs usually must be employed. Indeed, in some instances markedly anxious, depressed patients will respond to tranquilizers in the absence of any antidepressant drugs (Lesse, Hoch, and Malitz, 1957).

The technique of psychotherapy in combination with tranquilizers has much in common with the technique of combining psychotherapy with antidepressant medications. Indeed, the latter technique was a direct outgrowth of the former. Many of the technical procedures are similar or parallel, being modified primarily by the nature of the symptoms and signs that are present and, when patients are depressed, the omnipresent danger of suicide. Just as the psychotherapy-tranquilizer method of treatment may be an alternative to electroshock and/or hospitalization in the management of very severely anxious, psychotic patients, the combined psychotherapy-antidepressant technique is an alternative to ambulatory electroshock therapy or institutionalization in severely anxious, depressed patients.

Improved techniques for the treatment of patients with suicidal ideation and drives are urgently needed because none of our current methods has proven dependable on a long-term basis for a sizable number of patients in whom suicidal forces play a chronic role. Psychotherapy alone, drug therapy alone, electroshock treatment alone, employed in or outside an institution cannot guarantee long-term success in patients with strong suicidal propensities. In part, this combined drug therapy-psychotherapy technique attempts to evolve a superior technique for the treatment of such patients.

Finally, there are literally millions of severely anxious, depressed patients who receive antidepressant drugs combined with a mélange of psychotherapeutic procedures, most of which are unintended placebo aspects of the treatment process. Drug therapy is thus relegated to the realm of pill pushing, no matter how impressive the mechanisms of statistical evaluation. As I stated in Chapter 13, psychotherapy should always be intended if it is to be optimally beneficial to the patient. For more than eleven years I have used the antidepressant drugs in combination with psychotherapy as a planned psychotherapeutic approach in an attempt to formulate a rational, effective procedure that is superior to drug therapy or psychotherapy alone.

A review of Chapters 13 and 14 is necessary for a full appreciation of the material included in this chapter because they discuss so many points that pertain to the selection of patients and to an appreciation of the benefits, limitations, and dangers associated with combined therapy.

As in the case of the combined tranquilizer-psychotherapy procedure, psychotherapy in combination with antidepressant drugs in the treatment of anxious, depressed patients has its greatest and most effective application at the very onset of treatment. However, drugs can be introduced during the course of psychotherapy should a patient become increasingly anxious and depressed. Drugs may also be introduced during the course of a psychotherapeutic procedure in the management of patients who manifest an anxious, depressed state for the first time. Antidepressant drugs also have definite application as maintenance treatment in the management of chronically or recurrently anxious, depressed patients.

In this chapter I will limit my descriptions to a general plan in which psychotherapy is used in combination with antidepressant drugs from the very onset of the treatment process.

Although many severely anxious, depressed patients who previously would have required electroshock treatments obtain very striking remissions with antidepressant drugs, many others do not respond satisfactorily or have a rapid exacerbation of their symptoms. It was very evident in my experience that one of the major causes of these failures was the fact that the patients returned to their previous and often chaotic patterns of life. The combined antidepressant-psychotherapy technique that I will describe has proven to be, in my hands, as effective as electroshock therapy in the acute and subacute management of severely depressed patients. Thus far, my experience is based on the treatment of more than 400 patients who have been exposed to this procedure during the past eleven years.

I do not intend this chapter to serve as a comparison of the long-term results between electroshock treatment, drug therapy, and combined psychotherapy-antidepressant drug therapy, although a study of this nature would be of extreme importance. Rather, this chapter is intended primarily as a working outline of the technique of combined psychotherapy-antidepressant therapy.

DEFINITION OF A SEVERELY ANXIOUS, DEPRESSED PATIENT

A severely anxious, depressed patient can be described best phenomenologically and according to his capacities to adapt to his environment. These patients are either unable or extremely impaired in their capacities to function vocationally, socially, and sexually. With few exceptions, they all overtly appear very depressed and either have a marked increase or decrease in the level of pyschomotor activity. Most have at least inconstant suicidal preoccupations.

In some severely anxious, depressed patients, the depressions are masked behind a façade of hypochondriacal or, less often, psychosomatic syndromes, commonly called *masked depression* or *depression sine depression*. This veneer can readily be removed revealing the underlying depressive core.

I utilize this combined procedure in patients who are too ill to be treated on an ambulatory basis by psychoanalytic, psychoanalytically oriented, or supportive psychotherapy alone. Indeed, the use of these techniques, without antidepressant drugs in severely depressed ambulatory patients, is archaic and painful and needlessly exposes the patient to the omnipresent dangers of an impulsive suicidal act. Prior to the advent of the combined procedure, these individuals would have been started on electroshock therapy without delay, either on an outpatient or inpatient basis. Mildly depressed patients who are able to function vocationally and socially and are not plagued by feelings of hopelessness or suicidal preoccupations can be treated by psychotherapeutic methods alone.

Regressed schizophrenic patients in whom severe depression is a major factor are not good subjects for this combined technique because they are poor condidates in general for drug therapy and/or psychotherapy on an ambulatory basis. Electroshock therapy remains the preferred treatment in these instances. Finally, patients who manifest severe anxiety and depression in the matrix or an organic mental syndrome should not be treated by this combined technique on an outpatient basis.

Some severely anxious, depressed nonschizophrenic patients who have constant suicidal preoccupations are also too ill for treatment in an ambulatory fashion by this combined procedure. There is no one factor in every patient that determines this decision, which depends on one or more of the following findings:

1. Recent history of a suicidal gesture.
2. History of previous suicidal acts.
3. History of suicide in the family.
4. History of acting out as a prime expression of increased anxiety.
5. Intensity of guilt feelings.
6. Intensity of marked overt or covert hostility.
7. History of poor results from prior drug therapy or psychotherapy.
8. Hostility to psychotherapeutic procedures.
9. The absence of any responsible relative or friend.
10. The presence of a debilitating physical disorder.

These factors and others are reviewed very minutely before one proceeds with the combined technique. This meticulous pretherapeutic evaluation is a necessary precaution against a precipitous suicidal act. It goes without saying that each patient should have a thorough general and neurological examination before the therapeutic procedure begins. This examination is particularly important in view of the fact that the vast majority of severely depressed patients that were seen in my practice were forty years of age or older.

SELECTION OF DRUGS

It is beyond the scope of this chapter to enter into a detailed discussion of antidepressant drugs. As in the instance of the tranquilizing drugs, there are literally thousands of papers dealing with the various antidepressant drugs now available for clinical use. I extend the same words of caution with regard to the selection of drugs that were made in the last chapter, namely, that one should know his drug well before using it, particularly with regard to its benefits, limitations, and side effects. In an eleven years' study of more than 400 patients, I utilized three groups of antidepressant drugs: (1) iproniazid (prior to 1960), (2) imipramine hydrochloride, and (3) tranylcypromine in combination with a phenothiazine drug, usually trifluoperazine.

The proper selection of antidepressant drugs is important. On the basis of earlier studies I employed iproniazid and imipramine only in those patients who demonstrated decreased psychomotor activity in association with their depressions. Also on the basis of earlier studies I used tranylcypromine in combination with trifluoperazine in patients with agitated depressions. I am not implying in my discussion of these three preparations that other antidepressants of the same general chemical structure are not effective antidepressant medications. In general, I would say that, if a particular antidepressant drug of a given biochemical group is ineffective, an analog of this drug usually will also be ineffective. The literature is full of papers that will dispute this statement. However, placebo reactions can readily account for their claims.

EVALUATING IMPROVEMENT IN DEPRESSED PATIENTS

In order to follow severely depressed patients throughout the course of treatment, to compare the depths of illness between two patients, and especially to compare the results of various therapies, one must utilize a consistent method of evaluation. For the past eleven years I have employed a method that is readily adaptable for the clinical evaluation of depressed patients and that is independent of the nature of the therapeutic procedure.

This scheme stresses the patient's adaptation to routine vocational, social, and physical responsibilities. In addition, the degree of amelioration of the initial presenting symptoms is evaluated. The technique also stresses the degree of pride and pleasure that the patient obtains as a result of his adaptive capacities. It is possible to quantitate these various points on a four-point scale with the sum of all the factors representing the final improvement rating. This procedure permits a day-to-day, week-to-week, month-to-month comparison in a given patient and enables the clinical observer to compare the effectiveness of a given therapy in different patients.

MOOD

Mood, as used here, refers to the degree of depression as measured by facial expression; tone, quality, and volume of voice; and content of conversation. Improvement of mood is evaluated on the four-point scale as follows:

Key

1. Excellent: appropriate cheerfulness and optimism; depression, when it appears, is commensurate with the severity of the cause both in intensity and duration.

2. Good: appropriate cheerfulness and optimism in most instances, but in brief self-limited occasions is given to episodes of mild "blueness," pessimism, and diluted capacity for pleasure; depression, when it appears, may be slightly more severe than is commensurate with the cause in intensity and duration; feelings of hopelessness, if they occur, are mild and transient.

3. Fair: general feeling of "blueness," relative anhedonia; chronic pessimism; rare and brief periods of cheerfulness and/or optimism not commensurate with the cause; prone to frequent episodes of severe depression with marked feelings of hopelessness; suicidal preoccupations, if they occur, are transient and poorly organized.

4. Poor: continued profound depression, anhedonia; obsessed with feelings of hopelessness; dominated by suicidal preoccupations.

PSYCHOMOTOR ACTIVITY

Psychomotor activity refers to the motor activity that reflects the degree of emotional pressure. The following is the key for the measurement of psychomotor improvements for the hyperactive group.

Key

1. Excellent: activity appropriate in degree and duration to the environmental stimuli.

2. Good: appropriate motor activity in most instances, but brief, self-limiting periods of mild restlessness, possibly with short periods of pacing, all slightly more severe than is commensurate with severity of the cause in intensity and/or duration.

3. Fair: general restlessness; infrequent periods of being able to remain in one place; frequent pacing; prone to periods of extreme restlessness with marked pacing and moving about precipitated by minor stimuli.

4. Poor: extreme restlessness; constant pacing; incessant moving.

There may or may not be chronic complaints of fatigue among those diagnosed as fair or poor.

Improvement of psychomotor activity for the hypoactive group is evaluated as follows:

Key

1. Excellent: activity appropriate in degree and duration to the environmental stimuli.
2. Good: appropriate motor activity in most instances but given to brief self-limited periods of slowness associated usually with complaints of fatigue and tiredness (often described as "feeling lazy"); symptoms are more severe than is commensurate with the environmental stimuli in intensity and/or duration.
3. Fair: generalized slowness; difficulty initiating any activity; infrequent bursts of motor activity (constant complaints of fatigue); prone to periods of extreme slowness or even lack of activity with patients remaining in bed and unable to fulfill routine daily personal responsibilities.
4. Poor: immobile; vegetating; not fulfilling routine daily personal responsibilities.

PERFORMANCE

The key to evaluating improvement in vocational performance is as follows:

Key

1. Excellent: full-time employment; functioning efficiently without strain; deriving great pride and pleasure from achievements.
2. Good: full-time employment; greater effort required than was necessary prior to illness; moderate pride and pleasure in achievements.
3. Fair: works intermittently with considerable difficulty; frequent absences; faulty performance at times; lack of pride and pleasure in achievements.
4. Poor: unable to perform at all.

Social performance, that is, individual and group interpersonal relationships, were evaluated as follows:

Key

1. Excellent: active and comfortable; high level of pride and pleasure in achievements.
2. Good: active but with slight to moderate difficulty at times; limited pleasure capacity.
3. Fair: socializes with great difficulty; becomes anxious readily; lack of pride and limited infrequent pleasure.
4. Poor: seclusiveness or chaotic relations.

AMELIORATION OF ANXIETY

Anxiety is defined for our purposes here in its broadest sense, as it was in previous chapters. It is considered to be synonymous with fear, whether this fear is generated by unconscious conflict or actual difficulties. I attempted to quantitate anxiety according to a four-point scale after analyzing this psychophysiologic phenomenon into four components: motor, affective, autonomic, and verbal.

Key

1. Calm: no restlessness; overt expression of fear when it occurs is appropriate to the severity of the actual stress.
2. Slight: slight restlessness; slight affective expression of fear; slight pressure of speech.
3. Moderate: moderate restlessness; pacing; moderate overt affective expression of fear; often severe pressure of speech.
4. Panic: incessant movement; state of terror is denoted by facial expression, tone and quality of voice and pressure of speech.

AMELIORATION OF INITIAL SYMPTOMS

Key

1. Excellent: all symptoms completely gone.
2. Good: symptoms markedly reduced in intensity and frequency; patient able to cope.
3. Fair: slight improvement only, with symptoms continuing to plague patient most of the time and with marked impact.
4. Poor: symptoms unchanged or worse.

DREAMS

Whenever possible, dreams are sought out and studied in an attempt to gain additional information. The disappearance of nightmares, decrease in the frequency of rage dreams, and the increase in the frequency of pleasant dreams are among the points that are evaluated.

This particular technique of evaluation, in its very conception, makes it necessary for the pyschotherapist to investigate minutely the psychopathologic aspects of the depression, the presenting symptoms, and the patient's adaptation to his milieu. As a result of this method of evaluation, the therapist is able to remain sharply aware of the intensity of the patient's illness and of his capacities to adapt to his environment at any given moment. The evaluation is accomplished through the direct observation of the patient and by close contact with the patient's family or friends.

The final improvement rating is indicated on a four-point scale that takes into account all of the factors described above:

Key

1. Excellent: appropriate cheerfulness, optimism and motor activity; full-time employment; active and comfortable in social performance; marked pride and pleasure in vocational and social performance; all presenting symptoms absent.
2. Good: usually appropriate cheerfulness, optimism and motor activity, but with periods of mild "blueness" and periods of either slight slowness and listlessness; full-time employment but requiring slightly greater effort than usual; active socially but with

slight to moderate difficulties at times; slight residual anxiety; symptoms markedly reduced in intensity and in frequency; slightly limited pride and pleasure in performance.

3. Fair: general feeling of depression; relative anhedonia; chronic pessimism; prone to frequent periods of profound depressions; marked restlessness with pacing or marked motor inactivity; working but with considerable difficulties; frequent absences; socializing with great difficulty; moderate to marked residual anxiety; slight improvement, if any, in symptoms; minimal pride and pleasure in performance.

4. Poor: continued state of profound depression; anhedonia; obsessed with feelings of hopelessness; dominated by suicidal preoccupations; either incessant pacing and uncontrolled activity or immobility; unable to perform vocationally or socially; anxiety level severe and unchanged; symptoms unchanged or worse; absence of pride or pleasure in performance.

PSYCHOTHERAPEUTIC TECHNIQUES IN THE COMBINED
TREATMENT OF SEVERELY ANXIOUS, DEPRESSED PATIENTS

INITIAL PHASE

The initial psychotherapeutic aspect of combined therapy is supportive in nature. Its aims are to remove or blunt the suicidal drives and to produce a marked improvement in psychomotor activity and the depressed mood. This phase of therapy is brief, one to two weeks at the most. Suicide is the omnipresent danger in this stage of treatment and all patients are treated accordingly.

Therapy is conducted in a face-to-face setting. The treatment is strongly ego supportive in nature in this phase, with the therapist offering a type of psychiatric transfusion in an attempt to temporarily satisfy the infantile dependency and hopelessness displayed by the patients. Most of the patients cry out for help although many feel that they do not deserve help owing to an overpowering, obsessive guilt mechanism. This guilt is rage-linked in that the conscious and unconscious hostility that can be detected readily in almost every depressed patient serves as a constant source of fuel for the paralyzing guilt.

A deliberate attempt is made to foster a strong positive transference. In this manner, the therapist is able to counteract temporarily the effects of the patient's crushing, self-destructive superego. The therapist assumes the role of an all-powerful, all-wise, all-forgiving, protective parent substitute. He expiates real or imagined wrongs and repeatedly reassures the patient as to the satisfactory outcome of treatment. This reassurance is really not an idle boast, because the vast majority of depressed patients do obtain very satisfactory results spontaneously by means of the combined therapy technique or, if need be, through the use of electroshock treatment.

The patient's positive past performances and accomplishments are stressed. This is not difficult usually, for, in truth, most of these patients have been very capable people. Indeed, most of the patients with agitated depressions have been driving, meticulous, self-demanding accomplished persons. They are told initially that their illnesses are triggered by exhaustion due to their "excessive demands on themselves."

These patients are all plagued with insomnia, anorexia, feelings of exhaustion, inability to concentrate, loss of interest in their person and in their environment, and they are incapable of assuming any obligations. Their inability to perform heightens their guilt. The therapist relieves them temporarily of their duties, indeed orders them not to assume any obligations. This admonition in itself commonly results in a marked reduction in the patient's anxiety and guilt feelings.

During this phase of treatment the underlying psychodynamic mechanisms of the depression are not brought into focus or discussed, although they are commonly very obvious to the therapist at the time of the initial interview. I agree with those therapists who believe that one cannot deal with the psychodynamics of depression until the actual depression has been eliminated. At this phase of therapy the patient's ego capacities are too fragile to tolerate a discussion of any unconscious mechanisms that are vague and often overwhelmingly painful. To enter into a discussion of these mechanisms at this point is to court disaster by a precipitation of a free-floating anxiety state that would accentuate all the presenting symptoms and signs.

Some therapists are afraid that excessively "giving" to depressed patients may increase the patients' guilt and introjected aggression. The *ego transfusion technique*—the deliberate fostering of a very strong positive transference—is necessary in patients with very severe depressions. Indeed, if it is not accomplished, combined therapy on an ambulatory basis becomes precarious and must be rapidly terminated in favor of electroshock therapy or hospitalization. These patients have child-like, magical expectations, and it is necessary for the therapist to be the strong, all-wise, all-forgiving, protective parent substitute. These severely depressed patients require, and should receive, direct and repeated reassurance that they will get well. This reassurance is in most instances realistic, because more than 80 percent of these patients do experience satisfactory remissions from their depressions when the combined psychopharmacologic-psychotherapeutic technique is employed. In addition, most of those who fail to respond dramatically to the combined therapy will obtain satisfactory results with electroshock therapy. A hard core of patients, about 5 percent, fails to respond to any of the current therapies.

The family is usually a most imperfect, unreliable, and even negative assistant. However, it plays an intimate role in the initial phase of combined therapy. The various members are consulted closely to obtain detailed histories concerning the patient's background and personality matrix. More important, they must be sampled repeatedly to obtain a picture of the quality and intensity of the patient's current behavior patterns.

The family is informed clearly of the severity of the patient's illness. The omnipresent danger of suicide is stressed repeatedly. They are forewarned that if the patient does not demonstrate very specific improvement during the first seven to ten days, or if the patient's status becomes worse during the same period, then electroshock therapy or hospitalization will be recommended. The family is admonished to observe the patient closely. Medications during the initial phase are usually placed in the hands of the family. The possible side effects of the drugs are described in detail to the family and the patient. They family is permitted, indeed advised, to be in close telephone contact with the therapist. Specific times are scheduled when the family can report. They are also interviewed at each of the frequent visits made by the patient during the initial phase. As the patient improves, the reliance on his family is decreased and finally eliminated.

During the first few weeks, but especially during the first week, the patient is minutely observed and questioned and the family is interrogated. The family is given free rein to contact the therapist by telephone. The intensity of the depression, of the feelings of hopelessness, and of the suicidal preoccupations are kept in sharp focus. A clear evaluation of the degree of psychomotor activity is of particular importance, for I have found in almost all instances that a trend toward normalization in the degree of psychomotor activity is the first sign of improvement (Lesse, 1960, 1961b). Other factors, such as an increase or decrease in insomnia, anorexia, expressions of guilt or hostility, increase or decrease in obsessive-compulsive trends, hypochondriasis, referential trends, and the degree of interest shown by the patient in his environoment and in his personal habits, are probed minutely, for they are sensitive indications of change in the patient's clinical status.

I feel it worthwhile to repeat once again that *a knowledge of the psychodynamic mechanisms per se does not indicate the severity of the depression at any given time. The psychodynamic modus operandi may be the same in a patient in a mildly depressed state as in a patient with strong suicidal drives.*

As indicated previously, if the patient does not demonstrate definite improvement during the first seven to ten days, of if his clinical status worsens, then ambulatory electroshock or hospitalization is considered. These decisions must be made firmly, for prolonged procrastination on the part of the psychiatrist or the patient's family has permitted many decompensating depressed patients to attempt suicide.

The time limit of approximately seven to ten days allowed for the first symptoms and signs of improvement was established for valid reasons. It is my experience, gained during the past eleven years, that if depressed patients, treated on an ambulatory basis, did not begin to respond to imipramine in approximately one week, then there is little likelihood of a significant change occurring with this drug (Lesse, 1960). Similarly, if patients with severe agitated depressions do not begin to improve within seventy-two hours when given the tranylcypromine-trifluoperazine combination, it is usually of no avail to continue these medications (Lesse, 1961a, 1961b).

Some neuropsychoparmacologists will vigorously dispute the time factor stated with regard to the use of imipramine and the use of tranylcypromine. Some claim that even six weeks is too brief a period in which to test the efficacy of a drug. Other investigators have noted that if patients do not respond favorably after a relatively short period, then they would not respond favorably after longer periods. It is my impression that if patients do not respond to psychotropic drugs within a relatively short period of time it is most likely that improvements that occur only after a long period of time result from various placebo effects. In any case, I reiterate that ambulatory combined therapy is emergency treatment, and if evidences of improvement are not forthcoming within seven to ten days one jeopardizes the patient's very existence by further procrastination, particularly because there are other means available to effectively ameliorate suicidal drives.

Another reason why the initial emergency phase of the combined therapy technique is limited to a period of one or one and a half weeks is that the "magic" of supportive psychotherapy in markedly ill patients becomes very tenuous after a short period of time. If a severely depressed patient does not begin to feel relief in a short period of time a strongly negative attitude toward the psychiatrist and the treatment quickly replaces the positive transference relationship.

PSYCHOANALYTICALLY ORIENTED PHASE

When definite evidence exists that suicidal preoccupations have disappeared and that feelings of hopelessness and the intensity of the depression have decreased markedly, then the scope of the psychotherapeutic procedures can be broadened. It should be remembered that the patient's improvement at this point is owing to the effects of the drugs, the strong supportive psychotherapy, or placebo affects, and it is not possible at this point to determine the relative importance of these factors. Indeed, one must be cautious lest the improvement be more apparent than real. The psychotherapeutic process remains ego supportive in nature with the degree of support being decreased gradually in proportion to the increase in the patient's ego capacities. The patient has little or no insight at this point as to the cause of his illness; he is completely dependent on the drug and the therapist for his very existence, and any appearance that he has recovered is tenuous.

In some ways, this is the most precarious point in treatment. I must repeat that suicide attempts are not uncommon during states of apparent remission. I caution the therapist against being lulled into a false sense of security or relaxing his vigil too quickly.

This danger can be avoided in almost all instances if one will continue to probe for and heed the evidences of the residual symptoms and signs of depression in the patient. The extreme, positive transference relationship is reduced gradually to prevent a permanent atrophy of the ego. This pattern that simulates infantile dependency inhibits effective psychotherapy if permitted to remain. The therapist's support is removed cautiously, the rate dependent on the realistic evidences of an increase in the patient's adaptive capacities.

In general, the therapeutic goals for these patients are less extensive than they would be in intensive, reconstructive psychotherapeutic procedures with psychoneurotic patients. In part, this is owing to the patients' age group, for severe, nonschizophrenic depressions are relatively uncommon in patients under forty years of age.

With the combined therapy technique, drug treatment usually is maintained for many months. Many patients with a history of repeated depressions have been kept on maintenance doses for one or more years. There are some patients with a history of recurrent depression who literally require maintenance drug therapy for a lifetime as evidenced from our current experiences.

Psychotherapy is carried on in a face-to-face setting. Free association is encouraged, but it is controlled free association in which the therapist actively points out the psychodynamic relationships among the events, thoughts, and emotions that occur in the patient's daily pursuits, and their counterparts from the patient's past. Interpretations are given only when the therapist feels that the patient's ego capacities are sufficiently strong to tolerate them. This active interpretation is necessary to prevent the development of free-floating anxiety, which from experience I found could exacerbate the depression if the patient was permitted to ruminate too freely without tying the ruminations to the "here and now," more specifically to the patient's emotional reactions to his daily life.

Dreams are studied very intensively for they offer important information as a source of the patient's current status and as a source of basic psychodynamic mechanisms. As I have pointed out before, dream material can be a prime source of data heralding an exacerbation or improvement in the patient's clinical status.

After the patient attains a greater degree of stability, his unconscious hostility is gradually permitted to unfold. In some individuals this hostility is covert, whereas in others it is overt. In any case, hostility can be compared to an iceberg in that no matter how much is openly expressed, the greatest quantum remains hidden.

In most patients, as I intimated before, this anger is strongly linked to guilt mechanisms. This means that if the patient manifests any overt or covert anger, guilt feelings are experienced and this anger is then turned inward. Until all latent hostility is brought into consciousness and the patient is able to react appropriately to anger-producing situations without experiencing guilt, he remains extremely prone to a reoccurrence of depression. It is worthwhile to stress once again that exposure of the guilt-linked rage mechanism should be handled very cautiously. If not, explosive abreactions can occur, resulting in a severe exacerbation of the depression, and even suicide. As all experienced psychiatrists have found, some patients have been so terrified in their early formative years that they literally must be taught to express anger.

An understanding of the psychodynamic processes behind rage mechanisms is imperative for therapists who treat depressed patients by means of the combined technique; unfortunately this aspect of psychodynamics has been neglected in the literature. I believe that one of the main reasons for this is that most psychotherapists are either unable to tolerate their patients' rage mechanisms or tend to avoid or reject patients who display marked overt hostility.

Depressed patients in my experience are almost always extremely overtly or covertly hostile.

Covert Hostility

Covert hostility is most commonly seen in patients demonstrating a severe decrease in psychomotor activity. The psychodynamic mechanisms for this covert hostility appear to follow one of two patterns, both of which are related to early childhood traumas and traumas occurring in infancy. These are as follows:

1. In one pattern of covert hostility the parents literally deserted their children emotionally. This psychic abandonment led to fears of complete isolation together with feelings of worthlessness and inadequacy. The child reacted with anger to the abandonment and deprivation but did not express this anger for fear of becoming completely separated and isolated from the parents. These patients were unable to react with appropriate

anger in later life even when it was justified. This covert rage is often guilt-linked, either based on the cultural prohibition against anger directed toward parents or the martyring attitudes of the very parents who rejected the child.

2. Another psychodynamic mechanism seen in patients with covert rage is one that develops in patients whose parent (or parents) was extremely hostile, domineering, compulsive, or critical—even sadistic. In this situation, the child was terrified by the aggressive, punitive atmosphere. All attempts by the child to fight this massive psychic attrition were met with overwhelming punishment. In addition, this type of parent was usually a martyr who constantly reminded the child of how ungrateful he was for the bounty he had received from the parent. The child also was reminded that he had broken the most sacred rule of man, namely that he must honor his parents under any and all circumstances. In this manner, even repressed anger becomes guilt-linked, and in retroflex fashion self-punishment would occur in the absence of any overt anger.

Overt Hostility

Overt hostility, on the other hand, is most commonly noted in anxious, agitated depressed patients. The psychodynamic mechanisms in these patients parallels in great measure those described in the preceding paragraph. The dominant parent (in our culture it is usually the mother) was a very aggressive, meticulous, often opinionated, critical person, whose negative attitudes filled the child with anxiety and feelings of inadequacy and worthlessness. The patient often became quick-tempered, irritable, and opinionated in turn. This type of child commonly has temper tantrums.

In this type of patient, in contrast to the child fostering covert anger, the domineering critical parent did not completely destroy the child's compensatory capacities and did not block the patient from expressing his rage. At our present cultural development, this type of psychodynamic mechanism is enhanced by the competition between children demanded by many intellectually and emotionally frustrated urban and suburban mothers who live vicariously through their children. This type of mother, in most instances, gives a great deal of attention to the child. However, she demands a great deal in return in the form of superior performance by the child. If such performance is not forthcoming, the child is the recipient of various types of rejection.

In the early phase of combined therapy, though the depressed affect may readily be ameliorated in response to the antidepressant drugs, initial improvement does not affect the guilt-linked retroflex rage mechanism. This rage mechanism requires gentle, intensive patient psychotherapeutic help if it is to be substantially altered.

Much of the psychoanalytically oriented phase of treatment is spent in pointing out to the patient that his depression is the result of long-standing maladaptation to his environment. Therapy is directed primarily toward helping to alter these adverse habit patterns. The therapist emphasizes to the patient that drugs alone or a mere parroting of the psychodynamic formulations that have been quoted to him in treatment did not safeguard him from future illnesses. In addition to helping the patient to adapt more realistically to his environment, a pointed attempt is made to make the patient aware of the earliest manifestations of emotional decompensation as they occur in him and that often this process is readily reversible if the environmental stresses are confronted as soon as they become evident.

PROBLEMS OF COMBINED THERAPY

The problems and dangers that occur with the combined antidepressant-psychotherapy technique are very similar in nature to those described in detail for tranquilizers in combination with psychotherapy (see Chapter 14). The omnipresent danger of suicide is an additional and the most important hazard that the therapist faces in the treatment of depressed patients. As such, the omnipresent danger of suicide in severely anxious, depressed patients, particularly patients being treated on an outpatient basis, requires a discussion in depth.

Before entering on this discussion of suicide I would like to emphasize that it cannot be repeated too forcefully that psychiatrists undertaking this combined psychotherapy-antidepressant drug technique should have facilities available for outpatient electroshock treatment and facilities for emergency hospitalization.

SUICIDE AND APPARENT REMISSIONS IN ANXIOUS, DEPRESSED SUICIDAL PATIENTS

In a series of 402 severely depressed patients, treated by the combined therapeutic procedure over an eleven-year period, the danger of suicide was very pertinent in a large percentage of the cases. For example, 159 patients (110 women and 49 men), ranging in age from twenty-seven to sixty-seven years, had endogenous depressions characterized by a marked decrease in psychomotor activity. Sixty-four (40 percent) had either periodic or persistent suicidal ideas. Fourteen had a history of prior suicidal attempts. (All had occurred one or more months prior to the onset of treatment.)

Two hundred and forty-three patients (162 women and 81 men), ranging in age from thirty-two to sixty-nine years, had agitated depressions with a marked increase in psychomotor activity. One hundred and four (43 percent) had either periodic or constant suicidal ideas. Nineteen had a history of suicidal acts (once again, all had occurred one or two months prior to the onset of treatment).

Though it seems almost trite to repeat the statement that suicide represents a very common cause of death in many countries, I do not believe that these figures can be repeated too often. For example, in 1957, more than 16,000 persons took their own lives in the United States. The rates in Denmark and Sweden average approximately twenty per 100,000 per population. These rates are paralleled or exceeded in other European countries, such as Switzerland, Germany, and Austria, and they are equaled and exceeded by the suicide rates in Japan. Despite the published frequency of death by suicide, it is very probable that the true figures are higher than those recorded in official reports. Unfortunately, mass statistics, such as the genocide figures relating to the Nazi atrocities, are of such stupendous proportions and are so impersonal that they make little impact on physicians and laymen alike.

Despite statistical analysis and repeated warnings to the effect that all patients who are ill with severe overt or covert depressions are potential suicidal risks there has been no significant decrease in the number of deaths by suicide. Indeed the rate appears to be increasing.

The problem of apparent remissions in suicidal patients has received insufficient attention, particularly with reference to the manner in which such states can be recognized and avoided. I am referring to those patients with a history of suicidal preoccupations or suicidal attempts in whom the destructive preoccupations or drives appear to have been ameliorated.

The states of apparent remissions in suicidal patients are not infrequent. In one study, more than 90 percent of the patients who had a history of suicidal attempts had an exacerbation (reactivation phase) of suicidal drives after a period of apparent marked improvement (Moss and Hamilton, 1956). This occurred when hospitalized patients, with a history of previous suicidal attempts, were considered improved and had contact with the environment from which they originally came. Another team of research workers reported that 75 percent of suicides have a history of prior suicidal gestures (threats or attempts) (Shneidman and Farberow, 1957). They point out that almost half of the individuals who kill themselves after leaving a hospital did so within a period of ninety days.

Other authors have warned about the dangers inherent in patients with histories of suicidal gestures who are in an apparent remission. The earliest was probably Bleuler (1924) who admonished that this period was particularly dangerous because "the impulse to suicide is still present while the patient's energy is no longer very inhibited." More recently, other observers have extended similar warnings (Lesse, 1961c; Freedman, 1962; Stengel and Cook, 1958; Chapman, 1965; Litman, 1965a, 1965b; Meerloo, 1959; Szasz, 1963; Basescu, 1965; Kubier, 1964; and Lesse and Mathers, 1968).

In a recent paper on suicide occurring during hospitalization in one large psychiatric institution (Chapman, 1965), eighteen acts of self-destruction were reported among 23,006 admissions (seventy-eight per 100,000). Eight occurred in the hospital while the patients were on authorized leave. None of the patients who killed themselves in the hospital had a history of suicidal attempts prior to their admission. Seven of the ten patients who succeeded while on leave were actively suicidal at the time of admission but were considered as having responded well to treatment. Four died while on a three-day pass; four were on trial visits at home. None of those who committed suicide while on official leave ever attempted suicide while in the hospital.

Though exacerbations of suicidal drives commonly appear to be precipitous acts, they are no more acute than the original suicidal gestures. Both the original suicidal drives and the reactivation phases rest on a more chronic psychiatric illness, with the clinical pathologic manifestations of the recurrent episodes escaping detection by the psychiatrist, his assistants, and the patient's family and friends. The exacerbations that often terminate in the death of the patient are avoidable in most instances if the psychiatrists or nonmedical psychotherapists develop a diagnostic acumen sufficient to recognize the nidus of future suicidal drives and learn to appreciate the subtle manifestations of decompensation in patients with a history of depression.

The problems that occur in the management of patients who have a history of suicidal gestures and who appear to be in states of remission depend on several factors. These factors are related to the therapist, the patient, and the patient's environment. In most occasions, the difficulties that occur are related to a combination of all factors.

THE THERAPIST

In this day of electroshock therapy, psychotropic drugs, and the various types of psychotherapy, the psychiatrist is often lulled into a false sense of security purely on the basis that he feels he is doing something for the patient. Also, the psychiatrist who treats a patient with suicidal gestures frequently is so relieved to record some degree of improvement that he may overestimate the true degree of improvement, paralleling the reactions of some surgeons whose patients have survived massive or very delicate operations.

Similarly, psychotherapists who treat anxious, depressed patients with a history of prior suicidal gestures are prone to forget that *a knowledge of the psychodynamics of depression per se does not indicate the severity of the depression at a given moment, for the psychodynamic modus operandi may be the same in a mildly depressed patient as it is in a patient with intense suicidal drives.* A very meticulous investigation of the patient's daily environmental adaptation, his symptoms, and his affective behavior is necessay before one can ascertain the intensity of the depression at any given moment.

Problems occur if the therapist does not understand the meaning of suicidal preoccupations or attempts. Suicidal behavior does not always have death as its goal. Indeed, there is a great deal of ambivalence in most patients with suicidal preoccupations.

The suicidal gesture may be a means of verbal or nonverbal communication by the patient to a significant other person. It may be a cry for help by the patient who reacts as if he is not receiving the support, recognition, love, or understanding he feels he needs or to which he feels he is entitled. This is usually on an unconscious level. The suicidal gesture may also be a communication of overwhelming feelings of guilt or guilt-linked rage.

At times, problems result from inadequate response on the part of the psychiatrist or psychotherapist. Attention has been called to the fact that a patient's suicidal behavior may immobilize individuals who are close to the patient though they have been forewarned (Litman, 1965a). It has been pointed out that hostile partners at times may will the death of potential suicidal patients (Meerloo, 1959). Hostility on the part of a therapist toward a patient, particularly one who has a long-standing unyielding therapeutic problem, may blind the therapist to the urgency of the patient's psychic state. It is probable also that philosophic concepts held by various therapists may inhibit their ability to react to the emergency of an impending suicidal act (Lesse, 1961c). These philosophic concepts may be legalistic in nature, such as that proposed by Szasz (1963) to the effect that an individual must have the right to kill or injure himself. Other therapists (Basescu, 1965; Kubie, 1964) have expressed the opinion that overconcern with regard to the possibility of suicide might interfere with effective therapy. Some authors (Litman, 1965b) communicate their indifference with regard to the patients possible death by suicide.

At times, the therapist is unable to present an image that is sufficiently strong to give the ego support for which the patient is overtly or covertly appealing (Kubie, 1964). The treatment of severely depressed patients requires an ego transfusion technique that some therapists are emotionally unprepared to administer.

As mentioned above, the pyschiatrist may be lulled into a false sense of security by the early results obtained in suicidal patients following the use of various therapies. Electroshock therapy, though very effective in treating anxious, depressed patients with suicidal drives, may on occasions just blunt or mask the suicidal impulses, particularly if the frequency or number of treatments is inadequate. As a result the psychiatrist prematurely may lessen his careful vigil during the course of treatment; at times this may result in a tragedy. Similarly, as the organic mental syndrome secondary to electroshock therapy clears, residual self-destructive drives on occasion may mushroom rapidly and end in a suicide attempt if the psychiatrist is not on guard.

The psychiatrist also may be lulled into a false sense of security following the administration of psychotropic drugs with a resultant premature relaxing of clinical vigil. Some suicidal patients may demonstrate apparent remarkable remissions following the administration of a tranquilizer or an antidepressant drug. At times, this may be purely a tenuous placebo reaction (Lesse and Mathers, 1968) with the suicidal drives just being superficially masked. Any relaxation of clinical precautions during the early phase of treatment may result in a suicidal act.

THE PATIENT

There are many factors pertaining to the patient that should alert the observant psychiatrist or psychologist to the danger that suicidal drives may be exacerbating. The symptoms and signs may be expressed verbally or nonverbally, and they may be conscious or unconscious as far as the patient is concerned.

It should be noted that following a suicidal attempt the patient is often much less anxious and depressed. One might say facetiously that a suicidal attempt, in which the patient survives, serves as an excellent tranquilizer and antidepressant. Psychodynamically, this may be explained in several ways. On the one hand, the attention that is given the suicidal patient by significant others may satisfy the need for recognition and support that is so common in most suicidal patients. On the other hand, the pain and danger that the suicidal patient experiences may satisfy, in great measure, the guilt-linked retroflex rage prominent in most of these patients.

The therapist should not be deluded by this pseudoremission, for it will be usually very temporary. Most important of all, the therapist should not be deluded into believing that this improvement results from any of his therapeutic techniques.

Any person who has suicidal preoccupations or who has made a suicidal attempt must be considered as having very tenuous ego capacities. This is particularly true with schizoid or actively schizophrenic patients, who are potential prospects for repeated suicidal attempts until there are very definite evidences from symptomologic and adaptational standpoints of marked ego strengthening. In my opinion, actively schizophrenic patients with suicidal preoccupations should always be treated in a hospital setting.

Similarly, patients with organic mental syndromes who have a history of suicidal preoccupations or who have previously made suicidal attempts must be watched very closely. This is particularly true if the patients have an obsessive-compulsive personality matrix. Some who have demonstrated a need to dominate their environment may react with a precipitous suicidal attempt if they feel themselves unable to maintain their previous level of functioning secondary to a fading memory or failing intellectual capacity.

One must particularly be on guard if there is a fluctuation in the intensity of the organic mental syndrome, as commonly may occur with cerebrovascular decompensation. When these patients are in a marked state of confusion there may be a decrease in the intensity of depression and suicidal impulses. However, as they regain relative clarity and insight into the nature of their problems, a suicidal gesture may be forthcoming. For these reasons, patients with organic mental syndromes who have suicidal preoccupations should be treated in a hospital setting.

In general, anxious, depressed patients who have somatic illnesses pose a special problem. Much depends on whether the physical ailment is realistically severe or severe only in the mind of the patient. If one has a chronic, markedly incapacitating process, such as may occur with diabetus mellitus, repeated myocardial infarctions, repeated cerebrovascular episodes, or malignancies, the threat of further incapacities, impending death, or persistent pain may stimulate further suicidal preoccupations or another suicidal attempt. Also, there are some individuals with insight into their impending death who may as a last act of defiance want to control their own fate. A suicidal act, to some, is the crowning example of such control.

It is imperative that the therapist correctly evaluate the threshold of pain in these patients in whom pain is a major factor. Evidence of a low pain threshold may be a danger in one who has had previous suicidal gestures. In close relation to this point, when one is dealing with depressed persons, especially individuals with a prior history of suicidal preoccupations, one must be cognizant of the degree of anxiety or depression that occurs in patients awaiting surgery.

Patients who anticipate facial or other types of disfigurement or loss of sexual potency or sexual image as a result of surgery demand very careful observation. For example, a radical mastectomy in certain women implies an unbearable loss of femininity. The loss of sexual potency following a prostatectomy or injury to the genitals may be overwhelmingly threatening to some men. Also in this regard there are women in whom a hysterectomy represents the end of youth; some cannot tolerate the termination of the reproductive period even though they may not desire further children.

There has been considerable discussion during the past few years as to the advisability of informing a patient of the presence of a malignant disease or of the threat of impending death. The patient with a history of depression should not receive such information.

Alcohol is also a major problem in depressed patients, particularly in those who have a history of previous suicidal gestures. Chronic alcoholics commonly are very depressed. Indeed, the alcoholic habit may be viewed in some as an attempt to escape depression. Suicidal acts have occurred when a chronic alcoholic sobers up following a bout of heavy drinking. In some debilitated patients, the continued imbibing of alcohol in itself may be viewed as an attempt at suicide. In any depressed patient the lowering of the ego boundaries that occurs with an excessive intake of alcohol may permit the unbridled development of feelings of hopelessness, desertion, rejection; it may also permit dominance by an overwhelming feeling of retroflex rage. The author has noted similar reactions in patients who have received lysergic acid.

Depressed patients in whom homosexuality is a factor, either latent or overt, pose major therapeutic problems. Precipitous suicidal attempts have occurred following a homosexual act that has consumed the patient with guilt. Similarly, suicide attempts have been made by patients with latent homosexual drives when an overt homosexual act was considered as imminent.

Physicians, in general, have been insufficiently aware of the depression sine depression (masked depression) syndrome (Lesse and Mathers, 1968). In this syndrome even massive depressions may be masked by hypochondriacal complaints or psychosomatic disorders. The presence or increase of hypochondriacal manifestations or psychosomatic disorders following the remission of a suicidal gesture should be recognized as a continued expression of the underlying depression.

The type of practice in which the physician is engaged will determine in great measure the frequency with which the masked depressions will be encountered. Physicians specializing in organic medicine will find that patients with masked depressions will account for many, if not most, of the depressions with which they will be confronted. Most psychiatrists, as noted by Hochstetter (1959), find that this syndrome is seen in a more limited percentage of depressed patients. Hochstetter found it in twenty-seven of 258 patients (10.5 percent) with a depressive syndrome. Recently,

I reported (Lesse, 1967) that this type of illness was found in 100 of 324 (30.9 percent) of depressed patients studied during a period of two and a half years. The masked depression syndrome will be observed most commonly by neuropsychiatrists who are frequently consulted by internists and surgeons in a large general hospital.

Patients in the state of apparent suicidal remission may signal an exacerbation of their suicidal impulses in various ways. A shift in affect, particularly if it is sudden and persistent, is suspect. A depressed patient may appear calmer and less depressed if he has decided to take his life or if he has chosen the specific technique by which he plans to kill himself. An hallucinating schizophrenic patient may appear calmer if his voices have told him to commit suicide. In an opposite vein, a patient may react with increased anxiety and depression as he considers suicide.

The retroflex rage mechanism is of prime importance in a large number of patients who attempt suicide. The therapist should be very sensitive to the level of anger, overt or covert, present in his depressed patient. An increase in the rage mechanisms, as indicated by the patient's behavior or dream material, may be a forewarning of an impending suicidal act.

Increasing defiance by a patient, as demonstrated by his attempts to dominate his environment or by demands for changes, particularly if these are expressed with great bravado, may indicate a last expression of angry protest prior to a self-destructive act. In an opposite vein, dependent patients manifesting increasing discontent, who complain that nothing is being done for them, may be communicating their needs for increased recognition and support. Their problems are often made worse by the fact that they may alienate the physician, the family, or the hospital staff by their persistent nagging.

Patients with a history of impulsive, antisocial activity occurring whenever they encounter stressful situations, who again begin to act out, should be suspect of an impending suicidal attempt if they have a history of previous suicidal behavior.

There are a number of other symptoms that have particular importance in patients with a history of depression that indicate residual depression. Of course, a residue of depressed affect or feelings of hopelessness obviously may nurture the redevelopment of a severe depressive syndrome. Other symptoms, such as insomnia or anorexia, also may indicate that a depression has not cleared entirely. If there has been a marked decrease in weight, associated with a depression, and the patient is unable to regain this weight, this too should be viewed as suspect of a residual depression. A persistent increase or decrease in psychomotor activity from that which is normal for the patient may also be a residual symptom. A need for soporifics or sedatives, particularly if this need increases, is an adverse sign.

An awareness of the patient's dream material is of extreme importance in the treatment of depressed patients, because an exacerbation of a depression and suicidal drives are often heralded by changes in dream patterns. The manifest content of these dreams may be very direct, or they may be masked in complicated symbolism. In one of my patients a recurrence of suicidal drives was heralded by a dream in which the patient was lying quietly at the bottom of the lake. He became aware, consciously, of his suicidal preoccupations one week following this dream. In other patients a marked increase in their retroflex rage mechanisms may be heralded by dreams.

THE PATIENT'S ENVIRONMENT

There are a number of factors pertaining to the environment that may significantly affect the patient who has a history of suicidal gestures and who is in an apparent state of remission. A change in psychiatrists, as might occur with routine staff rotation in a hospital setting or as the result of a psychiatrist leaving on vacation, may stimulate a rapid exacerbation of suicidal drives. This occurs if the psychiatrist has become the significant other in the patient's life, his prime source of security and recognition.

An exacerbation of suicidal drives also may be precipitated by intercurrent problems, such as financial debts or losses. Rejections by a lover, friend, or relative may be other major sources of stress.

Very often patients with a history of suicidal gestures are permitted to return to work too soon or prematurely are permitted to take on responsibilities that overwhelm their ego capacities. This may precipitate a massive exacerbation of suicidal drives even if the patient experiences just a minor reverse. I have noted the occurrence of such situations when patients were promoted too soon following their return to work. On the other hand, if the patient is "punished" by being demoted after an absence due to his illness, he may feel overwhelmingly rejected. As a general rule, one must not permit patients to assume obligations that are beyond the ego capacities that they have firmly demonstrated.

During the postsuicidal period (which may vary from weeks to months) the therapist must be prepared to protect his vulnerable patient from untoward environmental stress either directly or by surrogates in the patient's community. If this is not possible on an ambulatory basis, the patient should be hospitalized.

RESULTS OF COMBINED THERAPY

This combined psychotherapy-antidepressant drug treatment in the ambulatory management of severely depressed patients produces very satisfactory results. In my series of 402 severely depressed patients 327 (82 percent) had excellent or good results as defined by the method of treatment of evaluation outlined earlier in this chapter in which results were based on remission of symptoms and the patient's ability to resume vocation and social responsibilities with a high degree of pride and pleasure.

These short-term results approach those obtained by electroshock therapy, in my experience, and have proven significantly more successful than antidepressant drug therapy alone. Attempts are now being made to ascertain whether exacerbations are more or less frequent following the use of combined therapy than when electroshock treatment is employed. This type of comparative evaluation is most difficult, and the results are usually unreliable for a variety of technical reasons.

If this book had been completed in 1965, I could have said that none of the patients in my study had made any suicidal attempts while under combined therapy. During the early part of 1966, one patient who was being treated by the combined technique attempted suicide by cutting her wrists. This was a forty-five-year-old woman who presented as a masked depression in the form of an atypical facial pain syndrome. She was under extreme stress caused in great measure by a son with extremely severe sociopathic behavior problems. The suicide attempt occurred when her husband was notified that he was to lose his job. Fortunately, in this instance, the physical damage to the patient was slight.

This one suicidal episode, from among a group of severely depressed patients treated by the combined technique that now numbers more than 400, illustrates how the danger of an actual suicidal attempt can be minimized if the precautions outlined in this chapter are observed closely. I call to your attention that electroshock therapy and hospitalization do not produce 100 percent deterrence to suicidal attempts.

Combined therapy is relatively new, and much more experience is necessary if it is to improve as a technique and if we are to obtain a clear understanding of the mechanisms by which it works. It offers to those who are technically and emotionally equipped a new and encouraging addition to our therapeutic armamentarium.

REFERENCES

Alexander, F. *Psychoanalysis and Psychotherapy*. New York: Norton, 1956.

Appel, K. E., Lhamon, W. T., Myers, J. M., and Harvey, W. A. *Long-Term Psychotherapy in Psychiatric Treatment*. A.R.N.M.D. Research Publication No. 31. Baltimore, Md.: Williams & Wilkins, 1953.

Apfelbaum, D. *Dimensions of Transference in Psychotherapy*. Berkeley, Cal.: University of California Press, 1968.

Balint, M. *The Doctor, His Patient, and the Illness*. New York: International Universities Press, 1957.

Basescu, S. The Threat of Suicide in Psychotherapy. *Amer. J. Psychother.*, 1965, 19:99.

Beecher, H. K. The Powerful Placebo. *J.A.M.A.*, 1955, 159:1602.

Bleuler, E. *Textbook of Psychiatry*. New York: Macmillan, 1924.

Blum, R. H. *Management of Doctor-Patient Relationship*. New York: McGraw-Hill, 1960.

Cartwright D. S. Effectiveness of Psychotherapy: Critique of Spontaneous Remission Argument. *J. Consult. Psychol.*, 1955, 2:290.

Cartwright, D. S., and Cartwright, R. D. Faith and Improvement in Psychotherapy. *J. Consult. Psychol.*, 1958, 5:174.

Cattell, R. B., and Scheier, I. V. *The Meaning and Measurement of Neuroticism and Anxiety*. New York: Ronald Press, 1961.

Chance, J. E. Personality Differences and Level of Aspiration. *J. Consult. Psychol.*, 1960, 24:111.

Chapman, R. F. Suicide During Psychiatric Hospitalization. *Bull. Menninger Clin.*, 1965, 29:35.

Dewey, E. R. Role of the Foundation for the Study of Cycles. *J. Cycle Res.*, 1961, 10:97.

Diehl, H. S. Medical Treatment of the Common Cold. *J.A.M.A.*, 1933, 101:2042.

Eysenck, H. J. The Effects of Psychotherapy—An Evaluation. *J. Consult. Psychol.*, 1952, 16:319.

Feldman, P. E. Clinical Evaluations of Chlorpromazine Therapy for Mental Illness. *J. Clin. Exp.Psychopath.*, 1957, 18:1.

Fischer, H. K., and Dlin, B. M. The Dynamics of Placebo Therapy. *Amer. J. Med. Sci.*, 1956, 232:504.

Frank, J. D. Dynamics of the Psychotherapeutic Relationship. *Psychiatry*, 1959, 22:17.

Frank, J. D., Gliedman, L. H., Imber, S. D., Stone, A. R., and Nash, E. H. Patients' Expectancies and Relearning as Factors Determining Improvements in Psychotherapy. *Amer. J. Psychiat.*, 1959, 115:961.

Freedman, P. Some Considerations in the Treatment of Suicidal, Depressed Patients. *Amer. J. Psychother.*, 1962, 16:379.

Friedman, H. J. Patient Expectancy and Symptom Reduction. *Arch. Gen. Psychiat.*, 1963, 8:61.

Goldstein, A. P. Therapist and Client Expectancies of Personality Change in Psychotherapy. *J. Consult. Psychol.*, 1960, 7:180.

Goldstein, A. P. *Therapist-Patient Expectancies in Psychotherapy.* New York: Macmillan, 1962.

Goldstein, K. *Human Nature in the Light of Psychotherapy.* Cambridge, Mass.: Harvard University Press, 1940.

Greenspan, J. Reinforcing Effect of Two Spoken Sounds on the Frequency of Two Responses. *Amer. J. Psychol.*, 1955, 68:409.

Gutheil, E. *The Handbook of Dream Analysis.* New York: Liveright, 1951.

Heller, K., and Goldstein, A. P. Client Dependency and Therapist Expectancy as Relationship-Maintaining Variables in Psychotherapy. *J. Consult. Psychol.*, 1961, 25:371.

Hinsie, L. E., and Campbell, R. J. *Psychiatric Dictionary.* New York: Oxford University Press, 1960.

Hochstetter, W. Depressive Syndromes. *Proc. Virchow Med. Soc., N.Y.*, 1959, 28:116.

Kansler, D. H. Aspiration Level as Determinant of Performance. *J. Personality*, 1959, 27:346.

Kelly, G. A. *Psychology of Personal Constructs.* New York: Norton, 1955.

Kolb, L. C., and Montgomery, J. Explanation for Transference Cure: Its Occurrence in Psychoanalysis and Psychotherapy. *Amer. J. Psychiat.*, 1958, 115:414.

Kurland, A. A. The Drug Placebo—Its Psychodynamic and Conditioned Reflex Action. *Behav. Sci.*, 1957, 2:101.

Kurland, A. A. "The Placebo," in *Progress in Psychotherapy.* J. H. Masserman and J. L. Moreno, eds., New York: Grune & Stratton, 1958. Vol. 3.

Kubie, L. S. Multiple Determinants of Suicidal Attempts. *J. Nerv. Ment. Dis.*, 1964, 138:3.

Lacey, J. E., and Lacey, B. C. LIV in Longitudinal Study of Autonomic Constitution: Four-Year Reproducibility of Intrastressor Thirty-Minute Stereotype. *Ann. N.Y. Acad. Sci.*, 1962, 98(Art. 4): 1257.

Lasagna, L., et al. Study of Placebo Response. *Amer. J. Med.*, 1954, 16:770.

Leonard, H. L., and Bernstein, A. *Anatomy of Psychotherapy.* New York: Columbia University Press, 1960.

Lesse, S. Psychotherapy and Ataraxics. *Amer. J. Psychother.*, 1956, 10:448.

Lesse, S. Combined Use of Psychotherapy with Ataractic Drugs. *Dis. Nerv. Syst.*, 1957, 18:334.

Lesse, S. Experimental Studies on the Relationship Between Anxiety, Dreams and Dream-like States. *Amer. J. Psychother.*, 1959, 133:440.

Lesse, S. The Evaluation of Imipramine Hydrochloride in the Ambulatory Treatment of Depressed Patients. *J. Neuropsychiat.*, 1960, 1:246.

Lesse, S. Combined Tranylcypromine-Trifluoperazine Therapy in the Treatment of Patients with Agitated Depressions. *Amer. J. Psychiat.*, 1961, 117:1038 (a).

Lesse, S. Combined Use of Tranylcypromine and Trifluoperazine in the Ambulatory Treatment of Patients with Agitated Depressions. *New York J. Med.*, 1961, 61:1898 (b).

Lesse, S. Psychotherapy and the Danger of Suicide. *Amer. J. Psychother.*, 1961, 15:181. (c)

Lesse, S. Placebo Reactions in Psychotherapy. *Dis. Nerv. Syst.*, 1962, 23:313 (a).

Lesse, S. Psychotherapy in Combination with Anti-Depressant Drugs. *J. Neuropsychiat*, 1962, 3:154 (b).

Lesse, S. Psychotherapy in Combination with Anti-Depressant Drugs. *Amer. J. Psychother.*, 1962, 16:407 (c).

Lesse, S. The Relationships Between Socioeconomic and Sociopolitical Practices and Psychotherapeutic Techniques. *Amer. J. Psychother.*, 1964, 18:574.

Lesse, S. Drugs in the Treatment of Neurotic Anxiety and Tension, in P. Solomon, ed., *Clinical Studies in Psychiatric Drugs*. New York: Grune and Stratton, 1966. Pp. 221–224 (a).

Lesse, S. Psychotherapy plus Drugs in Severe Depressions—Technique. *Compr. Psychiat.* 1966, 7:224 (b).

Lesse, S. Hypochondriasis and Psychosomatic Disorders Masking Depression. *Amer. J. Psychother.*, 1967, 21:607.

Lesse, S. Obsolescence in Psychotherapy—A Psychosocial View. *Amer. J. Pschother.*, 1969, 23:381.

Lesse, S., Hoch, P., and Malitz, S. Chlorpromazine Therapy in Private Practice. *J. Nerv. Ment. Dis.*, 1957, 125:25.

Lesse, S., and Mathers, J. Depression sine Depression (Masked Depression). *New York J. Med.*, 1968, 68:535.

Luborsky, L. Personality of the Psychotherapist. *Menninger Quart.*, 1952, 6:3.

Lipkin, S. Clients' Feelings and Attitudes in Relation to Outcome of Client-Centered Therapy. *Psychol. Monogr.*, 1964, 68, whole no. 376.

Litman, R. E. Immobilization Response to Suicidal Behavior. *Arch. Gen. Psychiat.*, 1965, 19:570 (a).

Litman, R. E. When Patients Suicide. *Amer. J. Psychother.*, 1965, 19:570 (b).

McLardy, T., and Davies, D. L. Clinical and Pathological Observations on Relapse after Successful Leukotomy. *J. Neurol. Neurosurg. Psychiat.*, 1949, 12:231.

Meerloo, J. A. Suicide, Menticide and Psychic Homicide. *Arch. Gen. Psychiat.*, 1959, 81:360.

Meyer, A., and Beck, E. *Prefrontal Leukotomy and Related Operations*. Springfield, Ill.: Thomas, 1954.

Moss, L. M., and Hamilton, D. M. Psychotherapy in the Suicidal Patient. *Amer. J. Psychiat.*, 1956, 112:814.

Pilowsky, I., and Speer, F. G. The Wordless Interview: Preliminary Communication. *Amer. J. Psychother.*, 1964, 18(suppl. 1):174.

Psychopharmacology Service Center Bulletin, 1964, Vol. 3, whole no. 1.

Rosenthal, D., and Frank, J. D. Psychotherapy and the Placebo Effect. *Psychol. Bull.*, 1956, 53:294.

Salzinger, K., and Pisoni, S. Reinforcement of Affect Responses of Schizophrenics During the Clinical Interview. *J. Abnorm. Soc. Pschol.*, 1958, 57:84.

Shapiro, A. K. The Placebo Effect in the History of Medical Treatment: Implications for Psychiatry. *Amer. J. Psychiat.*, 1959, 116:298.

Shneidman, E. S., and Farberow, N. L. Clues to Suicide. In E. S. Shneidman and N. L. Farberow, eds. *Clues to Suicide*. New York: McGraw-Hill, 1957. Pp. 5–12.

Snyder, W. U., and Snyder, B. J. *Psychotherapy Relationship*. New York: Macmillan, 1961.

Stengel, E., and Cook, N. G. *Attempted Suicide: Its Social Significance and Effects*, Maudsley Monograph No. 4. London: Chapman and Hall, 1958.

Storrow, H. A., and Spanner, M. Does Psychotherapy Change Patients' Attitudes? *J. Nerv. Ment. Dis.*, 1962, 134:440.

Szasz, T. S. *Law, Liberty and Psychiatry*. New York: Macmillan, 1963.

Tibbetts, R. W., and Hawkins, J. R. The Placebo Response. *J. Ment. Sci.*, 1956, 102:60.

Wilder, J. Law of Initial Value. *Z. Ges. Neurol. Psychiat.*, 1931, 137:317.

Wilder, J. The Law of Initial Value in Neurology and Psychiatry: Facts and Problems. *J. Nerv. Ment. Dis.*, 1956, 125:73.

Wolf, S., and Pensky, R. H. Effects of Placebo Administration and Occurrence of Toxic Reactions. *J.A.M.A.*, 1954, 155:339.

INDEX